What's So Liberal about the Liberal Arts?

FRAMEWORKS
Interdisciplinary Studies for Faith and Learning

What's So Liberal about the Liberal Arts?

Integrated Approaches to Christian Formation

EDITED BY
Paul W. Lewis and
Martin William Mittelstadt

☙PICKWICK *Publications* • Eugene, Oregon

WHAT'S SO LIBERAL ABOUT THE LIBERAL ARTS?
Integrated Approaches to Christian Formation

Frameworks: Interdisciplinary Studies for Faith and Learning 1

Copyright © 2016 Wipf and Stock Publishers. All rights reserved. Except for brief quotations in critical publications or reviews, no part of this book may be reproduced in any manner without prior written permission from the publisher. Write: Permissions, Wipf and Stock Publishers, 199 W. 8th Ave., Suite 3, Eugene, OR 97401.

Pickwick Publications
An Imprint of Wipf and Stock Publishers
199 W. 8th Ave., Suite 3
Eugene, OR 97401

www.wipfandstock.com

ISBN 13: 978-1-4982-3144-2

Cataloging-in-Publication data:

What's so liberal about the liberal arts? : integrated approaches to Christian formation / edited by Paul W. Lewis and Martin William Mittelstadt.

xvi + 252 p. ; 23 cm. —Includes bibliographical references and index(es).

Frameworks: Interdisciplinary Studies for Faith and Learning 1

ISBN 13: 978-1-4982-3144-2

1. Spiritual Formation. 2. Christian Education. I. Series. II. Title.

BV4511 W38 2016

Manufactured in the U.S.A.

These essays are in honor of James and Twila Edwards, exemplars of an integrative, multidisciplinary approach to liberal arts education

Contents

Series Preface ix
List of Contributors xiii
Acknowledgments xv

An Introduction to the Frameworks Series:
Why Frameworks? My Storied Explanation 1
Martin William Mittelstadt

Introduction: What's So Liberal about the Liberal Arts? 7
Paul W. Lewis

1 Watchers: James and Twila Edwards as Models
 of Integrated Faith and Learning 11
 Gary Liddle

HISTORICAL DEVELOPMENTS

2 Shaping Minds, Shaping Culture: The Story of Liberal Arts
 Education in the Middle Ages 23
 Michael Palmer

3 Global Pentecostal Renaissance? Reflections on Pentecostalism,
 Culture, and Higher Education 43
 Jeff Hittenberger

4 Liberal Arts and the Assemblies of God: A History and Analysis of a
 Strained Alliance 65
 Barry Corey

THE LIBERAL ARTS AS INTERDISCIPLINARY EXPERIENCE

5 "How Primitive!" The Modern Pentecostal Movement as a Reflection of Cultural "Primitivism" 85
  Robert Berg

6 "Teach me how to curse mine enemies": Subversive Female Power in Shakespeare's *Richard III* 107
  Diane Awbrey

7 Pioneering Missionary Women in Asia and the Pacific Rim 123
  Barbara Cavaness Parks

8 Herbert's Ratios of Psalmic Intertextuality in *The Temple*: A Prospectus for Further Study 141
  Nathan H. Nelson

9 Eat, Drink, and Include: A Theology of Hospitality in Luke-Acts and Beyond 154
  Martin William Mittelstadt

10 "The Truest, Least Selfish Heart": God's Childlikeness in George MacDonald's Fairy Tales 166
  LaDonna Friesen

11 Tolkien as Ethnographer: The Role of Culture in J. R. R. Tolkien's *The Lord of the Rings* 181
  Paul W. Lewis

THE LIBERAL ARTS IN PRACTICE

12 Study Abroad: A Transformative and Integrative Journey 203
  Robert Turnbull

13 Meeting at the Table: The Divine Intersection Between Writing Centers and the Discipline of Hospitality 218
  Jennifer Fenton

14 Complexities of Learning: From Jerusalem to *Shantistan* 230
  Ruth Burgess

Index of Authors Cited 247

Series Preface

Frameworks: Interdisciplinary Studies for Faith and Learning

WE AFFIRM THE VALUE of a Christian liberal arts education. We believe that lifelong development of a Christian worldview makes us more fully human. We attest that engagement in the liberal arts contributes to the process of integrating Christian spirituality with a broad range of disciplinary studies. This integrative process requires that we explore and reflect upon biblical and theological studies while learning effective communication, pursuing healthy relationships, and engaging our diverse global community. We believe that the convergence of academic disciplines opens the door to the good life with enlarged promise for worship of the living God, development of deeper communities, and preparation for service and witness.

Our contributors are dedicated to the integration of faith, life, and learning. We celebrate exposure to God's truth at work in the world not only through preachers, missionaries, and theologians, but also through the likes of poets, artists, musicians, lawyers, physicians, and scientists. We seek to explore issues of faith, increase self-awareness, foster diversity, cultivate societal engagement, explore the natural world, and encourage holistic service and witness. We offer these studies not only as our personal act of worship, but as liturgies to prepare readers for worship and as an opportunity to wrestle with faith and practice through the arts and sciences.

In this series, we proclaim our commitment to interdisciplinary studies. Interdisciplinary studies involves the methodological combination of two or more academic disciplines into one research project. Within a Christian worldview, we address complex questions of faith and life, promote cooperative learning, provide fresh opportunities to ask meaningful questions and address human needs. Given our broad approach to interdisciplinary studies, we seek contributors from diverse Christian traditions and disciplines. Possibilities for publication include but are not limited to the following examples: 1) We seek single or multiple author contributions that address Christian faith and life via convergence of two or more academic disciplines; 2) We seek edited volumes that stretch across interdisciplinary lines. Such volumes may be directed specifically at the convergence of two or more disciplines and address a specific topic or serve as a wide-ranging collection of essays across multiple disciplines unified by a single theme; 3) We seek contributors across all Christian traditions and encourage conversations among scholars regarding questions within a specific tradition or across multiple traditions. In so doing we welcome both theoretical and applied perspectives.

The vision for this project emerged among professors at Evangel University (Springfield, MO). Evangel University, owned and operated by the General Council of the Assemblies of God (AG), is the fellowship's national university of arts, sciences, and professions: the first college in the Pentecostal tradition founded as a liberal arts college (1955). Evangel University is a member institution of the Council for Christian Colleges and Universities (CCCU). Consistent with the values and mission of the AG and CCCU, Evangel University exists to educate and equip Christians from any tradition for life and service with particular attention to Pentecostal and Charismatic traditions. Evangel University employs a general education curriculum that includes required interdisciplinary courses for all students. The Evangel University representatives for this series continue to participate in the articulation and development of the Evangel University *ethos* and seek contributors that demonstrate and model confessional integration not only for the Evangel University community and Pentecostals, but all Christians committed to the integration of faith, learning, and life. We offer this series not only as a gift from the Evangel University community to other Christian communities interested in the intersection of intellectual integration and spiritual and societal transformation, but also as an invitation to walk with us on this journey. Finally, in order to ensure a broad conversation, our editorial committee includes a diverse collection of scholars not only from Evangel University but also from other traditions, disciplines, and academic institutions who share our vision.

Series Editors

- Paul W. Lewis (Associate Professor of Historical Theology and Intercultural Studies at Assemblies of God Theological Seminary)

- Martin William Mittelstadt (Professor of Biblical Studies at Evangel University)

Editorial Board
- Diane Awbrey (Professor of Humanities at Evangel University)
- Jeremy Begbie (Research Professor of Theology at Duke Divinity School)
- Robert Berg (Professor of Theology at Evangel University)
- Jonathan Kvanvig (Professor of Philosophy at Washington University-St. Louis)
- Joy Qualls (Chair & Assistant Professor of Communication Studies at Biola University)
- Brandon Schmidly (Assistant Professor of Philosophy at Evangel University)
- Geoffrey W. Sutton (Professor Emeritus of Psychology at Evangel University)
- Grant Wacker (Gilbert T. Rowe Professor of Christian History at Duke Divinity School)
- Michael Wilkinson (Professor of Sociology at Trinity Western University)
- Everett Worthington (Professor of Psychology at Virginia Commonwealth University)

Contributors

Diane Awbrey (PhD, University of Missouri-Columbia) is Professor of Humanities at Evangel University

Robert Berg (PhD, Drew University) is Professor of Theology at Evangel University

Ruth Vassar Burgess (PhD, University of Missouri—Columbia) is Professor Emeritus of Reading and Special Education at Missouri State University

Barry H. Corey (PhD, Boston College) is President at Biola University

Jennifer Fenton (MA, University of Missouri—Kansas City) is the Writing Studio specialist at Metropolitan Community College—Longview in Lee's Summit, MO

LaDonna Friesen (MA, Missouri State University) is Associate Professor of Humanities at Evangel University

Jeff Hittenberger (PhD, University of Southern California) is the Chief Academic Officer at Orange County (CA) Department of Education.

Paul W. Lewis (PhD, Baylor University) is Associate Professor of Historical Theology and Intercultural Studies and Admissions and Program Coordinator of Intercultural Doctoral Studies at Assemblies of God Theological Seminary

Gary Liddle (MA, Bethel Seminary) is Professor Emeritus of Theology at Evangel University.

Martin William Mittelstadt (PhD, Marquette University) is Professor of Biblical Studies at Evangel University

Nathan H. Nelson (PhD, University of Minnesota) is the Chair of Humanities and Professor of English at Evangel University

Michael Palmer (PhD, Marquette University) is Professor of Philosophy at Regent University Divinity School

Barbara Cavaness Parks (PhD, Fuller Seminary) is Missionary Educator with Assemblies of God World Missions (USA)

Robert Turnbull (PhD, New York University) is Professor Emeritus of French at Evangel University

Acknowledgments

We wish to thank of all of the contributors to this volume. They have waited patiently for publication of their work.

We appreciate the publishers for recognizing the merit of the Frameworks series and providing editorial guidance to us throughout the process.

We are grateful to our Frameworks editorial team. The idea for this series was the culmination of a long and delicate process. Over the years the "original" team members of this series, all of them from Evangel University, talked, dreamed, and charted (an ongoing) vision for interdisciplinary studies. When Chris Spinks at Pickwick Publications enthusiastically approved our vision for the series and called for a larger editorial team, our Evangel University colleagues answered the call and helped us bring together an outstanding group of scholars.

We are indebted to Evangel University students Ally Walsh and Anna Mitchell for their work in editing, checking, and double-checking various components of the project.

Finally, we wish to express our appreciation to our wives, Eveline Lewis and Evelyn Mittelstadt, for their kindness in affording us the time away from other tasks as we continually live out our academic dreams *and* meet deadlines!

—Paul and Marty

Why Frameworks? My Storied Explanation

MARTIN WILLIAM MITTELSTADT

As THIS IS THE inaugural volume of *Frameworks*, it seems fitting to elaborate briefly on the motivation and purpose behind this series. Given the dedication of the editorial team to the liberal arts, and specifically, to the integration of faith and learning, I propose not a thesis, but a story. Stories provide the foundation for the liberal arts. Our beliefs, values, rituals, and communities are based upon shared and evaluated stories. I cut my teeth on a Pentecostal pew and came to understand the importance of story early in my life.[1] In his *Thinking in Tongues*, James K. Smith recounts the days of his youth when his church would engage in a spontaneous ritual they called "God sightings"; congregants would respond to the question, "where did you see God this week?"[2] Whether at church or at home, work or the classroom, or the hockey rink, people would recount how God had enlivened daily activities. Such testimonies continue to function as an expected element of Pentecostal liturgy, typically unscripted (yet rather formulaic) narratives of conversion, sanctification, Spirit baptism, healing and deliverance, financial relief, and restoration of marred relationships. As I grew up in this tradition, I not only learned the rhetoric, but quickly came to value the desired outcomes of this practice. I gave praise to God, benefited from the shared experiences of my fellow believers, and eventually began to declare my own testimonies that had been "modeled" for our community. Though I continue to cherish this practice, my understanding of the value of storied testimony grew immensely during my educational journey.

1. I grew up in the Pentecostal Assemblies of Canada. Comparable denominations in the United States include the Assemblies of God, Church of God (Cleveland, TN), Church of God in Christ, International Church of the Foursquare Gospel, and International Pentecostal Holiness Church.

2. Smith, *Thinking in Tongues*, xxii.

Upon graduation from high school I began theological studies at a small Canadian Pentecostal college. As a young theologian in training, I began to discover technical language for my beliefs and practices. It came as no surprise to me that Pentecostals read the stories of the Bible not only as history, but as our stories. When we debated the historicity of people, places, and events in Kings and Chronicles or the Gospels and Acts (and we always landed emphatically on the side of historical reliability), we concluded that these stories were not merely to help us better read the propositional language of the Old Testament prophets or sayings of Jesus. I discovered that the biblical narratives served as a template for our contemporary testimonies.[3] Though "Evangelical" hermeneutics remained steeped in pursuit of historical critical questions, Pentecostals were surprisingly ahead of the curve. In the larger academic arena, biblical scholars of the late 1980s and beyond would produce the first generation of students and ensuing scholars to employ new methods such as literary criticism, narrative criticism, reader response theories, and emerging interdisciplinary approaches. As a Pentecostal, however, I came to realize that we were already reading the Bible *like* narrative critics and literary artists ahead of many other traditions and the academy. But herein is the irony; we were quasi-formalists and didn't know it. Our clergy typically entered church-related ministry with only a bachelor's degree (sometimes only a three year diploma in theology) from Pentecostal Bible colleges with a majority of their program focused upon theological studies. They typically received minimal engagement with other disciplines such as the humanities, behavioral sciences, social sciences, or hard sciences. Amazingly, while they knew little of the jargon, they played the game rather well. Though comfortable with the propositions of the OT prophets and NT letter writers, they often mined the epic stories of Abraham, Joseph, Moses, David, Elijah and Elisha, Daniel, Jesus, Paul, and the early church. Through these stories we discovered models to follow God's lead, to resist temptation and overcome adversity, to take down "Goliaths", to experience a personal "Damascus Road" conversion, to trust God, to preach under duress, and to reproduce miracles, healings, and deliverance like those "in the days of old."[4] We were in the game, but needed to learn a new set of rules.

I eventually entered Winnipeg Theological Seminary (now Providence Seminary), affectionately described as a "non-denominational seminary in the Mennonite tradition." I felt very much at home as I soon discovered that

---

3. Goldingay, "Biblical Story."

4. I understand that such preaching was not merely the domain of Pentecostals, but I have observed that Pentecostals capitalized on this in great measure.

my Anabaptist friends also employed story to stimulate meaning, rehearse and reenact their identity, and thereby encourage faithfulness to Jesus and their tradition. I remember well the first time I read Thielem J. von Bracht's *Martyrs' Mirror*, a seventeenth-century hagiographical collection of martyrological accounts from early Christianity to the emergence of Anabaptists.[5] Jan Luyken produced a subsequent edition with some one-hundred pictorial illustrations of which thirty survive. The account and illustration of Dirk Willems left an indelible mark on my life. Lukyen sketches Willems' dramatic prison escape from his religious opponents. As Willems runs to safety across a frozen river, his pursuer falls through the ice. Willems must make a split-second decision to continue his flight or save a life. In dramatic fashion, Luyken portrays Willems rescuing his pursuer. Willems is subsequently returned to town and burned at the stake. Like a Pentecostal testimony, Willems's story provides Anabaptists (and all Christians) a concrete story of Jesus' call to "love your enemies [and] do good to those who hate you" (Matt 6:27), "Blessed are those who are persecuted for righteousness' sake" (Matt 5:10) and "those who want to save their life will lose it, and those who lose their life for my sake, and for the sake of the gospel, will save it" (Mark 8:34). As I observed my Mennonite friends engage in deliberate reflection upon centuries-old narratives, I began to crave integration of my tradition not only with the larger Christian story, but with the human story.

I eventually made my way to MU and took another giant leap, this time into the rich tradition of Catholicism. Once again, I found my faith re-contextualized. As I read (and re-read) the Christian story, I found myself reading afresh the biblical stories and history of the church alongside people of faith with perspectives, experiences, interests, and methodologies different from my Pentecostal worldview. I came to MU in the early 1990s as a new wave of biblical studies began to reach its crest. Though not the end of the historical critical era, journals and monographs on biblical studies became flooded with the new formalism—hijacked from the hallways of humanities' departments. As a Lukan scholar in training, I began to encounter Luke-Acts not only as historiography, but fiction, novel, epic, biography, and a host of other genres. As I wrestled with scholars of competing genres, I found myself revisiting not only the writings and methodologies of ancient Jewish and Greco-Roman history, but the nature of story-telling (both oral and written) by way of contemporary approaches to literature, narrative, drama, and film. Furthermore, a second methodological shift

---

5. Originally published in Dutch. Translated by Joseph F. Thom in 1837 as *The Bloody Theatre, or Martyrs' Mirror, of the Defenceless Christians Who Baptized only upon Confession, and Who Suffered and Died for the Testimony of Jesus, Their Savior, from the Time of Christ until the Year A. D. 1660.*

of tsunamic import would converge literary and narratival waves with the likes of socio-political, economic, post-colonial, feminist, and Global South readings built upon the contexts of emerging scholars and their specific stories and concerns.

I am in my sixteenth year as Professor of New Testament at Evangel University, the national university of the liberal arts for the Assemblies of God. Barry Corey's essay in this volume tells of the tumultuous journey of the governing administrators of the Assemblies of God to bring Evangel University to fruition (founded as Evangel College in 1955).[6] The Assemblies of God (and the larger Pentecostal movement) is now into its second century of existence and only beginning to come of age. Though people of story, we are now only just beginning to explore "God sightings" in new venues. We have survived and thrived through our employment of biblical stories and pragmatic use of culture for the furtherance of missions, but the opening of Evangel College begged the question, how would "a college of arts and sciences" benefit the larger Pentecostal tradition. While early (and contemporary) Pentecostals often testified to minds delivered from a host of evils caused by addictions or dysfunctions by way of divine intervention, how might the disciplines of sociology, anthropology, and psychology contribute to long term individual and societal transformation? While Pentecostals employed a legion of "church growth" models, how might the church better understand and assimilate business and education models to disciple and shape the people of God toward holistic health, growth and societal reparation? While early Pentecostals such as Aimee Semple McPherson would take "worldly" stories and films such as *Gone with the Wind* and turn them into an illustrated sermon, is it possible to experience God through Shakespeare's plays, Herbert's poetry, or Spielberg's films?

An important work in the evolutionary ethos of Evangel University faculty has been the monumental volume of Wheaton College philosopher, Arthur Holmes. His *The Idea of a Christian College*, published in 1975, became the definitive work for a generation of educators that sought to integrate faith, learning, and life in confessional colleges and universities. If, according to Holmes, "all truth is God's truth," there can be no compartmentalization of sacred and secular, spiritual and the natural, or the church and the world. God's work must not be dichotomized. Though in full agreement with Holmes' efforts to lay a foundation for an entire generation of confessional scholars and practitioners, the Christian academy must once again adapt to new language and shifting methodologies. It is here that

---

6. Corey is an alumnus of Evangel University and current President of Biola University.

confessional academicians should find the rise of *interdisciplinary studies* attractive and beneficial. Allen Repko, a pioneer in interdisciplinary studies, describes the opportunity before those in higher education:

> For over two decades, major scientific organizations, funding agencies, and prominent educators have advocated for the need for interdisciplinary studies. The current interest in interdisciplinarity is widespread and increasing in intensity, motivated by the belief that it is now basic to education and research. To meet this perceived need, educators have developed a wide range of interdisciplinary courses and "studies" programs. Interdisciplinarity, it is fair to say, is becoming an integral part of higher education.[7]

Repko builds his case upon numerous factors including: the complexity of nature, society, and ourselves, the growing convolution of the globalized workplace; the need for systems thinking and contextual thinking; the public world and its pressing needs. Such challenges and opportunities call for a new kind of university research and education built upon *both* disciplinarity *and* interdisciplinarity.[8] To Repko's thesis, I must only add "how much more among confessional academicians!"

Though the faculty at Evangel University has always proclaimed the Christian liberal arts gospel of the integration of faith and learning, I (and other colleagues) often hear students say that this happened only some of the time; some teachers across campus do it well, but others do not. To address this concern, various faculty members (including a number of the Evangel University representatives of this series' editorial team) began to consider how we might more uniformly engage our students in connecting their faith with other fields of study. We imagined courses that actually brought together theology with literature, and with history, and with art and music, and the hard and behavioral sciences. Thus was born our interdisciplinary *Frameworks* courses. It is to this most recent wave of education and scholarship that I (and my fellow editorial team) hope the *Frameworks* series will contribute.

So what is the distinct motivation for this series? Though interdisciplinary studies continue to become increasingly popular and important among academicians, proponents recognize that a prevailing definition

---

7. Repko, *Introduction to Interdisciplinary Studies*, 3–4. Thanks to Robert Berg, my colleague and contributor to this volume for directing me to Repko. Repko is now retired, but led the way for a successful interdisciplinary studies program in the School of Urban and Public Affairs at the University of Texas at Arlington.

8. Ibid., 4.

remains rather elusive for *inter*disciplinarity in methodological infancy. Since I certainly do not intend to end the debate by way of a pithy and catchall definition, I simply bring my story full circle. Interdisciplinary studies prove to be fertile ground for even deeper personal and collective transformation. Given Jesus' command to "love God with heart, soul, mind, and strength", the time is ripe for confessional scholarship and education across the disciplines. We seek to integrate our faith, learning, and research through enlargement of our collective "pneumatological imagination."[9] We implore God's Spirit to change us through the great works of history and literature alongside developments in science, psychology, and economics— and all of this—through intense engagement with the Scriptures. I and the editors of this series invite you to join with us on a path of discovery. In this series, we seek to extend the role of testimony. We seek to enlarge the realm of "God sightings." We seek the likes of psychologists in conversation with philosophers, ethicists with historians, biblical scholars with rhetoricians, scientists with economists, environmentalists with neurologists. As these conversations continue across the disciplines, the "framework" from which to draw our individual and collective testimonies will only enlarge. We invite you to think, behave, preach, sing, pray, research, and indeed to live this multi-faceted journey with us. If indeed our stories are never complete, we invite future contributors and readers to share their "God sightings" with us.

BIBLIOGRAPHY

Goldingay, John "Biblical Story and the Way it Shapes Our Story" *Journal of the European Pentecostal Theological Association* 17 (1997) 5–15.

Repko, Allen. *Understanding Interdisciplinary Studies*. Part 1. Online: http://www.sagepub.com/upm-data/55817_Chapter_1_Repko_Intro_to_Interdisciplinary_Studies.pdf.

Smith, James K. *Thinking in Tongues: Pentecostal Contributions to Christian Philosophy*. Grand Rapids: Eerdmans, 2010.

Von Bracht, Thielem. *The Bloody Theatre, or Martyrs' Mirror, of the Defenceless Christians Who Baptized only upon Confession, and Who Suffered and Died for the Testimony of Jesus, Their Savior, from the Time of Christ until the Year A. D. 1660*. Translated by Joseph E. Thom. Scottsdale, PA: Herald, 1938.

Yong, Amos. *Discerning the Spirit(s): A Pentecostal-Charismatic Contribution to Christian Theology of Religions*. Sheffield: Sheffield University Press, 2000.

---

9. I am indebted to Amos Yong for this term. See *Discerning the Spirit(s)*, 102.

Introduction: What's So Liberal about the Liberal Arts?

Paul W. Lewis

WHAT'S SO LIBERAL ABOUT the liberal arts? This question highlights the diversity of understanding of the word "liberal." In modern usage, the term can have political, theological, social, or other connotations. However, this question cuts to the core of the liberal arts. What are the liberal arts? In this volume the contributors seek to further the discussion—historical studies, multidisciplinary application, and pedagogical employment of a liberating arts education.

A common emphasis in Christian liberal arts universities is the integration of faith and learning. The discussion of this integration has a storied history. Whereas Justin Martyr made full use of contemporary Greek philosophy in his defense of the Christian message in the mid-second century, by the early third century Tertullian proclaimed the oft quoted dictum, "What relationship does Jerusalem have with Athens?" While Tertullian (like Origen) certainly did not endorse the use of Greek philosophy, he definitely made use of his legal training and like Origen, made use of philosophical, rhetorical and legal traditions. Likewise, Augustine endorses the belief (also employed by Arthur Holmes, John Calvin and many others) "all truth is God's truth." He encouraged all learning to be applied alongside theological studies. Anselm and the Reformers subsequently discussed the nature of Christian life in terms of education in a multiplicity of fields. The importance of the integration of the Christian faith with education (including but not limited to theological education) has been a key concern in Christian schools in the West and for this volume mainly in North America. And though many American colleges and universities were founded on Christian values (e.g., Harvard, Princeton), many of these institutions have lost the traditional Christian components in the general education of the students. On the other hand, many Christian schools still endorse the integration of faith and learning (e.g., Baylor, Notre Dame, Pepperdine), and retain statements of such in their respective documents, and mission/vision statements. The Coalition of Christian Colleges and Universities (CCCU) likewise emphasizes the importance of the integration of faith and learning among its member schools.

The integration of faith and learning is an important common theme, but the tendency has been to focus on a certain bilateral integration of faith and learning, for example, the integration of faith and business, or faith and science. Interdisciplinary studies have become more prominent in recent years as the need for such has become increasingly obvious. This is due in part to the growing awareness that we live in a multi-disciplinary world. In a normal week, we must negotiate our way through a complex commercial, legal, musical, theatrical, rhetorical, scientific, and religious world. In the church, the multidisciplinary posture of the congregation is assumed (see Paul's discussion in 1 Corinthians 12 on being many diverse members in one body). Of course, the worlds of the marketplace and the church must not be dichotomized. We are called to live integrated and multidisciplinary lives at work and in worship.

When it comes to the multidisciplinary integration of faith and learning, there are two main ways to promote it: first, through description and analysis; and second, by application of integrative models and examples. Contributors to this volume recognize, celebrate, and honor the impact of Jim and Twila Edwards on our lives. Jim and Twila modeled multidisciplinary integration of faith and learning through their ongoing efforts to develop the liberal arts model at Evangel University and through their daily employment of integrated faith and learning. We dedicate this volume to them!

The first essay by Gary Liddle showcases the Edwards as concrete examples of the multidisciplinary integration of faith and learning in real life. Liddle narrates the educational development of the couple, and moves into their respective roles as teachers, mentors, and models at their college, at their church, and in the community.

The essays by Michael Palmer, Jeffrey Hittenberger, and Barry Corey explore the historical development of universities with special attention to the liberal arts and multidisciplinarity. Palmer tracks the development of education through the medieval period, namely the impact of the Monastic schools, the Cathedral schools, and the founding of the universities and thereby establishes a basis for ensuing liberal arts education. Hittenberger unpacks the philosophical understanding of education within Pentecostalism. He delineates key values and foci in Pentecostal education within the broader ecclesiastical context (with particular attention to the Moravian, Jan Amos Comenius). Corey charts the development of the first liberal arts school to develop in the Pentecostal tradition, Evangel College (est. 1955; later Evangel University). He tells a riveting story of the tumultuous efforts of the embryonic Assemblies of God (est. 1914) and its leadership in an attempt to enlarge their vision beyond the standard Bible institutions and colleges.

Robert Berg looks at a common thread among three influential figures at the turn of the twentieth century, namely Pablo Picasso, Igor Stravinsky, and William Seymour. Berg analyzes Picasso's, *Les Demoiselles D'Avignon*, Stravinsky's *The Rite of Spring*, and Seymour's leadership at the Azusa Street Mission. He charts their employment of art, music, and revival as a primitivistic response to cultural disillusionment.

Diane Awbrey and Barbara Cavaness Parks examine the value of women through their respective fields. Awbrey focuses on the noted Shakespearean play, *Richard III*. She contrasts Shakespeare's original characterization of women with the later revision by Restoration writer Colley Cibber (ca. 1700). Awbrey notes that while the Restoration theatre writers increase the frequency of women in their work, the breadth and depth of the female characters were greatly diminished. The transformation of the portrayal of women in *Richard III* from Shakespeare to Cibber's revision demonstrates a reductionistic move. Parks celebrates the important contributions of women to Assemblies of God missionary efforts, particularly, single women in Asia and the Pacific Rim. She traces the entrepreneurial spirit of these women in the early twentieth century. These pioneering women contributed greatly to the early growth of the young movement through church planting, social actions such as orphanages, and other ministries, often in hostile environments and dangerous situations.

Nathan Nelson looks specifically at the work of the noted Christian poet, George Herbert. Nelson explores Herbert's indebtedness to the Psalms in *The Temple*. He evaluates not only psalmic influence in Herbert's poetry, but discovers a similar statistical ratio of psalmic types between the canonical Psalter and Herbert's poetry.

Martin Mittelstadt examines the role of hospitality (or inhospitality) as a primary human virtue (or vice). He explores the primacy of hospitality in the ancient world, New Testament, Luke-Acts, and contemporary examples. Mittelstadt offers theological and ecclesiological implications for intentional hospitality. Hospitality makes Pentecost possible and successful. Hospitable people provide an environment for hurting people to experience transformation.

Two great literary figures, George MacDonald and J. R. R. Tolkien, are the focus of the essays by LaDonna Friesen and Paul Lewis, respectively. Friesen emphasizes the importance of divine "childlikeness" within the fairy tales of MacDonald. She expresses the key elements of love, divinely-guided imagination, and the centrality of childlikeness in order to understand MacDonald's contribution to Christian life. Lewis looks at the monumental work by Tolkien, *The Lord of the Rings*, through the lens of cultural anthropology. Lewis argues that Tolkien unpacks the cultures of the free peoples in this work by reflecting Clifford Geertz's "thick description." Tolkien clearly narrates cultural difference and distance; he refuses uniformity of cultures, but celebrates unity with diversity through friendship (the Fellowship of the Ring).

Robert Turnbull, Jennifer Fenton, and Ruth Burgess provide pedagogical examples of the liberal arts in action. Turnbull analyzes the importance of the study abroad program for a liberal arts school. Using the motif of the journey, he demonstrates the difficulties yet ultimate benefits for students who study abroad, in particular, for growth and transformation. Fenton assesses the impact of Writing Centers in schools, particularly the employment of hospitality as the primary posture for tutor / student relationships. She calls upon tutors not only to assist students in the development of writing skills, but to enact prophetic hospitality for mutual holistic transformation. Burgess enlarges the work of her mentor, Reuven Feuerstein, and his lifelong exploration of Mediated Learning Experience. According to Burgess, educators must pay particular attention to the multiple cultural and multigenerational contexts of the student and utilize pedagogical approaches that address the self-identity of the learner and her relationship to society.

In sum, the cumulative effect of this volume provides impetus for the ongoing development of integrated and multidisciplinary education. As proponents of Christian liberal arts continue to define and promote key values, their academic institutions will need to remain vigilant in their pursuit of multidisciplinary education. As proponents continue to employ their craft, some will be given to narratival description, others to modeling of multidisciplinary integration, and still others to pedagogical development. Contributors to this volume encourage such growth and conversation.

1

Watchers: James and Twila Edwards as Models of Integrated Faith and Learning

Gary Liddle

EVERY COLLEGE HAS THEM: watchers, keepers of the flame. Sometimes they are administrators but usually faculty and staff, who often have more longevity than top leaders. They are like long-serving civil servants in government at every level; they contain within their commitments and practices the institutional wisdom and ideals that propel and guide good procedures. When they leave, they take institutional memory with them, often to the detriment of their agency or school. They serve as examples and mentors to younger faculty, often unofficially and unintentionally. Others measure themselves by the best characteristics of these exemplars. In such ways is the school's mission defined, elaborated, embodied, and passed on to others. James (hereafter Jim) and Twila Edwards were such persons for forty years at a small, church-supported college in Missouri.

They had come from different parts of the country—he from Midwest prairies, she from northern Pennsylvania forests. Both from homes of modest means; his father was a Pentecostal preacher, her parents were dedicated church members in Erie. Their formative years were similar: small tightly-knit family life and religious experiences of intense Pentecostal and what-is-now-known-as fundamentalist variety—with the pluses and minuses associated with them, including legalism and sexism. Jim's father and Twila's mother seem to have had the greatest influence on them, respectively.

After successful high school years—including sports for Jim (football) and music for Twila (piano and accordion), they both made their way to

Central Bible Institute (CBI) in Springfield, Missouri in the mid-1950s. CBI was one of a score of Bible institutes sponsored by the Assemblies of God (AG). Such schools had been common among evangelical groups since the late 1800s. A.B. Simpson founded the first American example—now Nyack College—in 1882. The foci of Bible schools were English Bible studies, practical training for Christian service, and a disciplined life. They usually required practical ministry experience, such as teaching Sunday school, conducting street meetings *a la* Salvation Army bands, preaching at outstations, and personal evangelism (students turned in weekly reports of their ministry efforts). Their primary purpose was training for professional and lay church vocations, rather than so-called secular professions. Originally as brief as six-weeks, many Bible schools by the mid-twentieth century offered a three-year diploma.

At their best they produced pastors, evangelists and missionaries in large numbers. When coupled with indigenous church principles, Bible schools became for the AG and other groups the main educational tactic in missionary strategy (over one thousand schools overseas sponsored by the AG alone). Frank Gaebelein called Bible schools "nothing less than a new educational genre and . . . one of America's distinctive contributions to Christian education." He also praised the missionary movement "in which the teaching of the Bible and the establishment of schools has had a major part on an ecumenical scale reaching beyond the Western world to every continent."[1]

In a still relevant 1979 book, however, Richard Lovelace pointed out some downsides to the Bible school tradition in America. Perhaps epitomized in the name of Frank Sandford's Bible school "The Holy Spirit and Us" where the only textbook was the Bible, some schools were "addicted to experience and dismiss[ed] doctrine and any informed use of the mind as irrelevant to spiritual maturity."[2] In addition, while professing trust in the Holy Spirit's power to sanctify, some erected a "training-code morality" (Lovelace's phrase) comprised of Puritan taboos: no theatre, dance, cosmetics, novel clothing styles, playing cards, or religious graphic art. To these most Bible schools added tobacco and alcohol usage. Perhaps, Lovelace suggests, some evangelicals were actually teaching salvation by sanctification, and sanctification "by will power more than by grace."[3] John Ortberg calls this "boundary-marker Christianity," by which he means "highly visible, relatively superficial practices—matters of vocabulary or dress or

---

1. Gaebelein, "Education," 332–33
2. Lovelace, *Dynamics of Spiritual Life*, 183.
3. Ibid., 194.

style—whose purpose is to *distinguish* between those inside a group and those who are outside" (emphasis original).[4]

Another downside articulated by philosopher Arthur Holmes of Wheaton College is curricular. In *The Idea of a Christian College*, Holmes writes that Bible schools often achieve more of a conjunction of Christian witness with a minimum of general education "rather than the integration of faith and learning into an education that is itself Christian." He goes on to say that "[t]o enlarge a person's biblical and theological knowledge and to train him for Christian service is not the same thing as helping him to work in the arts and sciences and thereby to understand all of life from a Christian perspective."[5] A number of writers have traced the varied degrees of anti-intellectualism present in twentieth and twenty-first century American evangelical churches, so I won't belabor this point.[6]

A third area where the Edwards perceived a disconnect between Pentecostal theory and practice on one hand, and biblical truth on the other was the role of women. For most of its one hundred year history, the AG has been open to women in ministry in theory. In practice, however, opportunities for leadership at the local, regional, and national levels of the AG were difficult to find. For example, there has never been a female District Superintendent, and only in the most recent decade has there been a female member of the Executive Presbytery and the Executive Committee of AG World Missions. In the 1950s Twila herself had served in the Deaf Ministries Department of AG Home Missions, and was especially sensitive to the struggle of female students trying to reconcile their sense of God's call with the practical difficulty of finding a place of ministry.

One can only speculate about how much of these trends—code morality, intellectual defensiveness, and chauvinism—were present in their Pentecostal upbringing and at CBI in the 1950s. When I reflect on the subsequent themes of the Edwards' careers at Evangel College—later University—however, we can see their desire to change their tradition toward what they saw as holistic Christianity.

They met at CBI, courted, and married. Jim was credentialed with the AG and pastored for a short time in north Texas while working on a Master's degree in English. Graduate study itself was a risky venture for a Pentecostal pastor at the time—in English no less—since there was plenty of prejudice against graduate education in general, particularly for pastors. CBI was in the throes of a debate over adding a fourth year and enough

4. Ortberg, *Life You've Always Wanted*, 30–32.
5. Holmes, *Idea of a Christian College*, 8.
6. Noll, *Scandal* and Trueman, *Real Scandal*.

general education to warrant a Bachelor's degree and accreditation with the Accrediting Association of Bible Colleges (now the Association for Biblical Higher Education). Soon the debate widened to whether Central Bible College (CBC) could develop a Master's program and still retain its spiritual vitality. "Prophetic" voices said such a move would ruin CBC and quench the Spirit, but the College enjoyed a season of revival during the first year of the graduate program, and fears subsided. Nevertheless, the graduate program was abandoned after a few years.

In 1955, the AG founded Evangel College. Part of the impetus was a desire to educate young people from Pentecostal churches for professions other than church vocations. There was also alarm that many students from Pentecostal churches were attending state and private universities and, consequently, were leaving the church and the Christian faith altogether. So, despite considerable doubt within the churches, Ralph Riggs and other top leaders founded the first AG national college of arts and sciences, in an effort to educate more broadly than Bible schools intended, and to conserve young people who felt a calling toward a variety of professions. They were wary still of calling Evangel a "liberal arts" institution, due to prejudice and misunderstanding of the word "liberal" (some years later, a seminary was established in Springfield under the "graduate school" name, for similar reasons).[7]

During the next two or three years, the Edwards made a momentous decision, namely, that their ministry would be teaching, and at a fledgling college called Evangel—the first AG college of arts and sciences, housed in a remodeled army hospital in Springfield—across town from their *alma mater*, CBC. There they worked, she on staff and he in the classroom at first, and by 1976 both in the classroom, for some forty-five years. In the 1960s Jim began a doctorate in English at the University of Missouri.[8] Twila pursued a Master's in English at Southwest Missouri State and another Master's at the Assemblies of God Graduate School. By the late 1970s he was a veteran teacher in the Humanities Department and she a new-comer in the Department of Biblical Studies and Philosophy.

When a Humanities colleague, Ralph Kay, decided to start a new church on the Evangel College campus, the Edwards along with many other faculty and staff became charter members. This church aimed at offering an alternative in music, community life, preaching, and organization to older AG churches in the area. Evangel Temple Christian Center met in the

---

7. On the emergence of higher education in the Pentecostal tradition and AG, see the chapters by Jeff Hittenberger and Barry Corey.

8. The title of this dissertation is *English Narrative Backgrounds to Edmund Spenser's The Faerie Queene*.

newly constructed college library—the first new building on campus. Later the congregation moved south to a remodeled dairy barn complete with silo, and in 1974 to a new church building at 2020 East Battlefield Street. They remained active there until Twila's death in 2011. The congregation of Evangel Temple Christian Center celebrated fifty years in 2014.

Their church involvement was one area where they pushed for change. Their activities at their church were varied over four decades, but their most intense involvement was with Bible quizzing. Here was an effort to foster a marriage of spiritual development and intellectual rigor. They, George Edgerly, and the Andre Curtis' produced quiz materials which they distributed nationally. They also coached award-winning Bible quiz teams for several years, taking a team of their son Craig, Jennifer Curtis, and Paul Lewis (co-editor of this volume!) to within one question of winning a national championship. All three members had memorized the Gospel of Matthew by reference and by quotation.

Their involvement with teaching and Bible quiz were indicative of a larger theme of their professional lives, namely, the need to integrate faith, learning, and life. Soon after joining the Department of Biblical Studies and Philosophy, Twila wrote "What is Truth?", the opening chapter of a department-produced textbook, *Essential Christianity*[9] for use in a freshman class with the same name. Here she confidently and persuasively states her and Jim's convictions on the value of Christian liberal arts education. By this point in their careers, if not earlier, they had come a long way from the intellectual defensiveness often present in their Pentecostal tradition. Arguing against fragmentation, she wrote, "Loving God with the heart on Sunday in church, but fail[ing] to love Him with the mind in class on Monday is an example of fragmentation rather than integration."[10] She stated further that Christ's first command insists that the "entire self must be integrated in loving God," and the second "indicates a necessity for wholeness in relationships with others."[11] Her resources for the chapter are a who's who of Christian liberal arts proponents: C. S. Lewis, Frank Gaebelein, Arthur Holmes, Elton Trueblood, Dorothy Sayers, and John Milton. Here was a clear call for holistic Christian engagement of the mind and heart.

She taught in the Humanities Department after completing her graduate work in English, and continued to teach a Milton course until she retired. Widely read, she taught Charles Williams and C. S. Lewis to a generation of students in classes that were always full. With her literary skills she also

---

9. Edwards, "What is Truth?" 19–37.
10. Ibid., 20
11. Ibid.

explored and expounded the Psalms and the Book of Revelation to students' delight.

In the mid-1990s, philosophy professor and department head Michael Palmer edited a multi-author book, *Elements of a Christian Worldview*, which drew on Pentecostal scholars from across the nation and Canada. Twila wrote a masterful chapter as an example of integrating Christian faith and the arts, with a focus on literature.[12] She used four Christian doctrines—creation, sin, redemption, and Pentecost—as lenses to examine artistic works, including G. K. Chesterton, Madeline L'Engle, Milton, Shakespeare, T. S. Eliot, Dorothy Sayers, Flannery O'Connor, C. S. Lewis, and filmmaker Steven Spielberg.

She begins her defense of reading in the life of Christians by writing about the cornerstone of literature itself—the Word.[13] Following Michael Edwards, she develops a connection between God as the Word and the written word of literature.[14] Then in lucid prose she shows the importance of the creativity of the literary artist, literary representations of sin, hints and depictions of the need for redemption and the possibility of redemption, and the renewal of language begun on the Day of Pentecost. She uses examples from novels, short stories, and poems, as well as screenplays and plays to illustrate her argument. Although she said it more quietly, she set out clear reasons in support of the artistic discernment called for by Lovelace: "If we [evangelicals] do not set our own art free of moralistic overkill, we will lose our children again and again to the evangelizing force of non-Christian popular art."[15] Hers is a mature statement that is a long way from the code-morality, defensiveness, and chauvinism often present in her tradition.

Jim's interests led to courses in Shakespeare and other masterpieces of drama, as well as bread-and-butter composition and rhetoric classes. While a drama professor was on sabbatical leave, Jim directed a well-received performance of "Othello," complete with question and answer times after each performance with the cast (Desdemona revived quite well, thankfully). His and Twila's love of theatre led them every summer to Shakespeare festivals in Canada and the United States, reading in the car to one another and their son Craig, and tent-camping to save expenses. Often they led students on field trips to regional theatres to see professionals perform, and to churches

---

12. Edwards, "Place of Literature," 341–75. See the chapters by Michael Palmer, Jeff Hittenberger, and Barry Corey concerning historical development of Christian higher education.

13. Ibid., 340.

14. Michael Edwards, *Christian Poetics*, 217.

15. Lovelace, *Dynamics of Spiritual Life*, 347.

that were using drama and other fine arts to celebrate the gospel—in Chaucer's words, to "teach and delight."[16]

The Edwards were opposing in a mostly gentle way what Lovelace calls "socially conservative enculturation." They would agree with him that "[t]he church ought to be like a mobile sculpture in which fixed forms of truth and fellowship are constantly shifting their relationship to harmonize with the décor of the social and cultural environment. Enculturation freezes the form of the mobile until it becomes a static monument, a reminder of the past which appears to have no relevance for the present."[17] They believed with Lovelace that "[v]itality in the church of Christ gathers around centered groups of Christians who are interacting with one another . . . like cells or organs in a body."[18] They were exploring in their educational and church contexts how to change this enculturation in the direction of wholeness, while keeping the fervor of truth set on fire by the Spirit.

Jim did this in part by staying involved in an early-morning men's prayer meeting at Evangel Temple and a weekly prayer meeting with a few male faculty at the college. Twila was active in prayerful pastoral counseling with friends at church and especially female students at Evangel College. Both were active in coordinating an adult Sunday school class whose subject matter rotated between Scripture study and topical issues. To foster a community of "minded" if not like-minded Christian friends from various denominations, they started a Sunday evening reading circle. This group met for thirty years, and continues to meet in their absence to this day. Membership was always "whosoever will." The group would choose a novel, short story, poem, or anthology, members took turns reading aloud, and then they discussed. Food was always present along with gourmet coffee and tea. The location shifted among members' houses. Here was concrete Christian hospitality in action. They were also part of a movie group which met for some years to watch and discuss films. Summer tent-theatre and symphony concerts were also part of their integrative repertory. Teaching in Belgium and study tours in Europe and Israel enriched them and their students. They were always trying to demonstrate the congruence of Pentecostal spirituality and openness to the power of artistic expressions of truth.

Perhaps her greatest legacy, besides over twenty years of students most of whom will arise and call her blessed, is her project on women in ministry. Already in the early 1980s while chairperson of the Department of Biblical Studies and Philosophy, she organized a two-day colloquy on the

---

16. Paul Lewis comments on shared experiences in his essay.
17. Ibid., 197–98.
18. Ibid., 226.

role of women. Speakers lectured on the topic historically, biblically, and theologically from Protestant and Roman Catholic viewpoints. It made nary a splash, except in a few students and in Twila's own determination to dig deeper. She continued to read everything pertaining to the issue. Since she and Jim were a concrete example of an egalitarian marriage, she knew from experience that patriarchy in the home was not inevitable. Gradually she made herself an expert on the literature and issues, and decided to develop a syllabus for a seminar-style course. In a semester shared between Assemblies of God Theological Seminary students and Evangel College students, Barbara Cavaness (now Parks), a seminary professor, audited the class. Though Twila didn't write a book herself, Cavaness produced in many ways a distillation of Twila's formative work on the issues.[19] Her co-author Deborah Gill concentrated on the biblical/theological, and Cavaness on the historical/theological issues. Twila taught this course until her retirement in 2000.[20] Cavaness continues to teach it in Springfield, and in multiple locations around the world including Europe, Central and South America, and Asia. Already the book has been translated in several languages, so the historic position of the AG USA is being taught in missionary contexts.[21]

The late beloved church historian and ecumenist Gary B. McGee wrote concerning this book, "Pentecostalism owes a great debt of gratitude to the pioneering contributions of women preachers. Yet the fact that the Holy Spirit has been equally poured out on men and women still surprises many Christians. Gill and Cavaness provide an insightful biblical theology of women that is faithful to the test of Scripture and relevant for women in ministry in today's church."[22]

Perhaps it's no surprise to hear that Jim and Twila's push toward wholeness and excellence was not appreciated by all. Some saw them as pushy. To some they seemed elitist. And they themselves were not perfect in their attitudes or their way of expressing their ideas. Who of us is? On the other hand, they continued until their respective retirements to demonstrate in their work, as best they could, the Christian liberal arts ideal. They continued to call Evangel University and their church to the high ideals of an integrated and whole Christian life. This volume duly dedicated to them attests to their influence upon students, peers, scholars, and fellow congregants!

---

19. Gill and Cavaness, *God's Women*.
20. Martin Mittelstadt filled her position at Evangel University in 2000.
21. See further the contribution by Cavaness Parks to this volume.
22. Gary McGee, quoted in Gill and Cavaness, *God's Women*, 3.

Epilogue

Certainly one of their highest achievements is to have passed on to their son their Christian faith and educational ideals. Dr. Craig Edwards, also a PhD in English, currently serves as Associate Professor of Humanities at Indiana Wesleyan University in Marion, Indiana. (IWU is the largest member of the Council for Christian Colleges and Universities and the largest private university in Indiana). He is now another keeper of the flame on a bigger stage.

Twila moved "further up and further in" in 2011 after a long illness. Jim Edwards re-married in 2013 and now lives near Chicago with his new bride Patte, also a writer. They have several joint writing projects planned, working together toward the Edwards' lifelong themes.

BIBLIOGRAPHY

Edwards, James. "English Narrative Backgrounds to Edmund Spenser's The Faerie Queene." PhD diss., University of Missouri, 1972.

Edwards, Michael. *Towards a Christian Poetics*. Grand Rapids: Eerdmans, 1984.

Edwards, Twila. "What is Truth?" In *Essential Christianity: The Christian in Contemporary Society*, edited by Edward L. MacAlmon, 19–37. Springfield, MO: Evangel College Press, 1981.

Edwards, Twila Brown. "The Place of Literature in a Christian Worldview." In *Elements of a Christian Worldview*, edited by Michael D. Palmer, 341–75. Springfield, MO: Logion, 1998.

Gaebelein, Frank. "Education, Christian." In *The New International Dictionary of the Christian Church*, edited by J. D. Douglas, 330–33. Grand Rapids: Zondervan, 1978.

Gill, Deborah M. and Barbara Cavaness. *God's Women, Then and Now*. Springfield, MO: Grace & Truth, 2004.

Holmes, Arthur F. *The Idea of a Christian College*. Rev. ed. Grand Rapids: Eerdmans, 1987.

Lovelace, Richard F. *Dynamics of Spiritual Life*. Downers Grove, IL: InterVarsity, 1979.

Noll, Mark. *The Scandal of the Evangelical Mind*. Grand Rapids: Eerdmans, 1994.

Ortberg, John. *The Life You've Always Wanted*. Grand Rapids: Zondervan, 1997.

Trueman, Carl. *The Real Scandal of the Evangelical Mind*. Chicago: Moody, 2011.

HISTORICAL DEVELOPMENTS

2

Shaping Minds, Shaping Culture: The Story of Liberal Arts Education in the Middle Ages

MICHAEL PALMER

IN THE ANCIENT GRECO-ROMAN world the most prominent and influential schools were Plato's Academy, Aristotle's Lyceum, Zeno's Porch with the Painted Columns (Stoa), and Epicurus' Garden. Following the close of the last of these schools about 500 CE, educational institutions of similar prominence and influence—universities—did not emerge in the Christian West until the twelfth and thirteenth centuries. When they did emerge, their programs of study and the public proclamations of their leaders reflected the widely held belief that the liberal arts, the patrimony of antiquity, were central to their educational mission. In the words of one scholar, "The entire faculty structure, especially of the northern ecclesiastical universities, was based on the belief that the seven liberal arts were the foundation of all higher knowledge."[1] How did thirteenth-century universities, products of Christian Western Europe, come to embrace and champion a form of education whose origin in antiquity was pagan? And in what ways did the curriculum of the universities differ importantly from its medieval and classical antecedents? The answers to these questions lie in understanding the contributions of certain persons and institutions (including the monastic and cathedral schools) which sustained, perpetuated, and changed the liberal arts from the end of the classical period until the emergence of the first universities.

1. Leff, *Paris and Oxford Universities*, 118.

Christian Appropriation of the Liberal Arts

Beginning in late Antiquity and continuing throughout the Middle Ages, Christians in Western Europe organized the educational programs in their schools around the Roman system and curriculum of education, which in turn had its origin in the literature and liberal arts disciplines of the classical Greek world. Augustine (354–430), a master of the Latin language and teacher of rhetoric prior to his conversion to Christianity in 386 C.E., was the most prominent church leader of the period to urge broad Christian adoption of the Roman educational system. He did so not because he embraced the classical tradition uncritically—in many ways he was highly critical of it—but because he believed that its essential disciplines and content could serve the church. Drawing on the biblical imagery of the people of Israel taking whatever they needed as they fled Egyptian bondage, he urged Christians to "spoil the Egyptians." Christians, he believed, should appropriate from the pagan Greco-Roman tradition ("the Egyptians") whatever they found useful and disregard the rest. For Augustine, the useful elements of the classical tradition were those which fostered literacy in the church.[2]

Augustine's educational strategy had two related but distinct components. First, he believed that instruction in grammar and rhetoric should be foundational in the curriculum. This emphasis may well have reflected his professional background in rhetoric. But, if so, it also clearly spoke to the church's need for literate clergy and manuscript copyists. Second, he advocated providing instruction in the content of the liberal arts by way of compendia, easily read summaries of classical philosophical and literary works, which he believed were compatible with Christian doctrine. Whatever the merits of instruction in grammar and rhetoric—and they were substantial—the compendia and other short treatises which came into use were almost without exception pale substitutes for their classical antecedents. In any case, such was the force of Augustine's authority in the church that his educational strategy, built on a foundation of grammar and rhetoric and steeped in summaries of classical literature, profoundly impacted Christian education from the fifth to the eighth centuries.

The formal features of the liberal arts as well as their general content were not new in Augustine's time. But their number (seven) and arrangement were fixed by Martianus Capella, a fifth-century contemporary of Augustine. In a book entitled *The Marriage of Philology and Mercury*, which begins as an allegorical romance and ends as a didactic treatise on the liberal arts, Martianus divides the seven liberal arts into two groups, one consisting of three verbal or literary arts (grammar, rhetoric, and dialectic or logic),

---

2. Augustine, *On Christian Instruction*, 40.60–61.

the other consisting of four mathematical arts (arithmetic, music, geometry, and astronomy). Throughout the Middle Ages, these groupings were known respectively as the *trivium* and the *quadrivium*.

It is worth noting which disciplines Martianus did not count among the liberal arts and why. For instance, he specifically excluded medicine and law, because they were concerned with "earthly" things—or, as we might say, they were applied, not pure, sciences.[3] The distinction Martianus introduced held sway throughout the Middle Ages and eventually influenced the organization of European universities of the high medieval period. Specifically, medicine and law were not represented on the arts faculties of those universities, an organizational decision reflected even today in liberal arts colleges and universities.

Although Martianus fixed the number of liberal arts at seven and established the three-fold and four-fold groupings of arts, it was Anicius Manlius Severinus Boethius (ca. 480—ca. 526) who coined the term *quadrivium*. This term, meaning "four-fold path," was intended to capture the relation among the four mathematical disciplines. He interpreted them as "paths" because, as Boethius explained, they lead "from the senses . . . to the more certain things of the intelligence."[4] In the language of the Neoplatonic philosophy which influenced Boethius and many other medieval Christian intellectuals, the mathematical arts were believed to lead students from the realm of ever-changing, spatio-temporal objects to the realm of stable, enduring, intelligible (abstract or non-empirical) objects.[5]

Boethius's enduring influence on later medieval thinkers and educational curricula extended far beyond the way he framed the *quadrivium*. With his extensive knowledge of the Greek language and culture, Boethius, more than any other person, provided a bridge between the pagan Greco-Roman world of Antiquity and the Christian world of the high middle ages. Quite simply, he preserved a critical link to some of the most important works of the classical period in a time when that link could easily have been lost. For example, he preserved the connection to Plato and Aristotle, the two Greek intellectual luminaries of fourth century BCE. In Boethius's time, the Latin West had none of Plato's works except half of the *Timaeus* in a Latin version from Cicero; and it had virtually none of Aristotle's writings. Concerned that these seminal and irreplaceable works would be lost if they were not translated into Latin, Boethius set forth a breathtakingly ambitious plan to translate as many of them as possible and to write commentaries

---

3. Cantor, *Civilization in the Middle Ages*, 82.
4. Boethius, *Principles of Arithmetic*, 1.1.7, quoted in Marenbon, *Boethius*, 14.
5. Marenbon, *Boethius*, 14–16.

on all of Aristotle's works.⁶ Unfortunately, his ambitious plans were cut short by his imprisonment and execution.⁷ Still, during his relatively short life, he succeeded in translating at least two of Aristotle's logical works, *Categories* and *On Interpretation*, as well as the *Isagoge* by the Neoplatonist philosopher Porphyry, a work which functioned as a preface to Aristotle's logical writings. He also wrote a commentary on the *Categories*, two on *On Interpretation*, and two on Porphyry's *Isagoge*. Until the twelfth century, it is principally through these works that Western Christian scholars knew Aristotle.

Boethius, however, was much more than a Latin translator and commentator. He was also an original thinker who authored philosophical and theological works which engaged the imagination of subsequent generations of students and intellectuals. In the spirit of the "four-fold path" which formed the *quadrivium*, he wrote works on arithmetic (*De institutione arithmetica*) and music theory (*De institutione musica*), and is reported to have written on geometry and astronomy, though these works, if they ever existed, no longer survive. In what were his last years, he completed four theological tractates, collectively known as the *Opuscula sacra*, and two theological treatises, *De fide catholica* and *De disciplina scholarium*.⁸

The *Consolation of Philosophy*, written during Boethius's imprisonment while awaiting execution, is unquestionably his most important philosophical work. Medievalist scholar Ralph McInerny says, "What lifts Boethius to the front rank of cultural and literary importance is the *Consolation of Philosophy*." Without the *Consolation*, Boethius would remain a central bridge between the Greco-Roman world of Antiquity and the Medieval Latin West, and an important contributor to theological conversations. But the *Consolation*, says McInerny, "crowns his achievement."⁹

Boethius's influence on later medieval thinkers and Western educational curricula can hardly be exaggerated.¹⁰ John Marenbon describes it as immense: "Only Aristotle and Augustine had so great a direct influence over so wide a range of intellectual life."¹¹ Boethius's *Consolation*, *De musica*, and *De arithmetica* were widely available, housed in all of the important libraries in medieval Europe.¹² Empirical research on manuscripts demonstrates that

---

6. McInerny, *Boethius and Aquinas*, 3.
7. Moorhead, "Boethius's Life," 18.
8. McInerny, *Boethius*, 4.
9. Ibid., 14.
10. Marenbon, *Boethius*, 164–82.
11. Ibid., 164.
12. Patch, *Tradition of Boethius*, 21.

these three writings of Boethius were not only available but were comparable to the Bible and the works of Augustine in terms of the total number of copies, their age, and completeness.[13] Boethius was read, quoted, and commented on from shortly after his death until the high Middle Ages. As early as the sixth century, not long after the *Consolation* appeared, Boethius's contemporary, Cassiodorus, produced a learned edition which included Greek rhetorical glosses.[14] Seven hundred years later, Thomas Aquinas, the great Italian theologian of the thirteenth century, mentioned Boethius by name one hundred thirty-five times in his *Summa theologica*.[15] Undoubtedly the most acclaimed assessment of Boethius's contribution both as a mediator of the liberal arts and classical literature of Antiquity and as an original thinker in his own right, is the one offered by Lorenzo Valla, the fifteenth century Italian humanist, rhetorician, and educator, who described Boethius as the "[l]ast of the Romans, first of the scholastics."[16]

Monastic Schools

In 529, by the decree of Justinian the Great (the Byzantine Emperor), pagan schools were closed. This development left an educational gap which could not be, and was not, filled by the Church's episcopal schools, which were supervised and controlled by bishops in various cities and whose primary function was to prepare clergy for vocational service in the Church. Monastic schools gradually emerged as the Church's chief educational centers and principal expressions of its educational values.

The monastic schools grew out of monasticism, which began as a spiritual movement and evolved into an institution and form of community life.[17] As a spiritual movement, monasticism was initially inspired by the desert fathers of Egypt, men who gave themselves to prayer and lived an ascetic life, often in the extreme. As an institution and form of community life, monasticism was indebted to men such as John Cassian (ca. 360–435), an educated Christian, whose spiritual quest led him for a time to the Egyptian desert. Later, about 400, while in Rome, Cassian accepted an invitation to establish an Egyptian-style monastery in France, near Marseilles. The product of his effort, known as the Abbey of St. Victor, was a complex of

---

13. James Collins, "Progress and Problems," 8.
14. Marenbon, *Boethius*, 173.
15. McInerny, *Boethius*, 10.
16. Quoted in Chadwick, *Boethius: Consolations*, x.
17. Graves. *History of Education*, 4–9.

monasteries for both men and women. One of the first such institutions in Europe, it served as a model for later monastic development.

Christians who abandoned their families and homes in towns and cities to pursue the ascetic life in the deserts, often lived in isolation and solitude. In this sense they were true monks. (The word 'monk' derives from the Greek *monos*, meaning "alone.") But the monks who inhabited the Abbey of St. Victor and other similar institutions established throughout Western Europe during the Middle Ages were hardly loners; they lived in communities. Community life required guidelines for personal conduct and regulations for governing social interaction. In the sixth century, Benedict of Nursia (c. 480–547) addressed the need by writing a book of precepts for monks living in community under the authority of an abbot. The Rule of Benedict, as it was known, came to be regarded as an exemplar of balance and moderation. As a result, this Rule, which was originally intended to govern only a local community, was eventually adopted by most religious communities—monks as well as nuns—established in the Middle Ages.[18]

In Chapter 48 of the Rule, Benedict speaks to the care of books and even mentions a "library." It is not clear whether this term originally referred to a room specifically set aside to store books or to the monastery's cloister, the covered passage that bounded the central courtyard, where books would be easily available to the monks. In any case, as collections grew, special rooms were designated as libraries, and some monastic communities appointed a specific person to care for the library and the books. A few communities even allowed outsiders to borrow books.

Monastic libraries were always limited in two ways: the types of books they collected and the total number of books in the collection. Monks needed to be able to read in order to study the Scriptures, to write in order to copy manuscripts, and to calculate in order to ascertain the dates for Church festivals. Because reading, writing, and computing were essential pathways toward and expressions of study, monasteries became repositories of literature deemed important for transmitting the knowledge and skills associated with general literacy, including works on grammar, style, and elementary arithmetic. The writings of Boethius and Martianus Capella would have appeared in many, perhaps most, monastic libraries. Consistent with their mission of training monks, monasteries also collected books suited to nurturing religious, spiritual, and moral formation, including the Bible, theological tractates, the writings of Church fathers, and works on psalmody. They contained only rudimentary resources on other subjects, and seldom anything in languages other than Latin. The size of most collections was

18. Ibid., 9–10.

also quite small. Most monastic libraries held only a few hundred volumes. A few held one or two thousand. The monastic library at Novalese in Italy was the exception that proved the rule; by the tenth century when it was destroyed by fire, it is reported to have held sixty-five hundred volumes.[19]

What did education look like in medieval monasteries? First and foremost, its central purpose was to make monks. Through the rigorous discipline of the ascetic life, all aspects of monastic life aimed at instilling three monastic ideals: obedience, chastity, and poverty. Everyone who aspired to become a monk took a solemn vow to live by these ideals, and community life in the monastery was designed to inculcate and reinforce them.

Compared to the emphasis placed on submitting to the discipline of the ascetic life and embracing the three monastic ideals, educating the intellect had relatively low priority. But it did have some importance. Indeed, for the Benedictines and other orders of monks and nuns which adopted it, the Rule of Benedict established patterns not only of prayer and work but also of study.[20] The foundational portion of the curriculum roughly reflected the secular disciplines of the seven liberal arts, organized according to the *trivium* and the *quadrivium*. But the attention given to the various disciplines was uneven. For example, in the *trivium*, most monastery schools for much of the Middle Ages devoted more attention to grammar and rhetoric than to dialectic (logic).[21] This general emphasis, which is consistent with the need to be conversant with the Latin language and literature, changed only in the twelfth century with the rise of Scholasticism, which placed high value on the cogency of arguments and therefore gave preference to the study of logic. Similar unevenness is evident in the treatment of the disciplines comprising the *quadrivium*. Until the late tenth century when the Arabic system of computation was introduced, instruction in arithmetic was rudimentary, often consisting of little more than teaching students how to compute the dates associated with the liturgical calendar. Relatively more attention was devoted to music. But here, too, for much of the Middle Ages instruction in music centered on sacred compositions and only in the eleventh century did it begin to give more attention to the history and theory of music. Summarizing the status of the *quadrivium*, one historian says, "[B]etween 600 and 1000 the *quadrivium* was in eclipse as an educational syllabus, and was either omitted altogether or treated simply in a brief, factual way."[22]

19. Ibid., 10–12.
20. Gies and Gies, *Women in the Middle Ages*, 70.
21. Knowles, *Evolution of Medieval Thought*, 68.
22. Ibid., 68.

In the classical world, education in the liberal arts aimed at preparing young adults (usually the sons of aristocrats) to participate in public life as free, responsible citizens. For monks in the Middle Ages, education in the liberal arts did not generally serve this purpose. In the first place, monks aspired to ideals (obedience, chastity, and poverty) which differed markedly from, sometimes even clashed with, the ideals of citizens in the classical world (allegiance to the city/state, care of family, and provision for the future).[23] The respective ideals represent importantly different answers to how one ought to orient one's life. In the classical world, education in the liberal arts might prepare one to deliver a public oration, to think imaginatively about the meaning of images in poems, or to reason incisively about arguments. By contrast, medieval monks viewed liberal arts education as foundational for the study of theology.

Although there is good reason to exercise caution in applying the term "dark ages" to all or part of the Middle Ages, the seventh and eighth centuries come closest to deserving the appellation. Except in a few monasteries, educational and literary activity waned almost to the point of extinction during this period. "Public schools had long since ceased to be, and the study of letters was preserved only in monasteries and a few bishops' households; the enlightened bishops were in most cases themselves monks."[24] In the midst of this intellectual darkness, King Charles the Great—Charlemagne (742–814)—seeing the need for a better-educated clergy and aristocracy, issued an edict in 789, *Admonitio Generalis*, calling for schools to be established: "In every bishop's see, and in every monastery, instruction shall be given in the psalms, musical notation, chant, the composition of years and seasons, and in grammar, and all books shall be carefully corrected."[25] Documents issued later by Charlemagne reinforced and elaborated on the directives set forth in the edict of 789.[26]

Charlemagne's directives had two main effects on monasteries. First, they gave new life and technique to the monastic tradition of copying manuscripts. The minimal literacy of monks had, over time, generally yielded inferior quality in the copying of books. Working in the service of Charlemagne, English scholar Alcuin (ca. 735–804)[27] set up excellent *scriptoria* in many locations and established rigorous standards of accuracy as

---

23. Graves, *History of Education*, 14.

24. Knowles, *Evolution of Medieval Thought*, 85.

25. *Capitularia regum francorum*, quoted in Knowles, *Evolution of Medieval Thought*, 66.

26. Riché, *Daily Life*, 192.

27. Dales, *Alcuin*. See especially chapter 6.

well as a new script style (the so-called Carolingian minuscule) for copying manuscripts. "With Alcuin began the great age of the copying of Latin manuscripts."[28]

Second, Charlemagne's directives led to the establishment of two educational tracks in monasteries. According to a plan on which Charlemagne and Alcuin agreed, one track was designed for boys (some as young as eight or ten) who intended to enter a monastic order. They might already be living in the monastery where they would be educated, or they might come from a less well-equipped neighboring monastery. In either case, because they were preparing to enter a monastic order, they were called the *oblati* ("those offered"). Later, a second track was established for boys and young men who did not plan to enter an order but who did plan to become clerks. They were educated by the monks but were called *externi* ("outsiders"). Apart from monks and clerks, few would have received any formal education during the Carolingian period.[29]

Monasteries, ever-present institutions throughout the Middle Ages, developed and flourished in the wake of Charlemagne's directive of 789. Under Alcuin's supervision, they perpetuated the important tradition of copying manuscripts and in some cases emerged as important centers of learning. The Benedictine abbey in Fulda (in present-day Germany) exemplified all of these features. Founded in 744, thus pre-dating Charlemagne and Alcuin, it eventually gained attention for its *scriptorium*, which was an important center for copying manuscripts. The abbey's school, open not only to theological students but also to young men pursuing secular careers, became a prominent center of learning, and was celebrated throughout Europe. Fulda's curriculum included the core subjects usually taught during the Middle Ages: the seven liberal arts. But it included other subjects as well, including the different branches of theology and the German language. Its library, unlike the preponderance of monastery libraries, included both religious and classical literature.[30] Although the educational success of Fulda was replicated in a few other monasteries across Europe, the educational opportunities available in most monasteries were much more modest, partly due to insufficient resources, partly due to a paucity of qualified teachers, and partly due to the abbots' lack of vision. In any case, the prominence of monasteries as educational centers in Western Europe declined in the twelfth century with the emergence of universities.

28. Knowles, *Evolution of Medieval Thought*, 69.
29. Thompson, *Literacy of the Laity*, 27–52.
30. Lins, "Fulda."

Cathedral Schools

Cathedral schools began in the Early Middle Ages at roughly the same time as the monastic schools and served complementary, sometimes overlapping purposes. Like the monastic schools, which functioned under the authority of an abbot, cathedral schools, which functioned under the authority of a bishop, served as educational centers. Also, like monastic schools, cathedral schools provided basic literary and theological education. Finally, like monastic schools, the primary emphasis of cathedral schools was not academic but vocational: their purpose was to prepare men and women to serve the Church.

An early (perhaps the first) cathedral school of the sort described was the school chartered in Spain during the second quarter of the sixth century. In 527 the Second Council of Toledo approved several canons (authoritative decrees) referring to a bishop's seminary, which was attached to the cathedral.[31] During the remainder of the sixth century and continuing into seventh century, more than twenty cathedral schools came into existence in Spain and Gaul (France).[32]

Although their primary educational mission was to prepare men (and some women) to fill vocational roles in the church, cathedral schools gradually evolved to serve a wider constituency, people who wanted to prepare themselves not for clerical roles but for secular professions. Leander (ca. 534–600), while bishop of Seville, was the first to envision a cathedral-affiliated school for teaching the liberal arts. He himself supervised the teachers. Among his first students was his brother Isidore (560–636), who later became the Archbishop of Seville. Building on Leander's initial idea, Isidore expanded the curriculum, augmenting the liberal arts with courses of study in languages (Latin, Greek, and Hebrew), law, and medicine. In 633, he presided over the fourth Council of Toledo, at which all of the bishops of Spain were directed to establish schools modeled after the one in Seville.[33]

Despite Isidore's vision for expanding the curriculum to include professional studies, most cathedral schools continued to devote their primary attention to preparing men for vocational work in the Church. Moreover, even though the education these schools provided included instruction in the liberal arts, the pedagogical techniques of the teachers more often than not were anything but liberating. The regimen of study typically emphasized rote memory and recitation of ideas received from ancient authorities.

---

31. Riché, *Daily Life*, 126.
32. Ibid., 282–90.
33. Drane, *Christian Schools and Scholars*, 14.

Among the arts, grammar and style were routinely emphasized over dialectic. The prevailing mode of instruction offered little that exercised the imagination or promoted critical, integrative, or analytical thinking. Apart from the broader and more intensive educational opportunities provided by a few bishops (sometimes in their homes, sometimes in their churches) and at a few monasteries, this state of intellectual "darkness" continued during most of the seventh and eighth centuries. It changed only with the reforms mandated by Charlemagne in the late eighth century.[34]

By the eleventh century, cathedral schools existed in several important cities in Western Europe. In general, they continued the traditional practice of preparing clergy. However, some of them—including those at Orleans, Paris, Laon, Liege, Rheims, Rouen, and Utrecht—developed into prominent educational centers, attracting great scholars and offering advanced courses of study in mathematics, theology, and logic. The foundational teaching in cathedral schools during this period remained, as it had for centuries, centered on the traditional seven liberal arts. There were, however, differences among the schools on the emphasis given for each subject. For example, the school situated in Chartres, a small cathedral town about fifty miles southwest of Paris, emphasized the mathematical arts of the *quadrivium* and natural philosophy.[35]

Indeed, during the eleventh and twelfth centuries—just before the rise of the universities, which ultimately eclipsed cathedral schools and monastic schools as the most important institutions of higher learning in Western Europe—the school in Chartres became one of the most celebrated and influential of all the cathedral schools. The school's reputation as a center of learning began in the late tenth century under the leadership of Bishop Fulbert, who arrived in Chartres about 990 and who was known as an advocate of the liberal arts. In a poem, his protégé, Adelman of Liège, praised the Bishop, saying "You explained the secrets of higher learning!" A later commentator noted that the Bishop was "proclaimed throughout Francia for his preeminence in the liberal arts."[36] At his death in April, 1038, Fulbert's obituary described him as "a man most eloquent and wise both in the sacred books and in those of the liberal arts."[37]

What did it mean to say that Bishop Fulbert was "wise ... in the liberal arts"? To begin with, it did not mean that he knew Greek, or at least it did

34. Knowles, *Evolution of Medieval Thought*, 65–71.
35. Jeauneau, *Rethinking the School of Chartres*, 31.
36. David Wagner holds this widely held assessment of Chartres's status. See his "Seven Liberal Arts" 1–31. Southern argues against the traditional assessment of Chartres' status in "Humanism and the School of Chartres," 61–85.
37. MacKinney, *Bishop Fulbert*, 37.

not mean he knew it well. According to Fulbert himself, he learned the language of Virgil (Latin) not the language of Homer (Greek).[38] It also did not mean that he had anything approximating a first-hand acquaintance with the primary texts of classical thinkers such as Plato. While it is possible that Fulbert was aware of Cicero's Latin version of Plato's *Timaeus*, there is no evidence in his extant writings that he read it.

Fulbert's lack of familiarity with texts from the classical Greek period was not due simply to the fact that he was not fluent in Greek. In general, writings of the ancient Greeks were unavailable to Western European scholars in the eleventh century and would not become available to them until the twelfth century. Much of what Fulbert could have learned about the classical philosophers came from three widely available Latin works: Martianus Capella's *Marriage of Philology and Mercury*; Macrobius's commentary on Cicero's *Dream of Scipio*; and Boethius's *Consolation of Philosophy*. But here again Fulbert's extant writings contain no mention of these works. What his writings demonstrate clearly, and what those who knew him confirm, is that he was "a man of culture who wrote elegant Latin, both in prose and in verse."[39] He also is credited with being "in touch with the latest developments in the sciences of logic, arithmetic, and astronomy . . . and he wrote poems to familiarize his pupils with the processes of calculation and the Arabic names of the stars just coming into fashion."[40]

As a result of the foundation laid by Bishop Fulbert, the cathedral school at Chartres attracted gifted students and scholars during the first half of the twelfth century. Among the scholars was William of Conches (ca. 1090—after 1154), a philosopher whose interests ranged from the classics to empirical science, and later John of Salisbury (ca. 1120–1180), author, diplomat, eventually bishop of Chartres, and an eloquent spokesmen for one of the primary educational doctrines of western civilization: namely, that the goal of education is not primarily intellectual, but first and foremost moral. Schools, he believed, should provide instruction in the liberal arts and traditional morality with the aim of preparing people both to live virtuous lives and to resist the corrupting effects of economic and political forces and emerging intellectual trends.[41]

Most notably, the school at Chartres benefited during the first half of the twelfth century from the exceptional leadership of three chancellors: Bernard of Chartres (died ca. 1130), philosopher and humanist, who became

---

38. Jeauneau, *Rethinking the School of Chartres*, 32.
39. Ibid., 33.
40. Southern, *Making of the Middle Ages*, 201.
41. Cantor, *Civilization in the Middle Ages*, 325–26.

one of the principal representatives of twelfth-century Platonism; Gilbert of Poitiers (ca. 1075-1154), theologian and logician; and Bernard's brother, Thierry of Chartres (ca. 1100-ca. 1150), theologian and encyclopedist. Active participants in the conversation which led to what is now referred to as the twelfth-century renaissance, all of these intellectuals helped launch Scholasticism, the intellectual movement which came to dominate learned discourse during thirteenth and early fourteenth centuries.[42]

The school of Chartres reached its zenith during the first half of the twelfth century. Over the next fifty years its influence gradually waned for three main reasons. First, being affiliated with a cathedral and therefore falling under the control of a bishop, the school offered relatively less autonomy for scholars than was afforded them in the schools of Paris. Second, the school's reputation for scholarly excellence was achieved not because of, but rather in spite of (or at least in addition to), its primary mission: to prepare young men for the priesthood. Over the long term, and without the visionary leadership of its three most distinguished chancellors, the school's masters failed to integrate the school's vocational mission with its role in sponsoring outstanding scholarship. Finally, the school, which never enrolled large numbers of students, suffered from being located in Chartres. A small city—a town, really—Chartres simply could not support the number of students that the much larger Paris could support. By the end of the twelfth century the cathedral school at Chartres was eclipsed by the newly emerging University of Paris.

Universities

The word "university" does not seem to have been used before the thirteenth century.[43] In the twelfth century, institutions of higher learning were known by the purely descriptive appellation *studium generale*, meaning simply a place of learning for students from anywhere; i.e., not limited to local students. Near the close of the twelfth century, the term came to have a more determinant meaning, referring to those institutions which had not only an arts faculty but also a faculty in one or more advanced field of study: theology, law, or medicine; and in which a large but unspecified number of masters (professors) instructed students. In about 1200 another expression gained currency: *jus ubique docendi*, referring to the right of a master, who had taught and was registered in the Guild of Masters of a *studium generale*, to teach in any other *studium* without further examination. For a time, this

---

42. McInerny, *History of Western Philosophy Vol. II*.
43. Haskins, *Renaissance of the Twelfth Century*, 381.

privilege was granted only to masters of the oldest universities: Salerno, Bologna, and Paris. But by 1233 the pope began to grant the privilege to masters from other universities, probably as a means of elevating the prestige of those universities. He also reserved for himself the exclusive right to confer this privilege on universities. Gradually, these four features—a student body not limited to a local jurisdiction, one or more higher faculties, teaching by masters, and the right of masters to teach in other *studia*—emerged as primary distinguishing traits in most medieval universities. In other respects they might differ, but these features were both common and normative.[44]

Among medieval institutions of higher learning, the *studium* which emerged at Paris in the middle of the twelfth century was unquestionably one of the two or three greatest. In the High Middle Ages, only Bologna and Oxford were its near equals. Paris was also distinctive in certain respects. For one thing, its genealogy was distinctive: it grew directly out of the cathedral school of Notre Dame under the leadership of a chancellor representing the bishop of Paris.[45] While many medieval European universities—certainly most of those north of the Alps—had strong ecclesial connections, most were not the offspring of cathedral schools. Oxford, for example, was not.[46] Nor were the two earliest Italian institutions: Salerno in southern Italy and Bologna in northern Italy. Salerno, following its own historical trajectory as a center for the healing arts, developed into a prominent professional school, and later into a university, dedicated to the study of medicine.[47] The university at Bologna, with its historical interest in Roman civil law, became known for its law curriculum.[48] Given Paris' distinctive genealogy, it is not surprising that it developed an advanced program in theology.

Despite its distinctive history and focus on the advanced study of theology, Paris was similar to other universities in the way it adapted and modified the traditional liberal arts curriculum. In the twelfth century, the core arts curriculum in the universities, including Paris, was organized, at least superficially, to resemble what was taught in monastic and cathedral schools. Moreover, as late as the first quarter of the thirteenth century the liberal arts as traditionally understood still received public acclaim. Some of Paris' chancellors favorably compared the seven liberal arts with the gifts of the Holy Spirit.[49] Moreover, all seven of the arts, but especially those

44. Knowles, *Evolution of Medieval Thought*, 139–40, 148–49.
45. Leff, *Paris and Oxford Universities*, 15.
46. Ibid., 76.
47. Cantor, *Civilization in the Middle Ages*, 310.
48. Knowles, *Evolution of Medieval Thought*, 140.
49. Leff, *Paris and Oxford Universities*, 118.

comprising the *trivium*, were held forth as essential preparation for the study of theology: "The sword of God is forged by grammar, sharpened by logic, and burnished by rhetoric, but only theology can use it."[50] But honorific acclamations such as these aside, the universities from the beginning, gradually but also steadily and irrevocably, changed both the purpose and content of the arts curriculum. Its purpose was no longer primarily to undergird the vocational training of clerics and monks, but to prepare students for advanced academic studies in theology, law, and medicine. As a result, more emphasis was placed on disciplines which had a direct bearing on preparing students for these advanced studies. In particular, grammar and rhetoric waned in importance and dialectic soared. The *quadrivium*, as traditionally understood, virtually disappeared, eclipsed by other disciplines, especially philosophy.

How and why did these changes occur? The answers to both parts of this question lay not so much in the universities themselves as in the larger cultural and intellectual trends to which the universities were responding. These trends may be traced to the early years of the twelfth century. Prior to 1100, scholars interested in classical logic and philosophy had access to limited resources. Prominent among them were Boethius's translations of Aristotle's *Categories* and *On Interpretation*, his commentaries on these writings, and his translation of the Porphyry's *Isagoge*. After 1100 the situation changed dramatically. Western European scholars began to encounter ancient writings in Syria, Constantinople, Sicily, and Spain. Of these sites, Spain was by far the most fruitful for gaining access to the Aristotelian corpus.[51] Libraries in Spain contained logical treatises by Aristotle which had not been translated by Boethius (or, if translated, had been lost). By the middle decades of the twelfth century, the full complement of Aristotle's logical works became available to scholars in European universities. (The logical works translated by Boethius came to be referred to as the "Old Logic" and the newly recovered ones, the "New Logic.") Libraries in Spain also contained Aristotle's philosophical works, translations of which appeared in European universities gradually over the next century. Finally, the libraries in Spain gave European scholars access to the writings of Islamic and Jewish philosophers, who were both well-acquainted with Aristotle's works and had written sophisticated commentaries on them. So profound was the impact of Aristotle's thought on European intellectuals that Aristotle came to be known simply as "the philosopher."

50. Haskins, *Studies in Mediaeval Culture*, 44–46.
51. Haskins, *Studies in the History of Mediaeval Science*, 5.

Access to Aristotle's writings had two related but distinct effects on twelfth and thirteenth century intellectual trends in general and on the curricula of medieval universities in particular. First, his New Logic accelerated interest in the study and practice of dialectical as a method for conducting inquiry. Indeed, the recovery of these texts proved decisive in thrusting dialectic into a central, even dominant, role in the liberal arts curriculum of the new universities. It was regarded as essential preparation for all higher studies.[52]

The New Logic also had a significant impact on Scholasticism, the method of inquiry which employed dialectical reasoning to extend knowledge by inference and to resolve contradictory theses concerning disputed issues.[53] The New Logic did not give rise to Scholasticism. Anselm of Canterbury (1033–1109), sometimes called the Father of Scholasticism, predated the New Logic. But it unquestionably accelerated and intensified the practice of the Scholasticism, which was used by several generations of medieval intellectuals, among them Peter Abelard, Albert the Great, Bonaventure, Thomas Aquinas, John Duns Scotus, and William of Ockham.

Aristotle's major philosophical treatises—including *Metaphysics*, *Physics*, *On the Soul*, *Nicomachean Ethics*, and *Politics*—attracted attention in European universities somewhat later than did his logical works. Studied in the second half of the twelfth century mainly by a few curious scholars, the impact of his philosophical works on medieval intellectual life intensified when some of the masters of arts at Paris, and theologians there and elsewhere began to use them in their classes, public lectures, and academic disputations. For a time, the philosophical writings were viewed with suspicion. In Paris, first in 1210 and again in 1215, the arts faculty was banned from teaching them or lecturing publically on them. Several concerns motivated the ban. Aristotle was a pagan, not a Christian. His writings seemed to conflict at key points with doctrinal teachings dating back to Augustine. Recovered in the West mainly through once-Islamic-controlled Spain, Aristotle's works had been extensively (and favorably) commented on by Islamic scholars like Averroes. This fact made Aristotle suspect in the eyes of conservative Christian theologians. Finally, by the time Aristotle's philosophical treatises became available in European universities, church leaders were already more than a little uncomfortable with the impact of Aristotle's New Logic on the teaching of theology. Whereas the content of theology

---

52. Knowles, *Evolution of Medieval Thought*, 172.
53. See Turner, "Scholasticism."

was sacramental and moral, scholars using the New Logic had made it a subject of metaphysical and speculative dispute.[54]

Despite the misgivings of conservative academic leaders and church officials, and despite the off-and-on enforcement of the ban, teachers and students avidly engaged Aristotle's philosophical works throughout the thirteenth century. The effects of his writings on scholarly discussions were profound, as seen for instance in the epoch-making works of Aquinas.

Aristotle's philosophical writings also stood at the center of fundamental changes in the arts curriculum of universities. During the thirteenth century, philosophy stood front and center in the arts curriculum, rivaling dialectic and completely eclipsing rhetoric, grammar, and the *quadrivium*. As Gordon Leff observes, "By the time we read the first syllabus for Paris in Robert de Courçon's statutes of 1215, dialectic and philosophy had virtually displaced all the other liberal arts."[55]

Beginning in the second half of the twelfth century, universities gradually institutionalized higher education. This means that, far beyond anything done by the monastic and cathedral schools, the universities integrated the academic disciplines into a structured system. They established a governance process, made teaching a profession by examining and licensing masters, and determined academic terms.[56] They established a core arts curriculum, which differed importantly in content from the arts curriculum in the monastic and cathedral schools. They accommodated change and dramatic growth in the cumulative knowledge base (Aristotle's corpus, but much more as well) and adapted to new ways of expressing knowledge (e.g., Aristotle's New Logic). Finally, they prepared men (not women) for the professions.

To be sure, universities were not always the principal drivers of institutionalization. For example, the extensive use of dialectic was largely driven by social factors such as the desire by young men to pursue lucrative careers in law. Nevertheless, by institutionalizing education in the ways they did, universities came to dominate education from the thirteenth century onward. As Leff eloquently summarizes, "Whereas in the twelfth century an independent master could set up a school and take pupils, and a cathedral school like Chartres or Laon could dominate the study of philosophy or the Bible, in the thirteenth century this was not possible."[57] Monastic and cathedral schools continued to exist in the thirteenth century but their role

---

54. Leff, *Paris and Oxford Universities*, 187–270.
55. Ibid., 118–19.
56. Ibid., 182–84.
57. Ibid., 117–18.

was much diminished, not only in comparison to their former roles but especially in comparison to the universities. In the final analysis, the universities collectively came to represent the greatest intellectual heritage of the Middle Ages.[58]

Conclusion

Some of the deficiencies of education during the Middle Ages are obvious. From their inception, the monastic and cathedral schools mostly delivered limited content using a pedagogical method which relied heavily on rote memorization and recitation, and did little to inspire confidence that exposure to the arts would liberate the mind of the learner. Even in the twelfth and thirteenth centuries, when dialectic prevailed and the writings of Aristotle and other great intellectuals from Antiquity were becoming available, education in the universities continued to be limited in content, narrow in focus, and often dogmatic. Its most prominent disputes were almost all metaphysical or religious. Research was limited to the study of books, religious arguments involved appeals to authority, and empirical data were given little attention. If the purpose of liberal education is to nurture in the learner an attitude of attention to the object of study, then a case can be made (with only slight hyperbole) that the architects and craftsmen who built the cathedrals, and the shipwrights and mariners who built and sailed ships, engaged the empirical world with a more open and teachable posture than did the scholars in the universities of the twelfth and thirteenth centuries.

Throughout the Middle Ages, education in the liberal arts was subordinated to other purposes. In the monastic and cathedral schools, arts education was aimed at preparing learners to study theology and eventually to enter into vocational ministry. Later the liberal arts (different arts, as it turned out) were treated as preparation for professional training and a career. John of Salisbury was one of a few medieval educators and church leaders to advance a different view, arguing that the goal of education is first and foremost moral: the proper end of education is to shape not just the mind but the character of the learner. But this view, largely unrecognized in medieval educational institutions, appeared among Italian humanists in the fifteenth century. For them, the liberal arts should be viewed not as preparation for advanced studies but rather as the main concern of any educational institution.[59]

58. Knowles, *Evolution of Medieval Thought*, 159–60.
59. Cantor, *Civilization in the Middle Ages*, 560.

Deficiencies, though prevalent during the Middle Ages, are not the most enduring legacy of medieval education. In the monasteries, many unsung men and women learned what was available to learn and then devoted their lives to copying manuscripts. Their dedication to acquiring an education (rudimentary as it was) and to copying manuscripts preserved the Bible and much else for future generations. And the universities, despite their tendency to foster seemingly endless speculative disputations and despite their diffidence toward empirical inquiry, nurtured a climate of intellectual rigor, attention to detail, and willingness to set aside appeals to authority which eventually proved essential for advances in the empirical science (Copernicus, Galileo), the literary arts (Dante, Boccaccio), and theological studies (Wycliffe, Huss). Finally, universities became the places where difficult questions could be explored, disputed, and arbitrated.

BIBLIOGRAPHY

Chadwick, Henry. *Boethius: The Consolations of Music, Logic, Theology, and Philosophy.* Oxford: Oxford University Press, 1981.
Cantor, Norman F. *Civilization in the Middle Ages.* New York: HarperCollins, 1993.
Collins, James. "Progress and Problems in the Reassessment of Boethius." *Modern Schoolman* 33 (1945) 1–23.
Dales, Douglas. *Alcuin: His Life and Legacy.* Cambridge: James Clarke, 2012.
Drane, Frances Raphael. *Christian Schools and Scholars.* Edited by Walter Gumbly. New York: Benziger Brothers, 1924.
Gies, Joseph, and Frances Gies. *Women in the Middle Ages.* Reprint. New York: HarperPerennial, 1991.
Haskins, Charles H. *The Renaissance of the Twelfth Century.* New York: Meridian, 1957.
———. *Studies in Mediaeval Culture.* Oxford: Clarendon, 1929.
———. *Studies in the History of Mediaeval Science.* 2nd ed. Cambridge: Harvard University Press, 1927.
Jeauneau, Edouard. *Rethinking the School of Chartres.* Translated by Claude Paul Desmalrais. Toronto: University of Toronto Press, 2009.
Knowles, David. *The Evolution of Medieval Thought.* 2nd ed. Essex: Longman Group, 1988.
Leff, Gordon. *Paris and Oxford Universities in the Thirteenth and Fourteenth Centuries: An Institutional and Intellectual History.* New York: John Wiley & Sons, 1968.
Lins, Joseph. "Fulda." In *The Catholic Encyclopedia.* New York: Robert Appleton Company, 1912. Online: http://www.newadvent.org/cathen/06313b.htm.
MacKinney, Loren C. *Bishop Fulbert and Education at the School of Chartres.* Notre Dame, IN: The Mediaeval Institute, University of Notre Dame, 1957.
McInerny, Ralph. *Boethius and Aquinas.* Washington, DC: The Catholic University of America Press, 1990.
———. *A History of Western Philosophy Vol. II.* University of Notre Dame Press 1963. Online: www3.nd.edu/Departments/Maritain/etext/hwp.htm#II.
Marenbon, John. *Boethius.* New York: Oxford University Press, 2003.

Moorhead, John. "Boethius's Life and the World of Late Antique Philosophy." In *Cambridge Companion to Boethius*, edited by John Marenbon, 18–22. New York: Cambridge University Press, 2009.

Patch, Howard. *The Tradition of Boethius: A Study of His Importance in Medieval Culture*. New York: Oxford University Press, 1935.

Riché, Pierre. *Daily Life in the World of Charlemagne*. Philadelphia: University of Pennsylvania Press, 1978.

Southern, Richard W. "Humanism and the School of Chartres." In *Medieval Humanism*, 61–85. New York: Harper & Row, 1970.

———. *The Making of the Middle Ages*. London: Hutchinson, 1933.

Thompson, James W. *The Literacy of the Laity in the Middle Ages*. New York: Burt Franklin, 1963.

Turner, William. "Scholasticism." In *The Catholic Encyclopedia*. New York: Robert Appleton Company, 1912. Online: www.newadvent.org/cathen/13548a.htm.

Wagner, David. "The Seven Liberal Arts and Classical Scholarship." In *The Seven Liberal Arts in the Middle Ages*, edited by David L. Wagner, 1–31. Bloomington, IN: Indiana University Press, 1983.

3

Global Pentecostal Renaissance? Reflections on Pentecostalism, Culture, and Higher Education

Jeff Hittenberger

NOT LONG AGO, I attended commencement exercises at the University of California's Hastings College of Law in San Francisco. I was there to see a student named Kofi receive his law degree and to celebrate with his mother, Afi.[1]

Afi came to the United States from Togo with her husband more than twenty years ago so they could pursue graduate studies in Los Angeles. Her husband and I were classmates at the University of Southern California and they invited me to join them for a home-cooked African dinner. We became close friends. They had three children when they came from Togo, and two more were born after their arrival. Their fifth child, Mensah, has Down Syndrome.

In 1990, when Mensah was not yet a year old, Afi's husband completed his dissertation and traveled to Togo, stating his intention to get things ready for his family's reentry home. He never returned. Afi did everything in her power to find him, enlisting the support of friends to write letters and seek him out, but it became increasingly clear that he had abandoned his family. Prioritizing the needs of her children, Afi determined that she would stay in Los Angeles in order to find the support and education for Mensah that she would not be able to find in Togo. With five children ages thirteen and younger, living in an apartment in Los Angeles, Afi called on

---

1. Names in this story are pseudonyms.

God to help her. The journey of the next seventeen years was marked by hardships beyond description, including heart problems, battles with the Los Angeles Unified School District, immigration hearings, and threatened deportation. Her children faced all the issues confronting youth coming of age in urban America. Afi speaks to God with the same passion and honesty as the Psalmist David: "My children are Your children. Do not let them die. Don't abandon us, as my husband did. We trust in You. Deliver us and bless us and make us a blessing!"

Seventeen years after she was abandoned by her husband, Afi and her children and grandchildren watched Kofi walk across the stage, shake hands with the Dean of the Law School, and receive his Juris Doctor degree. God had answered. Kofi is not the only success story in this family. Afi's eldest daughter is a nurse. Her second daughter graduated from medical school at the University of California, San Francisco, and is now a surgeon. The son who follows Kofi graduated from an Ivy League university and is now in medical school. Mensah is now in his twenties and is thriving.

Afi embodies, for me, a kind of "Global Pentecostal Renaissance." She is a woman of profound and unshakable faith. She sees visions. She does battle in spiritual realms. She prays in tongues. She does not doubt that Satan is out to destroy her and her family, and that God is her shield and refuge. She can tell you stories of miracles without which she would be dead and her family would be lost.

Afi is also a woman of learning. She earned a PhD in French at UCLA and teaches at a community college. She demanded that her children take advantage of every educational opportunity and would not take "no" for an answer. When Kofi was fourteen, he decided not to go to school any more. She called the police. "I need you to make my son go to school." He relented. She refused to let her children be crippled by self-pity related to their father's departure. Her faith and her commitment to education are inextricably linked.

As an African, Afi embodies the trends in global Christianity in general and global Pentecostalism in particular. Her faith is not bound by any particular culture or national agenda, but draws on cultures from around the world. She is trilingual and teaches a language at the college level that is not even her first language. She finds ways to serve redemptively, whether as a professor in a community college classroom, an advocate for Mensah in public school, or a Christian neighbor praying with a friend in need.

Pentecostal Christianity, at its best, looks like Afi, integrating a passion for God with a passion for learning and a passion for loving service. In this extended reflective essay, I contemplate the potential of Pentecostalism as a global learning movement and the potential of Pentecostal higher education to be a catalyst for a Global Pentecostal Renaissance.[2] Global Pentecostal Renaissance is here defined as a Spirit-empowered awakening among Christians worldwide that integrates a passion for God, a passion for learning and creative expression, and a passion for redemptive service and mission.[3] In order to explore this idea, the study is organized around four essential questions:

1. What are Pentecostal attitudes toward learning?

In order to assess Pentecostal attitudes toward learning, one must reflect on how learning is related to education and to culture. Culture in the broadest sense has been described as "What we make of the world."[4] This includes how people interpret the world and tell stories of its meaning, as well as the products people create in the world, products like language, family systems, technological inventions, forms of art and music, and even pots and pans.

Education is the process by which we come to learn the cultures into which we are born and which surround us in the world. Education can be formal, as when we attend school and are introduced to elements of our culture through a formal curriculum, or informal, as when our parents read us a story, or teach us what clothes to wear in a particular setting, or non-formal, as when we participate in a structured learning experience, like Sunday School, not directly linked to a formal schooling system.

Learning is, in one sense, inevitable. We come into the world completely ill-equipped to navigate its demands, and must learn from our earliest moments in order to survive. Different societies structure learning experiences for children in various ways, whether in the home, in community

---

2. Throughout this paper, I use the terms Pentecostal and Pentecostalism in the broad sense, including classical Pentecostal denominations like the Assemblies of God, the Church of God (Cleveland, Tennessee), and the Church of God in Christ, as well as Charismatics and other Renewalists, all of whom share a belief in and experience of the baptism of the Holy Spirit and the supernatural gifts of the Spirit. I write from a classical Pentecostal perspective and in some cases highlight themes particular to classical Pentecostalism, but seek to identify trends that are relevant for all Renewalists.

3. This definition suggests the need for a Renaissance within global Pentecostalism, or a new awakening to the powerful connections between a passion for God, a passion for learning, and a passion for service. While these woven passions have always been at work in Pentecostalism, I suggest that more is possible and greater things are yet to come. This definition also suggests that Pentecostalism can be a catalyst for a broader awakening within global Christianity, in partnership with Christians of other streams, and that the resulting Renaissance can have significant impact on cultures around the world, even outside the church.

4. Crouch, *Culture Making*, 23.

associations, or in formal school settings. In the past two hundred years, formal schooling and literacy have become quasi-universal in much of the world. A nation's level of development is often measured by the percentage of its children who receive formal schooling and become literate, and by what levels of proficiency they achieve with regard to the objectives of formal schooling systems.

To ask about Pentecostals' attitudes toward learning, then, is to pose a complex question. Few people, if any, are opposed to learning, as such. Groups of people, and groups of religious people, differ, though, in how much they value formal education. One would be wrong to say that the Amish, for example, oppose learning. It would be accurate to say, however, that the Amish are suspicious of formal school systems, especially those run by the state, and consequently the Amish typically believe formal schooling through the eighth grade is sufficient. Amish theological views of the broader external culture, that it is generally hostile toward their faith and tends to lead their children astray, makes their skepticism about formal schooling understandable.

How then shall we assess Pentecostal attitudes toward learning (and, by extension, toward formal education and culture in general)? A full assessment of this kind is beyond the scope of this essay, but consider the following experience as possibly descriptive of what many young Pentecostals have encountered.

Following my graduation from Evangel College (an Assemblies of God [AG] institution now known as Evangel University), I received a Rotary Foundation Ambassadorial Scholarship to study for a year at l'Université Mohamed V in Rabat, Morocco. From an academic point of view, I felt well-prepared to begin my studies of international relations and beginning Arabic. I hoped to build friendships with my Moroccan Muslim classmates and perhaps have opportunities to share with them my faith in Christ.

I was not prepared, however, to be on the receiving end of *their* evangelistic efforts. In stark contrast to American stereotypes of the Arab world, the Moroccans I met were kind and hospitable. They invited me to their homes and shared their couscous and tagine cuisine. They wanted to know about life in America and were happy to show me the souks, the beaches, and the historical sites of their North African home. Regularly, they shared with me their deep feelings of faith and wondered if I believed in God.

My religious and cultural assumptions were challenged by this experience in a deeper way than they might have been had I encountered overt hostility to my Christian faith. As a twenty-two-year-old who had grown up in a missionary household, I had to ask myself whether my beliefs about God and about the exclusive claims of Christianity were really true and to what degree they were simply products of my subculture. My Moroccan friends wondered how Christians could be so shocked by Islamist violence when we ourselves had perpetrated violence against Muslims and others during the Crusades and the Inquisition. As Christians, we had not spoken out against European imperialism, but had in fact been complicit in the conquest, allowing the cross to accompany the flag during wars throughout the world. And what about the centuries of slavery, which many Christians had justified by reference to Scripture?

Their questions sent me on a new quest to understand my own beliefs and to try to sort out what was genuinely of Christ and what was bound up in uncritical cultural loyalties. During that year, I read books like Edward Said's *Orientalism*, which challenged Western scholarly characterizations of "the East." I read *La Rose de l'Imam* (The Rose of the Imam), written by Marius Garau, a Catholic priest who made it his mission to build bridges to Muslim neighbors.

It was a year of intense reflection, prayer, and uncertainty. At times, it felt like the pillars of my faith were crumbling. And yet I felt God was with me. My Pentecostal college had given me the intellectual and spiritual tools to dig deep, and had taught me that "All truth is God's truth, wherever it is found." So I did not shrink from exploration, or retreat to safe and unexamined assumptions. My Pentecostal faculty members at Evangel had embodied an integration of faith, learning, and life that I wanted to live out. They had encouraged me to believe that my mind was the ally of my spirit in the quest to be faithful to God. So I read. I thought. I prayed.

As I shared this quest with friends through letters (this was long before email), the reactions varied greatly. Two general orientations toward my situation are captured by two particular responses I received.

One missionary friend who will remain unnamed wrote: "Continue to inquire, to question yourself, to search again and always (and you will never finish doing so). But it is in this way that you will become yourself, that is infinitely more than simply the product of your milieu. . . . Be faithful to God." I would identify this as a generally positive orientation toward inquiry, toward learning, toward the formal education I was pursuing, even in a non-Christian setting, and toward the benefits that may arise when one's cultural assumptions are challenged.

Another missionary friend had a different perspective. With genuine affection and concern, she wrote: "Don't think so much. Have faith." I understood what she was getting at. Her comments drew on Prov 3:5-6, emphasizing trusting God in times of uncertainty. She was pointing out that our ability to understand the complexities of this world are limited. Faith involves a conversation with God in which we often come to the end of our understanding and learn to walk with him in the darkness. If we insist on having absolute answers to all our questions, we can end up fabricating answers that exclude God and these answers can be less credible than the ones we started with. While there was legitimate caution in her counsel, her letter brought back comments that I sometimes heard in Pentecostal churches as a child. "Your thoughts will lead you astray. If you try to figure things out, you'll lose your faith. Your mind will deceive you. Don't ask so many questions." This orientation might be described as a generally skeptical view of inquiry, which is often associated with skepticism about formal education and wariness about the influence of culture and cultures on our faith.

Both this generally positive orientation toward inquiry, education, and culture, and this generally skeptical orientation toward inquiry, education, and culture have been a part of Pentecostal discourse from its earliest years.

Some have characterized the skeptical orientation as "anti-intellectual," but I would suggest that this label oversimplifies what is a more complex response. Given that Pentecostalism was born in the era of the modernist-fundamentalist conflict, the education that Pentecostals were skeptical of was often hostile toward the supernatural in ways that contradicted what Pentecostals were experiencing of God's real and transformative presence in their lives. It should not be surprising, then, that Pentecostals would be skeptical of naturalistic, materialistic, and atheistic orientations in higher education. One could not accurately interpret this skepticism as being opposition to learning, or intellect, or to education, *per se*.[5]

Still, this skepticism, while well placed in certain contexts, sometimes became what Andy Crouch refers to as a "posture."[6] This skeptical posture may result in resistance to inquiry and to cultural phenomena that are not familiar to one's particular subculture.

In the years that followed my sojourn in Morocco, I was able to walk with God into a deeper faith that jettisoned many assumptions and cultural trappings and became even more profoundly committed to Christ.

This dichotomy between the generally positive orientation to inquiry, learning, culture, and education, on the one hand, and the skeptical

---

5. A lively debate has taken place over many years about the legitimacy of the "anti-intellectual" label in reference to Pentecostalism. Mark Noll's *The Scandal of the Evangelical Mind* tends to include Pentecostals with fundamentalists in his critique of dispensational and pietistic modes of thinking. Grant Wacker in *Heaven Below*, on the other hand, contends that the charge of anti-intellectualism often misses the point. "Typically the driving motivation was not anti-intellectualism but simple impatience, a determination to get on with the job rather than waste time on pointless theorizing" (31).

6. For a full discussion of postures and gestures, see Crouch, *Culture Making*, 78–99.

orientation, on the other, is illustrative of the divided attitudes toward learning within the Pentecostal movement.

2. What internal resources make Pentecostalism a learning movement (and what are some possible impediments)?

At its core, Pentecostalism has the resources to be a genuine "learning movement." Inherent in the Azusa Street revival, for example, are four orientations to life that might enable Pentecostalism to experience a kind of global renaissance. I think of these as the Azusa Street DNA, but they have also characterized other Pentecostal revivals both before and after.[7]

First, Pentecostalism is **exploratory**. Pentecostals at Azusa Street, like the first-century Christians who experienced the coming of the Holy Spirit, were willing to go out on a limb, to attempt the impossible, to seek God in new ways, to come to fresh understandings, and to challenge conventions.

Second, Pentecostalism is **global**. On the day of Pentecost, people who had gathered in Jerusalem from every nation heard the word of God being spoken in their own languages as the Spirit fell on the disciples. Three thousand came to faith that day, and millions since, from every nation, have joined. Likewise, Azusa Street was an inter-racial, cross-cultural, gender-inclusive revival that gathered people from many nations and sent them back out to the whole world. This global character brings with it a cultural pluralism that is evident in the indigenization of Pentecostal churches across nations and cultures, and the contextualization of Christian beliefs and experiences. Pentecostals have come to many different ways of understanding the world and even the supernatural phenomena that accompany the coming of the Holy Spirit. When Pentecostals met to establish fellowships, they sought common understandings that would allow them to organize themselves in the missionary-sending enterprise, but they were modest even in their claims about their agreements. No one in Pentecostalism spoke *ex cathedra*. The global diversity of Pentecostalism is such that today there are thousands of distinct Pentecostal groups sharing a common commitment to Christ, to the empowerment of the Holy Spirit, and to missions, while retaining the right to differ on the subpoints.

Third, Pentecostalism is, at its best, **holistic** or integrational. The Azusa Street revival encouraged people to engage their emotions, soul, and body with their mind in worship to God and in the quest to know him. At

---

7. For a rich exploration of the Azusa Street revival that began in Los Angeles in 1906, one of the key engines of the twentieth century Pentecostal movement, see Robeck, *Azusa Street Mission*.

their best, Pentecostals have attempted to build on their core faith commitments to understand all the dimensions of their lives in terms of the real and dynamic Lordship of Christ.

Finally, Pentecostalism is **Christ-centered**, rooted in a radical experience with God through the work of the Holy Spirit. This experience of Christ's real presence transforms and shapes our perspective of the world. All of life is animated by our experience of and core commitment to Jesus Christ as Savior and Lord. Pentecostals are characterized by a love of Scripture, and a commitment to the priesthood of all believers, both women and men, necessitating personal responsibility for searching the Scriptures, and bringing one's mind into alignment with the mind of Christ. There should be no domains of life where the Pentecostal believer puts his or her faith on the shelf.[8]

As an exploratory, global, holistic, and Christ-centered movement, Pentecostalism has encouraged learning and growth for generations of people, many of whom came into the movement and into the experience of the Holy Spirit from backgrounds with limited economic and educational opportunity.

Though these elements are all part of the Pentecostal *ethos*, they are not always evidenced in practice. Over time, movements can lose their exploratory dynamics, dichotomize mind and spirit, lose their rootedness in Christ, and adopt undiscerning postures toward culture and education. Impediments to Pentecostalism as a learning movement might include a loss of a passion for God, a lack of appreciation for learning and creative expression, and a growing indifference toward redemptive service and mission.

In order to better understand these dynamics, it is helpful to expand on the notion of orientations toward culture. Crouch offers a taxonomy of these orientations, or modes of engagement (he calls them "gestures") toward culture, and reflects on how Christians in the United States have lived out these various responses over the past century.[9] Note that Pentecostals at various times and in various settings have adopted each of these approaches.

Cultural condemnation is an approach adopted by many fundamentalists at the turn of the twentieth century, when modernism rose as a dominant force in many Christian institutions, including church-related colleges and universities, and even seminaries. The rise of modernism, with

---

8. These four elements of Pentecostal DNA draw on and "Pentecostalize" Arthur Holmes' description of four elements of a Christian worldview (exploratory, pluralistic, integrational, and confessional). See Holmes, *Idea of a Christian College*, 57–60.

9. Crouch's analysis (see note 6) updates and, I believe, improves upon the classic Christ and Culture taxonomy proposed by Niebuhr, *Christ and Culture*, which has been critiqued by, among others such as Carter, *Rethinking Christ and Culture*.

its accommodation to naturalist and materialist views of the world, was viewed by fundamentalists as undermining core ("fundamental") Christian commitments to the veracity of Scripture, the divinity of Christ, and the supernatural and miraculous presence of God in the world. As American and higher education cultures became increasingly hospitable to modernist views, it seemed increasingly inhospitable to Christian fundamentals, with the result that many conservative Christians, including numerous Pentecostals, withdrew from many domains of the larger culture (entertainment, higher education, politics, and the like). The focus of these Christians became to offer a lifeboat for those who would abandon the sinking ship of modern culture.

Cultural critique was a second approach, one that re-engaged evangelicals (who became uneasy with the connotations of withdrawal and condemnation associated with the term "fundamentalist") with culture. Evangelical thinkers like Carl F. H. Henry and Francis Schaeffer taught a new generation of post-fundamentalist evangelicals to take culture seriously, but to identify its assumptions, including its falsehoods and failings, so as to serve as more effective witnesses to those living without Christ and under the sway of mainstream cultures. Many Pentecostals, but perhaps not as often as other evangelicals, joined the project of cultural critique.

Cultural copying became much more common with the rise of the Jesus movement in the 1960s and 1970s, as young evangelicals (most of them Pentecostals) threw off the cultural condemnation approach, and adopted forms of popular music and dress so as to introduce the Christian message to a new generation. This approach resumed a practice that Christians had used for many centuries to advance the Gospel through the idiom and creative expression of the local culture.

Cultural consumption was the most common form of cultural engagement of modernist Christians in the early twentieth century and has become a very common approach among evangelicals (and many Pentecostals) in the early twenty-first century. Having seen the limitations of condemnation (which has often led to legalism), critique (which can seem intellectually arrogant and socially disengaged), and copying (which can seem superficial), many Christians adopt a more open, but too often uncritical, approach to culture and its goods and expressions.

Crouch argues that each of these four "gestures" toward culture has its appropriate time and place. Condemnation is the only reasonable response to cultural phenomena like pornography and sex-trafficking. Critique is a reasonable approach to works of art, film, philosophy, or literature that are meant to engage serious thought. Copying is an inevitable and often useful way to communicate the eternal ideas of the Gospel in accessible form.

Consumption is a reasonable response to all of the good things that remain a product of common grace in all its cultural forms, such as great cuisine, riding a bike, using an iPhone, or attending a baseball game.

The problem comes when these gestures become overzealous postures. When we condemn all things, or critique all things, or copy all things, or consume all things, we fail to draw important distinctions informed by biblical wisdom. Instead, the Christian should be discerning about what approach to culture is relevant in a given cultural situation.

According to Crouch, Christians should recapture two approaches too often neglected, especially in twentieth century American Christianity, which are at the heart of God's intention for humanity from the beginning (and, I would add, essential for a Global Pentecostal Renaissance): *creation* and *cultivation*.[10] As makers of culture, we commit ourselves to creating products, processes, designs, messages, mechanisms, institutions, and works of art that honor God, in whatever domain we work. As cultivators of culture, we seek out, nurture, and preserve cultural expressions that glorify God, and such expressions exist in cultures around the world because God's image is stamped on all people and their cultures, in spite of the distortions and evils brought about by sin. An example of cultural creativity arising from the Pentecostal movement is Teen Challenge, a ministry launched by David Wilkerson in 1958 to help people find freedom from drug addiction through faith in Christ. More than one thousand Teen Challenge centers now operate in more than ninety-three nations.[11]

Increasingly, Pentecostals are constructively engaged in virtually every domain of society in nations around the world: hundreds of thousands of teachers in both the public and private sector; school principals and superintendents at every level; doctors, nurses, and other health care professionals; responsible business people creating excellent products and services, building up their communities, and treating their employees with dignity; lawyers and government officials advocating for justice; social workers and community advocates seeking to strengthen families and cities; engineers, scientists, mathematicians, and technologists researching, discovering, and applying in all the domains of the physical world; professors and university administrators both in church-related and secular institutions mentoring the next generation of leaders; entertainers, media professionals, and other communicators bringing their faith to bear on the formation of people's hearts and minds; pastors, missionaries, and aid workers in every

---

10. For a full discussion of cultivation and creation, see Crouch, *Culture Making*, 65–76.

11. Teen Challenge, "History" and Global Teen Challenge, "Global Teen Challenge."

community of the nation and every nation of the world, extending the Gospel and sharing the Pentecostal experience of the empowerment of the Holy Spirit. Many Pentecostals embrace learning every day, both for the sheer joy of knowing God and God's world, and for practical preparation to serve in God's love.

3. What biblical and historical precedents are there for a Global Pentecostal Renaissance?

I have defined Global Pentecostal Renaissance as a Spirit-empowered awakening among Christians worldwide that integrates a passion for God, a passion for learning and creative expression, and a passion for redemptive service and mission.

How might the Pentecostal movement draw on the DNA that was evident at Azusa Street to grow as a learning movement that can impact the world in ever greater ways, including the domains of education, artistic and creative expression? To answer this question, it is important to look at biblical and historical precedents upon which we can draw as we move in this direction.

"In the beginning, God created" (Gen 1:1). Genesis 1 describes the breathtaking panorama of God's creative genius, a world which He assesses as good, good, good, good, good, good, and very good. God's creation culminates in the creation of human beings, male and female, created in God's image (*imago Dei*). The *imago Dei* has been variously and inexhaustibly interpreted, but given the context it must at least include sharing in God's creative impulse and genius. What do humans create? Humans create culture, and they do so from their earliest commissioning by God, Who sets them in a garden to cultivate it, gives them stewardship over the earth and all its living creatures, and invites them to use their new gift for culture making, language itself, to name the animals.[12]

This is an extraordinary vision of humanity called to culture making, sometimes called "the cultural mandate," in partnership with God. This mandate was violated when humanity sinned, but the mandate was never abrogated and continues to be our calling. This mandate, this calling to create and cultivate in partnership with God, begins at birth when a child begins to learn the language and cultural patterns of his or her family and continues with education in the home, in the community, through the media, and at school.

12. See Gen 1:27–28.

Pentecostal theologian Frank Macchia has written: "The biblical precedent for linking pneumatology and learning is vast."[13] The literary forms of Scripture themselves bear powerful witness to the calling to learning and culture-making. Under the inspiration of the Spirit, the writers of Scripture employed genres of many kinds (such as poetry, history, epistle, parable, and proverb) to communicate the messages of God to humans in their languages and cultural settings.

Many other examples could be offered to illustrate this cultural mandate in action, but I will highlight the story of Bezalel, in whose case artistic expression and teaching are explicitly shown to be a means of living out God's mandate under the anointing of the Holy Spirit.[14] Filled with the Holy Spirit, and with wisdom, understanding, knowledge, and artistic genius, Bezalel and his colleagues created the Tabernacle, a place for the presence of God among God's people. The relevance for a Global Pentecostal Renaissance is that the infilling of the Spirit of God awakens followers of Christ to works of creativity across the entire spectrum of human activity and God is glorified in the fulfillment of our cultural mandate as well as our missionary mandate.

For historical precedent, one could choose myriad instances of God's empowering presence enlivening followers of Christ to integrate vibrant faith with avid learning, creative expression, and redemptive service. I will focus here on one such example: Jan Amos Comenius and the *Unitas Fratrum*, also known as the Moravian Brethren, a movement that was also exploratory, global, holistic, and rooted in a transformative experience of Christ. The Moravians foreshadowed and laid spiritual groundwork for the Pentecostal movement in ways that merit our attention.

Key figures of the Protestant Reformation were advocates for learning and education and laid groundwork upon which Comenius built. John Wycliffe (c. 1320–1384) was an Oxford professor who completed the first translation of the Bible into English and called for an end to the corruption and political dominion of the Church. John Hus was born to peasant parents near Prague in Bohemia, in the present day Czech Republic, around 1370 and eventually became the leader of the University of Prague. When he embraced the ideas of Wycliffe, Hus was excommunicated and then burned at the stake when he refused to recant in 1415.

Czech reformers who followed Hus kept alive his reformation message and from that movement was born the *Unitas Fratrum*, an early Protestant church (predating Luther by two generations) centered in the twin Czech

---

13. Personal correspondence, 1/12/03.
14. Exod 35:30–35, NIV.

provinces of Bohemia and Moravia. This church was one of the first to advocate education for all children.

The leader of the *Unitas Fratrum* in the first half of the seventeenth century was Comenius (1592–1670). Comenius was a product of both the Renaissance and Reformation, and his work and that of his Moravian church initiated a global renewal of education and a global missionary movement.

Comenius pursued higher education in Heidelberg, and returned to Moravia to become a pastor, teacher, and principal of a Christian school. The Counter Reformation was in full force, however, and the armies of the Catholic Church defeated a Protestant army at White Mountain at the beginning of The Thirty Years War in 1620. The Moravian Brethren and other Protestants in the region were imprisoned, scattered into exile, or forced to go underground. As the spiritual and educational leader of this community, Comenius led a group of the Brethren out of Moravia and into exile in Poland.

It was in the early years of persecution and exile that Comenius wrote *The Labyrinth of the World and the Paradise of the Heart*, an autobiographical allegory along the lines of *Pilgrim's Progress*, in which he examines the ways of humanity, and finds corruption and suffering in all his endeavors, until he comes to Christ and finds there the peace, the hope, and the purpose for which he had been searching. The book ends with this statement of faith:

> Lord, lead me, hold me, that I may not stray and fall. Grant that I may love you with an eternal love and love nothing beside yourself except in you and for your sake, O endless love! But what else shall I say, my Lord? Here I am, I am yours; I am your own, yours eternally. I renounce heaven and earth that I may have you alone. Only do not withhold yourself from me, and I have enough. To all eternity, unchangeably, I have enough in you alone.[15]

Drawing on the love and empowerment of God, Comenius became a teacher and leader of extraordinary influence during his forty-two years in exile. During those years, he moved frequently from nation to nation in Europe, serving as an educational counselor to princes and kings, writing 154 books in the process. He introduced a fresh approach to education focused on the inherent value and preciousness of each student, in contrast to the heavy-handed and often brutal methods of previous generations. His book entitled *The Great Didactic* brought this new pedagogy to teachers, influencing systems of education around the world. His book *Orbis Sensualium*

15. Comenius, *John Comenius*, 224–25.

Pictus [The Visible World in Pictures] was the first textbook to incorporate illustrations, a phenomenon we take for granted, but which was a revolutionary idea at the time. Such was his influence that Comenius was invited to be the first President of Harvard College, but refused the invitation in order to remain with his people in exile.

Comenius believed that all truth was God's and that Christians should eagerly seek to understand God's world. He encouraged an experimental, empirical, and scientific approach to learning that incorporated all the senses. He attempted a grand synthesis of ideas by gathering knowledge from all domains into a "pansophic" (all wisdom) encyclopedia. Another battle of The Thirty Years War destroyed the encyclopedia and many of his unfinished manuscripts when he was in his sixties.

He served as a mediator between warring Catholics and Protestants, and called for peace and unity among all Christians, decrying the idea of war in Christ's name. Comenius influenced all subsequent generations of European and world education with his holistic methods of education. No less an educator than Jean Piaget wrote the introduction to a collection of Comenius's works published by *Unesco* in the 1950s.[16]

Comenius, serving as Bishop, kept the Moravian Church alive in spite of great personal suffering. He died in 1670, with the Moravian believers still in exile. To fully appreciate Comenius's contributions, and appreciate the relevance of his work for the idea of a Global Pentecostal Renaissance, one must describe the ways in which his influence extended into subsequent generations and centuries.

Fifty years after Comenius's death, a nineteen-year-old count from Germany named Nicolas von Zinzendorf invited the scattered Moravians and other persecuted Christians to take up residence on his vast lands in Germany. The Moravians established a community called "Herrnhut," or "The Lord's Watch."

Zinzendorf helped the Moravians, who had survived in small groups and were suspicious of others, to begin to live together and establish a renewed sense of Christian community. Zinzendorf read Comenius's *Ratio Disciplinae*, which informed the development of a "new brotherly agreement" to guide the life and faith of the Moravian church. The Moravians began to pray together with Zinzendorf as their leader. In 1727, during a communion service, the gathered believers at Herrnhut experienced a powerful visitation of the Holy Spirit, and what is described as "the Moravian Pentecost" followed, including glossolalia, healings, a calling to missionary

---

16. Piaget, *John Amos Comenius on Education*. See also Piaget, "Jan Amos Comenius," 173–96.

service, and a round-the-clock prayer vigil that lasted for one hundred years.[17]

Out of this Moravian Pentecost arose one of the earliest Protestant missionary movements, with emissaries of Herrnhut circling the globe in missionary work, including ministry among the people enslaved in the Americas and the establishment of thriving churches in Africa.

Zinzendorf became known as an advocate for a "heart religion" that went beyond what he perceived as dry intellectualism in the state Lutheran church. Just as an emotional religious experience that does not affect the mind or behavior can become a distortion, so an intellectual faith that makes no room for emotion and no impact on behavior can become like "a whitewashed tomb."

Zinzendorf, like Comenius, encouraged an exploratory approach to life and a holistic Christian faith that integrated heart, mind, soul, and strength through the power of the Holy Spirit. The Moravians experienced the transformative power of Christ, which became the basis for all their actions. The results were stunning and global. George Whitefield, who along with Jonathan Edwards was the most notable preacher in the American First Great Awakening, housed the Moravians as they established themselves as missionary communities in America. Whitefield and Edwards were the fathers of the Evangelical movement in the United States. John and Charles Wesley, fathers of the Methodist revival and churches, were discipled by the Moravians. The Evangelical and Wesleyan movements laid the foundations for the Pentecostal revival that began in the early years of the twentieth century and mirrored the experience of the Moravians at Herrnhut.

In what sense does Comenius serve as a model for a "Global Pentecostal Renaissance"? Note the ways in which Comenius embodied what is referred to above as the Azusa Street DNA.

- First, Comenius embodied an **exploratory** approach to life and faith. He saw education and learning as an expression of love for Christ and faithfulness to his calling. Comenius advocated for the education and development of all people, giving special opportunity and attention to women. Consequently, women came to occupy key leadership roles in the Moravian movement.

- Second, the scope of Comenius's mission and the character of his movement were **global**, as he sought to give witness to Christ and mediate conflicts across Europe. Comenius worked to build a Christian community of love and trust that welcomed the hurting, the exile, and the stranger and reconciled all within the body of Christ.

17. See "Zinzendorf the Ecumenical Pioneer" and "Moravians" for further details.

The Moravians became the forerunners of the modern missionary movement.

- Third, Comenius's approach to education was **holistic** and integrational. He advocated for education and learning as keys both to understanding God's world and to serving that world through acts of compassion, witness, and artistic and literary expression.

- Fourth, his life, philosophy and work were **Christ-centered**, rooted in a passionate love of Jesus Christ, and a desire to obey and serve Him. Comenius laid the groundwork that encouraged the Moravians to receive the empowerment of the Holy Spirit as the basis for community and service. Comenius modeled for the Moravians and the whole church a spirituality that integrated body, mind, and spirit under the Lordship of Christ, enduring hardship without losing faith.

Ultimately, Comenius's interest was not in building the Moravian Church, *per se*, or in spreading Moravianism. He loved his people and served as their bishop, but he had a larger vision rooted in his global perspective and his faith in Jesus Christ as Lord. He wrote:

> To all Christian churches together I bequeath a lively desire for unanimity of opinion and for reconciliation among themselves, and for union in faith, and love of the unity of spirit. May the spirit which was given to me from the very beginning by the Father of spirits be shed upon you all, so that you would desire as sincerely as I did the union of all who call upon the name of Christ in truth.[18]

The Moravian Church is only a small part of the legacy of Comenius (and Zinzendorf). The far greater part of their legacy belongs to the whole church of Christ, in the form of an integrated faith, empowered by the Spirit, reaching the whole world, and even to the world beyond the church, in the form of education systems that consider every child to be precious and worthy of our best efforts (even where societies have lost the underlying faith that every human is created in the image of God).

This also is a lesson for Pentecostalism from Comenius: the purpose of Pentecostalism is not its own perpetuation or institutionalization. The purpose of Pentecostalism is, like the purpose of Pentecost, to bring the reality, redemption, and reconciliation of God in Christ to the world, empowering all who call on him to fully become the people He created them to be. A

---

18. John Comenius, *Bequest of the Unity of Brethren*, quoted in Comenius, *John Comenius*, 16–17.

Global Pentecostal Renaissance will help us remember our core identity and our core mission.

4. How might Pentecostal higher education contribute to a Global Pentecostal Renaissance?

Though the Pentecostal movement was born among people of few means and, in general, little formal education, it has had remarkable success in establishing institutions of higher education, and these institutions have played a major role in the development of the movement, as I have described elsewhere.[19]

Pentecostals in higher education seek to cultivate more than a cognitive worldview. Pentecostal integration seeks to weave faith, learning, and life together in all dimensions of our humanity, such that they constitute a "life way" and not merely a worldview, shaping not only the mind, but also the affections.[20] Drawing on the empowerment of the Holy Spirit, Pentecostals have the resources to live holistic and exploratory lives in communities that are global and diverse, and to experience a transformative relationship to Christ that reshapes all facets of life through the guidance of the Holy Spirit who leads us into all truth.

A few examples will suffice to illustrate how Pentecostal colleges and universities are, in fact, contributing to a Global Pentecostal Renaissance in a variety of domains. These are just a few of the myriad examples that could be provided. The brief descriptions below are accompanied by references to websites where the reader can learn more about these institutions and their initiatives.

Pentecostal colleges contribute to Global Pentecostal Renaissance through theology and ministry preparation. Pentecostal colleges and universities of all kinds have a rich history of preparing ministers and contributing to theological reflection in institutions around the world. These range from the powerful preparation being provided in two-year programs like the Associate degree program in Bible and Ministry at Latin American Bible Institute in La Puente, California[21] to the internationally influential scholarship being carried out by faculty in programs like Regent University's PhD in Renewal Studies.[22] Global University is pioneering the use of Kindle devices

---

19. For an analysis and taxonomy of Pentecostal institutions of higher education, see Hittenberger, "Future of Pentecostal Higher Education," 83–104.

20. For a rich analysis of shaping the affections, see Smith, *Desiring the Kingdom.*

21. "Degree Offered."

22. "PhD in Renewal Studies."

to provide full theological libraries and programs of study in e-book format for pastors in nations with limited or no access to theological libraries or seminaries.[23]

Pentecostal colleges contribute to Global Pentecostal Renaissance through the liberal arts. Many Pentecostal colleges and universities offer strong liberal arts programs, such as the newly revised "Frameworks" curriculum at Evangel University, which features thematic, interdisciplinary courses including one entitled simply "Pentecost."[24] Humanities faculties at Pentecostal institutions include notable poets, playwrights, fiction writers, and historians.

Pentecostal colleges contribute to Global Pentecostal Renaissance through music and fine arts. Many outstanding music programs are making an impact on students' lives and on the world at Pentecostal colleges and universities. The highly-regarded Lee University choir was invited to sing at the 2013 Presidential inauguration.[25] Vanguard University's Theatre program is one of only two Council of Christian Colleges and Universities (CCCU) institutions accredited by the National Association of Schools of Theatre.[26] Vanguard's Music program frequently ministers internationally and travels regularly to China for concerts.[27] Increasingly, Pentecostal universities are also offering programs in film production and digital media.

Pentecostal colleges contribute to Global Pentecostal Renaissance through science and technology. Regent University College of Science and Technology in Accra, Ghana, is perhaps the first Pentecostal institution launched specifically to prepare students in the sciences. Scientific research is being carried out at a number of Pentecostal institutions, as is deep reflection on the interface between science and Pentecostal Christianity, as evidenced by the publication of *Science and Spirit: A Pentecostal Engagement with the Sciences.*[28] A number of Pentecostal institutions such as Northwest University, Oral Roberts University (ORU), and Vanguard University are leading the way in preparing nurses and other students who seek to serve in health fields. ORU's engineering program is sending engineering students on international missions trips.[29]

23. "Library Announces Availability of e-books."
24. "Frameworks."
25. "Senator Lamar Alexander."
26. "Perfect Blend."
27. "International Tours."
28. Yong and Smith, *Science and Spirit*.
29. "ORU Engineering."

Pentecostal colleges contribute to Global Pentecostal Renaissance through social and behavioral sciences. Graduates of Bethany University and Vanguard University were instrumental in launching Latin American ChildCare (which educates tens of thousands of children in Christian schools) and Enlace (which has created a powerful model of church-based community development in El Salvador). Convoy of Hope (an international relief agency) was launched by brothers who graduated from Evangel University and Bethany University. Vanguard's Global Center for Women and Justice[30] is leading the way in AG efforts to combat human trafficking. Outstanding programs in Psychology prepare counselors at many Pentecostal institutions and a number of these engage students in service in the United States through organizations like Royal Family Kids Camps (an organization ministering to thousands of foster children, founded by an alumnus of a Pentecostal institution), and internationally.[31]

Pentecostal colleges are also contributing to Global Pentecostal Renaissance through programs in business, education, student development, spiritual formation and many other programs too numerous to catalog here.[32] More information is available from the website of the Alliance for AG Higher Education (colleges.ag.org) and the individual websites of Pentecostal colleges and universities not mentioned above, such as the Assemblies of God Theological Seminary (Springfield, MO), Pentecostal Theological Seminary (Cleveland, TN), Emmanuel College (Franklin Springs, GA), Life Pacific College (San Dimas, CA), North Central University (Minneapolis, MN), Southeastern University (Lakeland, FL), Southwest Assemblies of God University (Waxahachie, TX), University of Valley Forge (Phoenixville, PA), and many others, as well as those in other countries like Hansei University (Gunpo, South Korea), West Africa Advanced School of Theology (Lomé, Togo), Universidad Cristiana de las Asambleas de Dios (San Salvador, El Salvador), and Asia Pacific Theological Seminary (Baguio, Philippines). Pentecostal institutions of higher education offer a unique environment for integrating a passion for God with a passion for learning and creative expression, and a passion for redemptive service and mission.

In the midst of the significant challenges they must navigate, Pentecostal institutions of higher education continue to equip students to commit their lives and God-given gifts to His glory and for the transformation

---

30. "Global Center for Women & Justice Home."

31. E.g., Evangel University Psychology Professor E. Grant Jones has led multiple teams to Africa to train grief counselors and provide counseling for victims of trauma.

32. See, for an example of entrepreneurship that combines preparation in business and anthropology: "Vanguard Alums Winners of the American Giving Awards."

of people's lives, whatever their field and wherever they serve around the world.

One final reflection on the contribution of Pentecostal colleges and universities has to do with a possible objection to the use of the term "Renaissance" and the emphasis of this essay on higher education. One might suspect that this term implies a kind of elitism. Given that Pentecostals now have opportunities to participate in higher education, and other social and cultural institutions from which they were previously excluded, the temptation to status consciousness is real. Drawing on *The Lord of the Rings* imagery, I have elsewhere referred to this as the temptation of the Ring, or the temptation to grasp at educational achievement as a pathway to social power on terms defined by secular society rather than as an opportunity to serve Christ and His kingdom.[33]

A true Global Pentecostal Renaissance, however, must be inclusive of all, recognizing in authentic Pentecostal fashion that all people receive gifts to share and must be welcomed and encouraged to do so. A Global Pentecostal Renaissance encourages all believers to express their gifts with confidence, as illustrated by this personal example.

My son Ben, like Afi's son Mensah, is a young man with Down Syndrome. Ben is also on the autistic spectrum, and for him participation in regular church settings is difficult. Ben has many gifts to share, but the conditions under which he is able to share them must be sensitively designed. When Ben became a teenager, my wife and I needed help from our local AG church in order to facilitate Ben's participation in the church community. Ultimately, that help came from two graduates of an AG college, one in special education and the other in nursing, who volunteered to create a special needs Sunday School class for teenagers who are not able to thrive in regular classes or services. By integrating their learning with their faith in their domains of study and service, these women creatively opened doors for Ben and other teens with special needs, so that they, too, could share their gifts with the people of God. Multiply this local expression of the Spirit's empowerment for redemptive service a hundred thousand times over in churches and communities around the world, and one can imagine what Global Pentecostal Renaissance looks like in a very practical sense.

Conclusion

Pentecostals have experienced the presence, love, and power of God in a life-transforming way. The natural response to that experience is to seek to

---

33. Hittenberger, "Future of Pentecostal Higher Education," 83.

follow God in all facets of one's life. A passion for God can and should be integrated with a passion for learning and creative expression, and a passion for redemptive service and mission.

While Pentecostals have sometimes been leery of higher education, this essay suggests that Pentecostalism, a truly global movement, has within its DNA the resources to be a learning movement. Pentecostalism, as exemplified by the Azusa Street revival, is exploratory, global, holistic, and Christ-centered. Pentecostal institutions of higher education play a vital role in encouraging these characteristics among Pentecostals and are contributing to a Global Pentecostal Renaissance, defined as a Spirit-empowered awakening among Christians worldwide that integrates a passion for God, a passion for learning and creative expression, and a passion for redemptive service and mission. Such an awakening will bless not only Pentecostals, but may also encourage and inspire Christians from other traditions with whom we partner to bless the world.

The future of global Pentecostalism will be bright if Pentecostal educators will partner with churches and families to bring that passion for God, passion for learning and creative expression, and passion for redemptive service and mission to bear on all human relationships across cultures and in all domains of life.

BIBLIOGRAPHY

Carter, Craig. *Rethinking Christ and Culture: A Post-Christendom Perspective*. Grand Rapids: Brazos, 2006.

Comenius, John Amos. *John Comenius: The Labyrinth of the World and the Paradise of the Heart*. Translated by Howard Louthan and Andrea Sterk. The Classics of Western Spirituality Series. New York: Paulist, 1998.

Crouch, Andy *Culture Making: Recovering our Creative Calling*. Downers Grove, IL: InterVarsity, 2008.

"Degree Offered." *Latin America Bible Institute*. Online: http://www.labi.edu/academics/degrees-offered/.

"Frameworks." *Evangel University*. Online: http:// www.evangel.edu/academics/undergraduate/core-curriculum.

Global Teen Challenge. "Global Teen Challenge." Online: http://www.globaltc.org.

Global University. "Library Announces Availability of e-books." Online: http://www.globaluniversity.edu/news_article.cfm?id=234.

Hittenberger, Jeff. "The Future of Pentecostal Higher Education in the United States: The Ring, the Shire, or the Redemption of Middle Earth?" In *The Future of Pentecostalism in the United States*, edited by Eric Patterson and Edmund Rybarczyk, 83–104. Lexington: Rowman and Littlefield, 2007.

Holmes, Arthur. *The Idea of a Christian College*. Grand Rapids: Eerdmans, 1987.

Niebuhr, H. Richard. *Christ and Culture*. San Francisco: Harper and Row, 1951.

Noll, Mark. *The Scandal of the Evangelical Mind*. Grand Rapids: Eerdmans, 1994.

"ORU Engineering Team Prepares for Missions Trip to Ghana." *Oral Roberts University.* Online: http://www.oru.edu/news/oru_news/20120420_oru_engineering_missions.php.

"PhD in Renewal Studies." *Regent University.* Online: www.regent.edu/acad/schdiv/academics/phd/home.shtml.

Piaget, Jean. "Jan Amos Comenius." *Prospects* (UNESCO, International Bureau of Education) 23.1/2 (1993) 173–96. Online: www.ibe.unesco.org/publications/ThinkersPdf/comeniuse.PDF.

———. *John Amos Comenius on Education.* Classics in Education, no. 33. New York: Teachers College Press, 1967.

Robeck, Cecil M. *The Azusa Street Mission and Revival: The Birth of the Global Pentecostal Movement.* Nashville, TN: Thomas Nelson, 2006.

"Senator Lamar Alexander Announces Lee Festival Choir To Sing at US Presidential Inauguration." *Lee University.* Online: www.leeuniversity.edu/newsdetail.aspx?id=2644.

Smith, James K. A. *Desiring the Kingdom: Worship, Worldview, and Cultural Formation.* Grand Rapids: Baker, 2009.

Teen Challenge. "History." Online: http://teenchallengeusa.com/about/history.

Vanguard University. "Global Center for Women & Justice Home." Online: http://www.vanguard.edu/gcwj/.

———. "International Tours." Online: http://www.vanguard.edu/music/about/events/international-tours/.

———. "Perfect Blend of Academics and Entertainment." Online: http://www.vanguard.edu/theatre/education/.

———. "Vanguard Alums Winners of the American Giving Awards." Online: www.vanguard.edu/about/vanguard-news/winners-of-the-american-giving-awards-2.

Wacker, Grant. *Heaven Below.* Cambridge: Harvard University Press, 2001.

Yong, Amos and James Smith, eds. *Science and Spirit: A Pentecostal Engagement with the Sciences.* Bloomington, IN: Indiana University Press, 2010.

4

Liberal Arts and the Assemblies of God: A History and Analysis of a Strained Alliance

BARRY COREY

THE ANNOUNCEMENT WENT OUT a few days before Christmas in 1913. A group of Pentecostals sensed that the time had come to organize its grassroots movement into a loosely-structured cooperative. This cooperative would become the General Council of the Assemblies of God (AG). The group circulated news of the forthcoming April 1914 meeting via word of mouth and through the tabloids of various Pentecostal publications. The printed notice listed five reasons for the united meeting of Pentecostals. It stated that the final purpose for the assembly of Pentecostal believers would be to act on a proposition "for a general Bible Training School with a literary department for our young people."[1] E. N. Bell and the other founding fathers of the AG made it clear that at least Bible training, and possibly a college of general education, would be intrinsic to the educational structure of the new denomination.[2] However, what was meant by "literary department" would remain a source of debate. Fulfillment of this would prove to be a tumultuous journey.[3]

1. Bell, "General Convention," 1. The first four reasons for the meeting included: 1) a better articulation of the doctrines of Pentecostal people in order to alleviate divisions; 2) better service of home and foreign mission fields; 3) better vision for financial accountability and expansion of foreign fields; and 4) better internal and legal governance as a result of consolidated efforts.

2. Chase, "Evangel College Buildings," 8–9.

3. For more substantive details concerning this journey, see my earlier work, *From Opposition to Opening*.

65

Laying the Foundation: Liberal Arts in the AG

The 1914 debut of the General Council of the AG in Hot Springs, Arkansas, passed without any serious mention of the establishment of any Bible school, let alone a literary department. Instead, founding participants were encouraged "to attend faithfully to a diligent search of the Scriptures, and if possible to attend some properly and scripturally accredited Bible Training School."[4] However, with the growth of the Pentecostal movement, T. K. Leonard's Pentecostal school in Ohio and a few others scattered across the country were not enough to train pastors, missionaries, and evangelists. To address this issue, leaders of the new church encouraged the creation of "Ten Day Bible Conferences" or "Itinerary Bible Schools" to be held in different regions of the country. The content of these courses gave "due attention to evangelistic work for the unsaved, and solid scriptural teaching for the saints."[5] Clearly a concern existed to train believers in sound Pentecostal teaching; however, organizing this effort was not an initial priority. Instead, church leaders were engaged in defining doctrine, building an organizational base, and creating a publishing center, Gospel Publishing House.

The earliest years of the AG were known more for their evangelistic initiatives than their educational initiatives. Although there were those who envisioned a college with a general education program in the AG, the creation of Bible schools such as Central Bible Institute (CBI) and others across the country were deemed more important by church officials. The standardization and centralization of the church's educational programs were also important to the new AG. In 1925, 1937, and 1939, the General Council passed motions which established the Springfield headquarters as the consummate authority of all educational institutions affiliated with the AG.

In 1943, Assistant General Superintendent Ralph Riggs, concerned with reforming Bible schools, standardizing and centralizing church educational programs, and establishing a denominational liberal arts college, emerged as the principle education advocate in the AG. His work was sanctioned by self-appointed educational committees and the General Presbytery; however, in 1945, the delegates of the General Council, the church's largest policy-making body, forbade Riggs to continue his work towards a liberal arts college without its approval. At the 1947 Grand Rapids General Council, the college issue first came to a vote, and the delegates—stirred by a message in tongues and a word of prophecy—overwhelmingly defeated the motion.

4. *General Council Minutes*, 23–24.
5. Ibid.

After the jolting rebuff by the delegates in 1947, Riggs retreated from his ardent campaign for a liberal arts college and began to work on revising and enforcing the church's educational criteria for its Bible schools. Riggs and several other AG educators also participated in the founding of the American Association of Bible Institutes and Bible Colleges (AABIBC) as an interdenominational accreditation body. During the motion to approve accreditation steps for CBI in the 1949 General Council in Seattle, the Great Educational Debate was unleashed when pastors and evangelists retaliated against the educational reform measures of the church. The emotional harangues, however, failed to convince the majority of the delegates that secular accreditation was ungodly. The sentiment of the church started to shift away from its anti-education stance of only two years earlier.

By the early 1950s, petitions for an AG liberal arts college began to come from across the country; this reflected broad-based support of the idea. At the Milwaukee General Council in 1953, delegates overwhelmingly approved the establishment of a liberal arts college. Riggs' forbearance and determination had finally been rewarded. After the victory in Milwaukee, a new cast of players arose to assist Riggs in preparations for the institution which would become Evangel College. J. Robert Ashcroft was selected as Education Secretary and Thomas Zimmerman was elected to the post of Assistant General Superintendent. In December, the planning committee met to flesh out a strategy for creating the college, but the meeting quickly turned into a fiasco. Many of the Bible school representatives were hostile to the idea of a church-supported liberal arts college, and they insisted that the new college not contain any competing academic programs. Because of this hostility, Riggs and his associates decided to create a Board of Directors. Despite these structural advances, however, the school still lacked the financial resources that it desperately needed. When Evangel College opened its doors in 1955, these fiduciary troubles plagued the college all throughout its early years, and its fiscal crises overshadowed the progress that the young school had made in other ways, such as increased enrollment and momentum to secure proper accreditation. In 1958, Ralph Riggs retracted his promise that no General Council funding would be used to support the liberal arts college, and a year later the administrations of Evangel College and CBI were merged to cut spending. That same year Riggs was voted out of office, and Thomas F. Zimmerman was elected in his place.

Evangel College: A Developing Institution

The story of the founding of Evangel College is about the process of change in a religious or social movement. It is about the passage traveled by the infant AG from its charismatic origins to its emergence as an organized ecclesiastical structure, a structure which accommodated a collegiate institutional form.[6] An understanding of this process helps explain why the church made certain decisions. A single collegiate liberal arts model was certainly not the only viable option in which these leaders could invest years of the church's time and resources. Various alternatives were argued by the gainsayers, but church leaders leveraged their authority in favor of the creation of a liberal arts college. One might wonder *why* the decision to adopt this model prevailed. The answer is by every means complex and lies in an indiscrete sociological web of external influences and internal choices, both inextricable from the process of institutionalization. It follows that the decision to establish Evangel College corresponded to the church's institutionalization process and was rooted in the belief that a rationalized form of education was a socially legitimate means of survivability.

Given the historical data in the decision to found Evangel College, it is argued that the formation of the college was a result of an institutionalization process at work within the church. In making sense of the decision, it is necessary to begin with the charismatic origins of the church and the sense of crisis and isolation out of which the church was born. As the church matured, it began to routinize its functions into bureaucratic forms, and this led to an ambiguity among leaders of the fledgling church. At the core of this ambiguity was the question as to what form of organized, ecclesiastical structure would be necessary for the church's survival. This gave rise to certain actors, specifically Ralph Riggs, who were profoundly affected by the notion of routinization and the need for the containment of charisma. These actors, who surveyed and copied what they understood to be successful means of containment in other religious movements, convinced the church that a collegiate structure *was* a legitimate means of survivability. Convincing the church's constituencies necessitated a calculated use of symbols and norms in the distribution of information. Ultimately, out of these processes of institutionalization, the collegiate structure of Evangel College emerged.

---

6. Among Pentecostal scholars, the term "charismatic" is popularly associated with the charismatic renewal movement of the mid-1960s when liturgical churches such as the Roman Catholics and Episcopalians infused the personal activity of the Holy Spirit into their traditions. Though this renewal movement encompassed many characteristics of charisma, or the charismatic, a sociological definition is significantly broader and will be defined further in this essay.

Analysis

1. The Church, Crisis, and Charisma

The origins of the AG are rooted in what some sociologists call "the charismatic," and followed a discrete pattern known among scholars in the same field as "the routinization of charisma."[7] A basic understanding of the phenomena of the charismatic as the entry point toward institutionalization is fundamental to discussions of decision-making theory as it relates to the establishment of Evangel College.

The institutionalization of religion grows out of the need for stability and continuity, the need to preserve the content of religious beliefs, and concern for safeguarding doctrines and teachings from distortion. When routinization of charisma has begun to take hold within a religious movement, the ecclesiastical organization emerges. Sociologically, the institutionalization of religious movements simply and yet necessarily *happens*. It is fundamental for transmission of the church's beliefs to others and critical for the church's very survival. It provides continuity, identity, stability, and social legitimacy.[8] Few dispute the reality of the institutionalization phenomena evolving from within a charismatic movement. It is inherent to virtually all religious movements; in varying degrees, it has occurred in Catholicism, Methodism, and Pentecostalism.

As a rule, religious movements begin as charismatic experiences. Charisma serves as a quality imputed to a person or movement because of a connection with ultimate and transcendent powers. The charismatic has something to do with what Emile Durkheim, who espoused purely social origins of religion, calls the sacred—something other than this "utilitarian sphere."[9] Rudolf Otto identifies these universal elements of the religious experience as the "the holy" or "the numinous," which he implies is a guiding force or spirit beyond rational and ethical conceptions.[10] Max Weber, a pioneer in the sociology of religion, treats charisma as the breaking point in the world of everydayness; it is extraordinary as opposed to mundane. Weber applies the qualities of charisma not only to individuals, but he recognizes the existence of these same charismatic qualities in organizations or movements.[11]

---

7. Parts of this discussion of the institutionalization of religion have been supplemented by O'Dea and Aviad, *Sociology of Religion*, 38–64.
8. O'Dea and Aviad, *Sociology of Religion*, 49–53.
9. Durkheim, *Forms of Religious Life*, 72–79.
10. Otto, *Idea of the Holy*.
11. See Weber's monumental two volume work, *Economics and Society*.

Charisma has its roots in crisis. A charismatic movement begins as a counter-movement to the establishment and is fundamentally at odds with society. Within ecclesiastical systems, religious controversies or ideological fissions over such matters as doctrine or governance are prone to occur. If unreconciled, the result is a schism. The new religious movement displays a break with the past and reflects a new spirit of coherence and unity.[12] How the new group grapples with its relationship to the established social order is often its foremost dilemma. The movement's leaders might ask themselves, "What is our relationship to the established society? Interaction or isolation?" The answer usually unfolds through a gradual evolution of choices in which leaders move toward a more rationalized form of organizational structure. Sociologically, charismatic movements tend to gravitate toward the functional and, consequently, the routinized. This is defined by Weber as the "routinization of charisma," namely, charismatic movements evolve or are transformed from their grass-roots beginnings into more stable forms of thought and practice legitimized by society. This certainly characterized the origins of the young AG. Routinization was stalled in the church's early years because there existed no need to interact with its larger religious and social environments. The church was content to be self-contained. As the church matured in years and created more and more bureaucracies to support its actions, interaction with new environments resulted, and routinization ensued.

The AG emerged out of a crisis of religious order. During the last quarter of the nineteenth century, there was a growing dissatisfaction with many traditional churches among holiness believers. They watched the church's increasing affinity with an industrial society which they believed to be corrupt and uninterested in spiritual matters. They lamented nineteenth-century church experiments with liberal ideologies that made room for relativistic frameworks, allowed doctrines of Social Darwinism and individualism to undermine the literal-minded biblicism of holiness followers. This trajectory claimed holiness believers, detracted from the supernatural, and marginalized the deity of Christ.

With the increasingly complex nature of nineteenth-century Protestantism came the need to institutionalize. Here again those of the devout holiness persuasion accused the church of allowing bureaucracy, education, wealth, and a growing power and prestige to displace personal piety and social service. For them, the assumed role of the church was "friendship with the world" and thus "enmity with God." At the same time, leaders of the established Protestant churches were leveling criticisms at the holiness

---

12. Wach, *Sociology of Religion*, 110.

movement for its disregard of authority, organization, and "established usages" within the church.

Early Pentecostalism harbored an enmity toward ecclesiasticism, and as a result, it considered religious organizations dubious. Mainline denominations had failed because they had allowed structure to obscure the zeal and passion for Christ evident in these churches' founders. Pentecostals were convinced these denominations' proclivity toward secularism had detracted those such as the Methodists and Presbyterians from an absolute trust in God for all things. The nineteenth-century secular drift of the mainline churches instilled a distrust of organized religion among Pentecostals.

From its earliest days, the AG adherents believed that the world was a dangerous environment for the believer because it was under Satan's domain; therefore, while Christians were in the world, they were to be withdrawn and aloof from it. Further, the church's four dominant ideological norms alienated it from pursuing interactions with external environments. Specifically, an enmity toward ecclesiasticism, belief in the imminent rapture of the church, personal asceticism, and an emphasis on the supernatural as an everyday phenomenon placed their church at odds with the American religious mainstream as well as the larger society.

In the period beginning in 1914, the decision-makers within the church were engrossed in last-days evangelism to the extent that adopting permanent auxiliary institutions seemed superfluous. If the coming of the Lord was indeed at hand, the urgency to spread the gospel as quickly as possible demanded the attention of ministers and missionaries. To accomplish this mission, the church's leaders devoted their attention to establishing Bible training schools, formalizing doctrinal positions, commissioning missionaries to evangelize overseas, planting new churches, and building a publishing house. The church was not ready at this time to establish a liberal arts collegiate structure. Although at its General Council sessions in 1914, 1929, and 1935, the church had expressed itself favorably on the idea of creating a liberal arts college, those in the position to initiate the process did not do so because of more immediate claims on their attention. The erratic character of decision-making during the 1910s, 1920s, and 1930s is more explicable by placing it in the context of the church's multiple and changing claims of attention.

"Problems, solutions, and decision makers come together," James G. March explains, "because they are available at the same time and the same place."[13] As the decades passed and the Lord did not return, those in leadership positions began to sense the need to construct support systems

13. March, "Emerging Developments," 4.

within the structure of the church. Clearly articulated by the top levels of the church's leadership, these support systems were constructed to strengthen the denomination for the upcoming generations. With this came some of the earliest tangible signs that the church was undergoing a process of institutionalization and routinization.

2. Routinization and Increased Ambiguity

If the first phase of the church's existence may be characterized in terms of the charismatic, the second can be characterized in terms of routinization. As time passed, the supernatural characteristics of the church needed to be grounded in the very natural framework of organizational structure. During this period, which is difficult to isolate in specific chronological dimensions, church leaders began to explore and implement new formal functions. As they did, the church became increasingly institutionalized. AG leadership argued that the essence of Pentecostalism had to be contained and preserved for upcoming generations. The ways in which the charisma happened to be contained was manifested in rational forms of institutionalization. As the church matured and began to routinize its functions into bureaucracies, uncertainties among the leadership resulted. Ambiguity centered around the issue of what form of ecclesiastical structure would be necessary to ensure the church's survival.

In its earliest stages of growth, the church was bound by a doctrinaire position that kept it secluded from other denominations or elements of society. The first generation of leadership emphasized the imminent return of Christ and the urgent need for evangelism. Consequently, itinerant ministerial training schools and regional Bible institutes were the first practical means of containing charisma. These educational institutions boasted a succinct mission and curriculum designed to prepare church members in an expedient manner to evangelize the lost. Additionally, AG leaders began a publishing house to print gospel tracts and training literature to supplement the church's mission of spreading the "good news" as quickly and as widely as possible. The principal emphasis of the church during these initial years was to save the lost, not to educate the saved. Because of this system of prioritizing, the occasional mention of creating a liberal arts college for the church's young people was disregarded.

Institutionalization of the AG included changes in response to conditions *internal* to the religious movement, while at the same time it included adjustments precipitated by *external* environments. H. E. Aldrich and Jeffrey Pfeffer study the relationship between organizations and their environments and argue that organizations aggressively seek to manage or strategically adapt to their environment.[14] While this was not true early in the life of the AG, by examining the movement longitudinally, it becomes clearer that adaptation *did* occur. Because the early AG did not sense a need for acceptance by its environment(s) and because it did not respond to environmental demands, the AG bore no substantive adaptations in its formal structure. When in later years it began to prospect its environment for acceptance, environmental demands were inevitably heeded. Also, the specific characteristics of the form to which the church adapted depended on the demands of the environment in relation to the proximity of the organization *to* its environment.

Various environments of the AG became increasingly important over time, and they began assuming a dominant role in its organizational structures and decisions. This was due in part to the conscious decisions of the church leadership to extend the denomination beyond its early ideologically-imposed boundaries. Nearly one generation old in 1942, the AG ventured outside its denominational security and became a founding member of the National Association of Evangelicals (NAE). In order to broaden the affiliations of church's higher educational institutions, five years later administrators of AG Bible schools allied their institutions with the new AABIBC. Because the progressive decisions of the church leadership outpaced the accepted position of most local churches, the result was a string of mild insurrections from the rank and file pastors. Mayer Zald explains that this conflict might occur when a denomination's leadership, due to interests or value preferences, justifies involvement in an environment as part of its moral or ideological beliefs.[15]

At the same time AG church leaders were aggressively affiliating with associations such as the NAE and the AABIBC, the church was also being affected by trends of societal change. After World War II, more and more ministers wanted to serve as chaplains in the armed forces, and the church responded by abridging its Bible school standards and beginning programs to accommodate government requirements. At this time, the sudden availability of O'Reilly General Hospital in Springfield, Missouri and the decision to create Evangel College forced the church's leadership into daily negotiations with federal bureaucracies, state agencies, and municipal boards. The result was a more cosmopolitan breed of leadership.

The advent of Evangel College compounded the demands on the AG church. With its first Bible colleges and earliest educational programs, the

14. Aldrich and Pfeffer, "Environments of Organizations," 79.
15. Zald, "Theological Crucibles," 328.

church was not obligated to abide by formal criteria in order to maintain operations. As demographic changes took place in the larger societal environment produced a growing need nationwide for higher education (such as the GI Bill's educational assistance and military chaplaincy requirements), AG leaders responded with motions toward accreditation of Bible schools, as well as establishment of a liberal arts college and a seminary. Suddenly, the church had to obtain academic credentials for faculty and administrators, practice strict adherence to accreditation standards, and become accountable to state and federal educational bureaus. As the church relied on these secondary controlling agencies in the creation and early years of Evangel College, the college began to adopt a similar model to like-minded institutions.[16]

As they were planning the college, church leaders were incapable of generating the necessary internal resources or functions for self-sustainability. Consequently, they engaged in relations and transactions with other potential partners to acquire the needed resources and services. The result was a stabilization of relationships within the environment and a mechanism to aid in the survival of the organization itself.[17]

Not only did the college adapt to external forces, its planners adapted to external standards of organizational structure modeled by other denominations. The inexperience of the men who accepted the responsibility of designing the college resulted in their imitating similar organizations outside of the AG. In the stages of planning during the 1940s, none of the college planning committee members had the advantage of prior experience in higher education administration in the secular sphere. None had ever before been involved in discussions concerning the creation of a liberal arts college. Most, in fact, had never attended a college other than one of the many Pentecostal Bible institutes. There were some like J. Roswell Flower, Irving J. Harrison, Klaude Kendrick, and J. Robert Ashcroft who had completed or nearly completed their graduate studies, but the large majority had attained an education of only a high school diploma and three years of Bible school. Consequently, most of these men approached the planning table with few skills and no background in designing a liberal arts collegiate institution. The greater their uncertainty between the means of designing a college and the end product of the college itself, the greater the inclination

---

16. Examples included well-established colleges such as Wheaton, Gordon, Anderson, Taylor, Houghton, Asbury, and Westmont.

17. Aldrich and Pfeffer, "Environments of Organizations," 84.

to model the proposed college after other organizations they perceived to be successful.[18] Yet to fulfill this purpose, new leadership had to rise up.

3. *The Rise of New Leaders*

Given the need created by the natural ambiguity among leaders of the young church and the precipitous growth of the AG during the 1940s and 1950s, certain players emerged who profoundly affected the institutionalization of the church. Most prominent among these were Riggs, Ashcroft, Zimmerman, and Kendrick. The patterns of behavior evident among Riggs and his colleagues in their quest for ways to contain charisma make it apparent that collective rationality, the notion that uncertain organizations imitate stable organizations, was preferred over ingenuity. These men surveyed and copied what they perceived to be successful means of containment in other religious movements and argued for a similar collegiate structure as a legitimate mechanism for the church's survivability.

After the charismatic stage moved toward formation and identity, a process of differentiation occurred. This was caused by those who first realized that charismatic authority was inherently unstable and that its transformation into institutionalized leadership was necessary for the survival of the group. As the first few decades passed, a new cadre of church leadership emerged which was more concerned with preserving the Pentecostal faith for future generations than its predecessors had been. If Christ did not return and the church was to survive beyond its first generation of believers, it would have to implement a strategy of reproduction. About this time, Riggs emerged as an AG leader who was deeply concerned about the survivability of the church. Not long after, others who shared with Riggs the vision for perpetuating the Pentecostal tradition were positioned in similar leadership roles. In their discussions as to various strategies for routinizing charisma within the church, these leaders concentrated their efforts on one option—the creation of the liberal arts college which would become Evangel College.

Riggs and his colleagues emphasized that this contingent college would be the bastion of orthodoxy for the church's children bound for non-ministerial careers. The retention and transmission of knowledge from one generation to the next became the goal of this second wave of leadership. As the denomination matured, it followed a trend toward rationalization; it more widely accepted means of transmitting information or doctrine. This rationalized process of retention manifested itself in the AG in terms of fraternal affiliations with other evangelical denominations, greater

18. Ibid., 154.

involvement in the local community, and the pursuit of financial and accreditation backing for Evangel College.

The 1940s and 1950s marked a period of development when the young church was facing uncertainties about its future. To confront these uncertainties, the decision-makers within the AG looked to religious organizations within the American religious mainstream they perceived to be orthodox and successful. Affiliation with the NAE and AABIBC provided the church leadership an alliance with other organizations within its own arena. In response to this crisis of routinization, the church leaders began to mimic structures of other denominations. James G. March and J. P. Olsen argue that when organizational technologies are poorly understood, when goals are ambiguous, or when the environment creates symbolic uncertainty, organizations model themselves after other organizations.[19] Similarly, Richard Cyert and James March link mimicking within organizational fields to uncertainty; when an organization faces a situation with ambiguous causes or unclear solutions, it may respond by modeling itself after those who have faced similar problems.[20] Finally, R. R. Nelson and S. G. Winter argue that weaker, younger, and more vulnerable organizations are compelled to imitate those organizations within their field they perceive to be more successful and legitimate.[21]

The process of imitating organizational developmental mechanisms might have made the AG more similar to other denominations, but in retrospect did not necessarily result in optimum efficiency. In the absence of evidence that mimicking other colleges within its field would increase organizational efficiency, church leaders nevertheless modeled the proposed college after other colleges within the other peer denomination's respective religious niches.[22] Instead of undertaking financial analyses and feasibility studies, it seemed most prudent to the leaders of the church to deal with their uncertainty by adapting the form of other evangelical denominations' liberal arts colleges which they perceived to be successful. In the mid-1940s Riggs gathered information from other colleges—colleges which were decried by Riggs for their anti-Pentecostal philosophies—to use in modeling the contingent AG liberal arts college. During the earliest stages of his planning, Riggs cursorily gathered information from the catalogs and bulletins of conservative evangelical colleges such as Wheaton, Gordon, Anderson, Taylor, Houghton, Asbury, and Westmont to use as models for the proposed

---

19. March and Olsen, "Uncertainty of the Past," 150.
20. Cyert and March, cited in DiMaggio and Powell, *Behavioral Theory*, 150.
21. Nelson and Winter, quoted in Youn and Loscocco, "Institutional History," 2.
22. DiMaggio and Powell, "Iron Cage Revisited," 147–50.

liberal arts college. In-depth discussion and analysis of any of this information, however, never materialized. He also frequently noted such religious movements as the Catholics, Mormons, and Seventh Day Adventists who established colleges as a means of their preserving their respective religious traditions. To justify the steps that were being taken to plan the new college, Riggs and his associates had to find a way to legitimize their actions.[23]

4. Information to Legitimize Routinization

The new leadership helped add to the institutionalization in the young AG by collecting information to rationalize their decision processes. In the process of lobbying for the college and subsequently planning the college, the decisions seemed based on a surveillance strategy; decisions were not embraced by a systematic in-depth strategy. What is meant by surveillance is that the information gathered was not necessarily characteristic of what would be most economically or ideologically prudent for the college.[24] Although a considerable amount of data and documents was amassed by men like Riggs and Ashcroft, and circulated among the members of the planning committees, no systematic process followed between the information gathered and the choices made. As AG leaders began to make decisions regarding the feasibility of a denominational liberal arts college, they had already reached their conclusion: the AG *needed* a college. Other religious movements had come to similar crossroads in their development, most of which had responded to the crisis of survival by creating collegiate structures. The arbitrary ways in which information was gathered substantiates the notion that the decision to create Evangel College was based on proponents responding to an evolutionary routinization within the church. Had information been collected which was vital to a particular decision, then it may be argued that the founding of the college was legitimized by proven needs. However, the insubstantial amount of information collected by the decision-makers had no correlation to the decisions made. Instead, planners gathered information to legitimize what they perceived to be successful methods of survivability implemented by other denominations. Arbitrary information was sought and considered, but the final decisions invariably disregarded the data in favor of the original opinion of the decision-makers. It can be concluded, therefore, that the link between information and decisions was weak.

23. See Corey, *From Opposition to Opening*, 49.
24. Feldman and March, "Information in Organizations," 173.

Although a collection of information by the college planners proved to have little value in the final decisions, the fact that information *was* collected engendered a belief among the planners and constituency that establishing the college was a necessity. In part, the decision-makers established their legitimacy by a ceremonial accumulation of information. For them, it was better to have information and not use it than not to have information at all. Martha S. Feldman and James March conclude that using information, asking for information, and justifying decisions in terms of information all come to be significant ways in which individuals and organizations symbolize that the process is legitimate, that they are good decision-makers, and that the organization is well-managed.[25] Within the AG, the college's most ardent proponents were not the rank and file members but those situated in the church's executive offices. From their positions of status, these college proponents accessed church publications, established committees, channeled funding, and adjusted agenda in hope of bettering the chances of an expeditious ratification by the General Council. By the time the motion came to the floor for the 1953 election, the church's several thousand voting delegates had been saturated by many forms of information detailing the church leadership's unequivocal position in favor of the college. Had the movement for the college been mobilized by those who did not enjoy access to Springfield's leverage, the college most likely would not have been authorized in 1953.

The historical narrative of the founding of Evangel College exposes ways in which information was manipulated so as to make the decision appear to be made within the bounds of careful planning. Regardless of the rationale underlying the decision, the college planners had little choice but to offer incentives in order to placate those skeptics who believed secular education would have a detrimental effect on the young church. Those who were most involved in the college's planning were those associated with the church's senior leadership. The incentives they offered accentuated attributes of the decision which were rooted in the purpose of the church. Zald refers to these as purposive incentives.[26] When the proposed liberal arts college was being considered, its supporters communicated to the local churches that the college would be an institution to preserve the morally and socially redemptive rudiments of the AG. Parents who enrolled students in Evangel College could expect their children to be educated in a thoroughly Pentecostal environment; the college would be an agent of the church created to contain the charisma of Pentecostalism. The planners pointed to

---

25. Ibid., 177–78.
26. Zald, "Theological Crucibles," 326–27.

programs, daily chapel services, admission criteria, non-academic faculty requirements, and various rules of behavior. These symbolic mechanisms were intended to be evidence of the college's ability to transmit values and beliefs, and proof to the constituency that the students would acquire these values and beliefs.

Given the uncertainty of leaders as to successful ways of continuing the institutionalization process, they looked next to other organizations for bureaucratic models. These leaders undertook no in-depth analysis on their data, and the data they did collect were negligible. Data were collected by the planners merely to legitimate their already-made decision, a method common among organizations uncertain about successful planning strategies. The leading men of the church were ambiguous as to what direction the denomination should take. Since the idea of the need for a college certainly did not originate out of a feasibility study, it stands to reason that the idea originated in what the leaders perceived to be successful in other organizations. The outcome was a liberal arts college founded as a means of perpetuating Pentecostalism.

Summary: The Emergence of a Collegiate Structure

The AG began in 1914 as a religious movement detached from virtually all interaction with elements of the formal academy. As the denomination grew in numbers and years, however, so did its involvement in the affairs of its external environments. This is often explained in sociological terms in that religious movements, in order to survive, follow discrete patterns of institutionalization. In many ways, the case of the AG and its decision to create Evangel College confirms the principles of institutionalization hypothesized by Weber, Durkheim, H. Richard Niebuhr, and others noted above. Specifically why and how the AG followed Weber's routinization of charisma is unclear. The answer lies in a complex web of external influences and internal choices, both interrelated with the issue of institutionalization and survivability.

As the AG matured, routinization proved inevitable. Although spokesmen at every level often lashed out against the suffocating effects of structure and bureaucracy, the creation of new offices increased precipitously within the church from 1920 to 1950. The church chose to, or was obligated to, form alliances with external elements which resulted in further adaption to a more routinized structure. These relationships resulted from environmental forces such as the nationwide increase in the number of college matriculants, particularly by way of the GI Bill of Rights and the educational requirements for chaplaincy in the armed forces. Finally, Evangel College came to fruition due to choices made within the ranks of the church's leadership which were based on surveillance of other denominations. AG leaders identified and imitated what they considered to be successful models of survival within other similar organizations. Churches which had adopted collegiate programs as a method of indoctrinating the rising generations became paradigmatic for the AG leaders.

The result of this routinization and ambiguity was the decision to establish a market-driven collegiate institution. This decision could be classified as rational because the college's academic programs were not principally based on philosophical models but mirrored the strategies of similar institutions within the church's organizational field. The popular and economically profitable academic majors in education, nursing, and business were included in Evangel College's first-year curriculum, making the college appear at first more like a professional school than a liberal arts college. Planners were packaging a product to sell to consumers which promised an institution where students could prepare for a profession, protected from the hazards of society, with others of similar beliefs.

Based on the historical data behind the decision to found Evangel College, it is clear that certain patterns of choice were linked to the church's position in the institutionalization process at a given time. The factors that played into the creation of the AG—the charismatic origins of the church, the sense of crisis, and the isolation due to the holiness movement—gave way to routinization as the need for new functions and legitimacy grew. Out of the maturation and routinization of the new church, a sense of ambiguity as to what form of ecclesiastical structure would be best for the survival of the church arose among the leadership. Because of the need for clear leadership, Riggs and other leaders arose and became profoundly affected by the notion of routinization and the need for the containment of the charisma. By imitating what they understood to be successful means of containment in other religious movements and gathering information to support their decisions, these leaders convinced the church that a collegiate structure was a necessary means of survival.

BIBLIOGRAPHY

Aldrich, H. E. and Jeffrey Pfeffer. "Environments of Organizations." *Annual Review of Sociology* 2 (1976) 79–105.

Bell, E. N. "General Convention of Pentecostal Saints and Churches of God in Christ." *Word and Witness* 9.12 (December 1913) 1.

Chase, Betty. "Evangel College Buildings and the Pioneers for Whom They Were Named." 1989. Manuscript found in Betty A. Chase Archives, Evangel University, Springfield, MO.

Corey, Barry. *From Opposition to Opening, the Story of How Evangel College Came to be: 1914-1955*. Springfield, MO: Evangel, 2005.

Cyert, Richard M. and James G. March. *A Behavioral Theory of the Firm*. Englewood Cliffs, NJ: Prentice-Hall, 1963.

DiMaggio, Paul J., and Walter W. Powell, "The Iron Cage Revisited: Institutional Isomorphism and Collective Rationality in Organizational Fields." *American Sociological Review* 48 (1983) 147–60.

Durkheim, Emile. *The Elementary Forms of Religious Life*. Translated by Joseph Ward Swain. Glencoe, IL: Free Press, 1954.

Feldman, Martha S. and James G. March. "Information in Organizations as Signal and Symbol." *Administrative Science Quarterly* 26 (1981) 171–86.

General Council of the Assemblies of God: Minutes. September 9–14, 1917. Held in Bethel Chapel, St. Louis, MO.

March, James G. "Emerging Developments in the Study of Organizations." *The Review of Higher Education* 6 (1982) 1–18.

March James G. and J. P. Olsen. "The Uncertainty of the Past: Organizational Learning Under Ambiguity." *European Journal of Political Research* 3 (1975) 147–71.

Niebuhr, H. Richard. *The Social Sources of Denominationalism*. Cleveland, OH: The World, 1967.

O'Dea, Thomas F., and Janet O'Dea Aviad. *The Sociology of Religion*. 2nd ed. Englewood Cliffs, NJ: Prentice Hall, 1983.

Otto, Rudolf. *The Idea of the Holy*. 2nd ed. Translated by J. W. Harvey. London: Oxford University Press, 1950.

Wach, Joachim. *The Sociology of Religion*. Chicago: University of Chicago Press, 1944.

Weber, Max. *Economy and Society*. 2 Vols. Edited by Guenther Roth and Claus Wittich. Translated by Ephraim Fischoff, et. al. Berkeley, CA: University of California Press, 2013.

Youn, Ted I. K., and Karyn Loscocco. "Institutional History, Ideology, and Organizational Decision Making: A Comparison of Two Women's Colleges." *History of Higher Education Annual* 11 (1991) 21–45.

Zald, Mayer N. "Theological Crucibles: Social Movements In and Of Religion." *Review of Religious Research* 23 (1982) 317–36.

THE LIBERAL ARTS AS INTERDISCIPLINARY EXPERIENCE

5

"How Primitive!" The Modern Pentecostal Movement as a Reflection of Cultural "Primitivism"

Robert Berg

Pablo Picasso, Igor Stravinsky, and William Seymour walk into a bar. Wait—this joke only works if you know who these men are. Since Picasso was probably the most important Western artist of the twentieth century, you may have heard of him. Stravinsky was one of the most important Western musicians of the twentieth century, but you might guess that he played hockey or chess. And only a very few will not be clueless about William Seymour, one of the leading figures of the modern Pentecostal movement. So I offer the following essay on cultural primitivism, after which I promise to bring the enlightened reader back to our bar scene.

Jacques Barzun claims that the West has had periodic attacks of primitivism, which he defines as the "longing to shuffle off the complex arrangements of an advanced culture."[1] Primitivism appears at the turn of the twentieth century driven by "emancipation" and "populism," both of which challenge the authorities and standards of centuries past.[2] I propose that like Picasso and Stravinsky, Seymour, as a representative of the modern Pentecostal revival, sought emancipation from cultural shackles and a reversion to something more "primitive."[3]

1. Jacque Barzun, *From Dawn to Decadence*, xix.

2. Ibid., 643–79.

3. The term "primitivism" was first used in France in the nineteenth century primarily to refer to fourteenth- and fifteenth-century Italian and Flemish paintings (Rubin,

Les Demoiselles D'Avignon

The young Pablo Picasso spent the summer of 1906 in Gosol, in the Catalonia region of northern Spain, in the Pyrenees. It was a critically important period of development for him artistically. Stimulation came in part from what was happening on the Paris artistic scene. In 1905, a group labeled the *Fauves* ("Wild Beasts") had provoked a scandal at a major exhibition by their shocking and seemingly unsophisticated use of vibrant color. The young artist first met the leading figure of this group, Henri Matisse, that next year. Picasso was also influenced by exhibitions of the work of Cezanne and Gauguin,[4] each presenting paintings challenging to a young artist searching for his own style.

In addition, Picasso was greatly affected by his study of ancient Iberian sculpture on display in the Louvre. In particular, he observed artifacts discovered in 1903, in Osuna, in southern Spain. His work during the summer and fall of 1906 reflects their influence. He increasingly strove to simplify the human form, stripping it down to its essentials. Bodies became less naturalistic and more block-like.[5]

In that fall of 1906, Picasso also began to work on what would become arguably the most important painting of the twentieth century.[6] Over the next three-quarters of a year, he made no less than 809 preliminary studies[7] for what would become known as *Les Demoiselles D'Avignon* (LDD).[8] Given how important the work has been in modern Western culture, it is not surprising that it has been the subject of many studies and interpretations.[9]

Primitivism, 2). Scholars are increasingly uncomfortable with the term "primitivism," since it often connotes a stereotypical and patronizing view of "the Other." See Diepeveen and Van Laar, *Art with a Difference*, 34–46.

4. Paul Gauguin represented a type of "primitivism," but it was more philosophical than artistic. That is, he advocated living apart from Europe, but depicted Tahitians, for example, in rather traditional European ways.

5. Picasso's *Portrait of Gertrude Stein* (1906) with its Iberian oversized head and eyes, demonstrates the change.

6. This work has been "long seen as a canonical work of modern primitivism," Perry, *Primitivism*, 4. "No twentieth century painting has attracted more attention; it bears unprecedented iconic fame." Richardson, *Life of Picasso*, 11.

7. That is, drawings working toward an ultimate painting. This is a number "unparalleled in the history of art." See Warncke, *Pablo Picasso*, 146.

8. As a rule Picasso did not name his paintings. He referred to this work as "The Avignon Brothel." The eventual title was given by André Salmon when it was first exhibited in 1916, apparently to minimize the offensive subject matter; *demoiselle* means young woman, not prostitute.

9. I lack the space to elaborate on how early sketches of the worked included two men, one with a skull in his hand. Picasso may have had in mind a sort of morality tale,

One of the most significant things about LDD is that it radically transformed a standard Western art form. The female nude had been a mainstay of European painting for centuries. Of course, taste had dictated that the nudes be removed from the immediate context; most acceptable were scenes from mythology, history, and the Bible. Only in recent times had this tradition been challenged, to the horror of refined tastes. Edouard Manet had dared to desentimentalize the female nude by depicting common French women of the time, unclothed and uncomfortably close to home. Picasso dared even further to challenge the underlying representational character of Western art. The sheer size of the canvas Picasso had made for the project—eight by seven and a half feet—indicates that he had significant goals in mind.

The viewer can perceive five women, whose bodies are done in tones that at least suggest skin color. The figures are set off by the burnt umber curtain to the left, and the white and blue segments that blatantly defy any sense of depth. Compositionally, the painting can be seen in either two or three parts horizontally. The top corner of the table at the bottom is precisely centered, and the triangle formed by the table is mirrored by the triangle formed by the arms of the figure in the middle. This would mean two parts. Yet the backgrounds to the figures suggest an irregular division with one figure on the left, two figures in the middle, and two to the right. The viewer is left uncertain.

What is most striking is the severity of the lines; the picture seems harsh, violent, and severe. The classical Western nude provided males with an acceptable means of dwelling on the beauty and desirability of the female body. There is none of that in this composition. The shape of the bodies appears to owe more to sculpture than to painting, ranging from merely block-like to monumental to downright contorted. Generally, scholars find that the central figures most resemble the Iberian sculpture Picasso had recently studied. We find here early characteristics of Cubist art: faces that are depicted from more than one perspective, with the face mostly straight on, but the nose from the side. The figure on the left is reminiscent of Egyptian art. But the infamous figures on the right are the most radical innovations. The lower figure sits as a prostitute might who is inviting the eye of a customer, but her head faces in the opposite direction. The upper figure occupies a nether world between representation and cubist abstraction.

The places where Picasso last reworked the painting have always demanded the viewer's eye and critical attention over the last century. Close examination shows that he reworked the head of the figure on the left,

---

given his fear of venereal disease.

making it darker, and reshaped the awkward hand holding back the curtain. And, most significantly, Picasso painted onto the figures on the right masks nearly as shocking today as in 1907.[10] Critics have battled for the last century over the origins and implications of these faces, but most believe that they were influenced by African masks that Picasso had viewed prior to or during his work on LDD. Picasso in later years denied this, but his protestations are usually regarded as unreliable.

The Iberian and African influence in the painting has led to its being considered an example of "primitivism." Scholars are agreed that artists of the time had little to no understanding of the original context and usage of the objects that captured Picasso's imagination. The masks that Picasso himself bought were in all likelihood less than a few decades old,[11] though he would not have realized that they were in no sense "ancient." Here is how Picasso described things about twenty years later:

> The masks weren't like other kinds of sculpture. Not at all. They were magical things.... The Negroes' sculptures were intercessors, I've known the French word ever since. Against everything; against unknown, threatening spirits.... They were weapons. To help people stop being dominated by spirits, to become independent. The spirits, the unconscious (which wasn't yet much spoken of then), emotion, it's the same thing.... *Les Demoiselles D'Avignon* must have come to me that day, but not at all because of the forms: but because it was my first canvas of exorcism—yes, absolutely![12]

Ultimately, it does not matter how old the masks were or even if they actually were made in Africa. What matters is that Picasso found in these objects the inspiration for a breathtakingly new approach to making art. These objects reflected a supernatural presence; as Picasso writes, we are here in the spiritual realm. But further, they exemplified "the freedom to distort anatomy for the sake of creating a rhythmic structure that can merge solids and voids and invent new shapes."[13] Undoubtedly, Picasso's perceptions

---

10. André Salmon, a good friend of Picasso, wrote in 1912: "It was the hideousness of the faces that froze with horror the half converted" (Salmon, *André Salmon*, 53).

11. Rubin, *Primitivism*, 243.

12. Cited in Flam and Deutch, *Primitivism and Twentieth-Century Art*, 33. Salmon reflects the same spirit: "Praise be the cannibal gods who gave us the courage of salutary massacres!" In Salmon, *André Salmon*, 145.

13. Rosenblum, *Cubism*, 26.

were colored by the paternalistic colonialism of Europeans toward places like Africa, but he was clearly more liberal in his views than most.[14]

What is pertinent is that Picasso used what he perceived to be "primitive" art as a revolutionary challenge to the culture of his time. Here was new life, a connection to the primal elements that had been lost in Europe. Renewal was possible only if artists reverted to an "earlier" time, before Europe had been paralyzed by tradition and propriety.[15] Whether the Iberian and African sculpture and masks were in any real sense the work of those who lived in an ancient time and were more in touch with the primal elements of life is not the point. The point is that Picasso thought (perhaps better: *felt*) that they were. "Picasso re-conceived the entirety of the European tradition from the roots up, and used its constituents to create a new visual language. It was not his intention to break with tradition. Rather, he was out to destroy convention—an altogether different undertaking."[16]

Herein lies the significance of LDD. It is "old" in that it follows the European tradition of the female nude, and still utilizes an array of standards of painting; there is even a still life of fruit! Yet it is radically new in its presentation. In contrast to the comfortable paintings of his main rival, Matisse, LDD is intentionally offensive, turning the female form into something terrifying. This is how LDD is a reflection of the cultural time. Dangerous times demand dangerous art. Picasso "stares into the abyss of the twentieth century and the social consequences of both its inventiveness and its self-destructive urges."[17]

LDD was not seen outside Picasso's studio until 1916. Even those privileged to see the canvas which had been rolled up against the wall—and thus only the artistically sophisticated—were as a rule shocked by it. Gertrude Stein, who supported the early Picasso and bought many of his works, apparently found it "ugly." Friends were horrified by how crude and offensive it was. Georges Braque, who within a year would be co-creating

---

14. Reports of abuse of Africans were in the news; some have suggested that Picasso intended the prostitutes to represent the oppressed in colonial rule. For example, Leighten, "White Peril," 621–30.

15. "As the new century approached, it was more and more broadly recognized that the ways human intelligence, society, and history worked were fundamentally *un* 'natural...'" and thus society must strive for what is natural, the "primitive." Kirk Varnedoe in Rubin, *Primitivism*, 183.

16. Warncke, *Pablo Picasso*, 163.

17. Joachimides and Rosenthal, *Age of Modernism*; "In essence, modernism, that was arguably inaugurated by Les Demoiselles D'Avignon, belongs to an irrecoverable past, as much the last outburst of a dying tradition as the beginning of a new age" (52).

Cubism with Picasso, said that the picture "made [me] feel as if someone were drinking gasoline and spitting fire."[18]

The Rite of Spring

When Sergei Diaghilev invited Igor Stravinsky to compose the music for the ballet *The Firebird* to be performed in Paris in 1910, he was taking a chance on a relatively unknown quantity. Diaghilev was riding high on a series of successes. He had mounted artistic exhibitions in Moscow and Paris, and in 1909 produced musical performances of Russian music in Paris that had been a smashing success. When mounting and moving entire opera companies and orchestras to Paris proved to be too costly, he hit upon the idea of what became the famous *Ballet Russes*, perhaps the most influential company of the twentieth century. Stravinsky proved to be more than up to the challenge. The ballets *The Firebird* in 1910 and *Petrushka* in 1911 were great successes both musically and dramatically. Part of the appeal to the Parisian audience was the subject matter: the strangely alien Russia, so far removed from the increasingly tiresome French cultural environment. Russia was in vogue. France, which had been isolated politically, signed a peace treaty with Russia in 1893. France celebrated and became culturally enamored of its new ally, and Stravinsky effectively created music that depicted the enchanting stories of what was deemed at the time the romantic "Orient."

Stravinsky maintained that the original idea for what was to become the culturally iconic *The Rite of Spring* (TROS)[19] came to him in 1909 when he was composing *The Firebird*. "I had dreamed of a scene of pagan ritual in which a chosen sacrificial virgin danced herself to death. The vision was not accompanied by concrete musical ideas . . . "[20] But the original idea for a ballet based on ancient pagan Russian practices probably came from Nicholas Roerich, the eventual artistic director, and "Russia's acknowledged specialist in the art of paganistic antiquity, both real and imaginary."[21] "Ro-

---

18. Hunter, Jacobus, and Wheeler, *Modern Art*, 136. Given that Picasso and his friends had anarchistic tendencies, the violent connotations of Braque's language is interesting.

19. "The *Rite* is universally viewed as an icon of modernism, dominating the twentieth century as Beethoven's Ninth Symphony did the nineteenth." Hill, *Stravinsky*, vii.

20. Stravinsky and Craft, *Memories*, 87. Stravinsky's "memories" are so varied and contradictory that in his recent, exhaustive study, Tarushkin refused to consider his narratives for documentary purposes, citing Stravinsky's "Orwellian memory hole." Tarushkin, *Stravinsky*, 12.

21. Ibid., 851. Roerich had worked with Diaghilev on his previous successes in Paris.

erich's mystic, spiritual experiences made him strangely susceptible to the charm of this ancient world. He felt in it something primordial and weird, something that was intimately linked with nature."[22]

Roerich reflected a Russian neo-nationalism in the late nineteenth century that corresponds with the cultural primitivism associated with Picasso at the turn of the century. Both Peter the Great (1672–1725) and Catherine the Great (1729–1796) reflected a trend toward European cultural development that at times involved a disparagement of the relative backwardness and coarseness of Russian culture. The nineteenth century brought a reaction that highlighted the distinctive glories of Russian culture.[23] For Roerich, the popular myth and, further back, the primordial state of man embodied "an archaic and cohesive strength lacking in the disruptive society of pre-Revolutionary Russia."[24]

> The fancied spiritual wholeness of primeval man was something after which many in Russia were hankering in the decades following emancipation[25] and (belated) industrialization, when the educated minority was forced to confront the cultural and spiritual implications of the forced uprooting of the peasantry. ... The urgent task of art was to renounce *kultura* and embrace *stikhiya* (elemental spontaneity) and thus transform itself into an amulet for restoring wholeness to the battered soul of contemporary man.[26]

Roerich's primitivism, then, was focused on the peasantry of ancient pagan Russia and, more fundamentally, primal man prior to any national identity. Scenery was minimal. Costumes were uniform and rustic. This would have been shockingly different from ballet as Parisians knew it and no doubt contributed to the negative reaction to its "primitivism."

Choreography for TROS was assigned to Vaslav Nijinsky, known widely for his performance as a dancer but limited in his experience as a choreographer. His version of primitivism led him to defy all standards of ballet form in order to match the primal subject matter. Witnesses describe

---

22. This was the judgment of Alexandre Benois, a painter involved with Diaghilev productions, Benois, *Reminiscences of the Russian*, 347.

23. "Going primitive" (*oproshcheniye*) dominated the Russian artistic scene at the time, with peasant arts colonies becoming influential, Tarushkin, *Stravinsky*, 855.

24. Bowlt, *Moscow and St. Petersburg*, 172; Life in a peasant village was probably not the idealized picture of Roerich or Tolstoy, but closer to that depicted by Anton Chekhov in his 1897 short story, "Peasants," which describes Russian peasants as "rough, dishonest, filthy, drunken" (221).

25. That is, emancipation of the serfs in 1861.

26. Tarushkin, *Stravinsky*, 850.

how the dancers in groups hopped around the stage, as if earthbound, defying the classical effort of ballet to soar in the air: head turned, feet awkwardly turned in, knees bent, arms tucked in. "In other words, the classical pose was contradicted entirely by what appeared to many as knock-kneed contortion."[27] One recalls seeing the woman playing The Chosen One "standing in her trance, her heels out. A sudden convulsion projects her body sideways in space. . . . She writhes and shrivels in an ecstatic seizure. And this primitive hysteria, terribly ludicrous, fascinates and overwhelms the helpless onlooker."[28]

For Diaghilev, ballet, as everything else, was a show; "art was not meant to teach or imitate reality; above all, it was to produce experience."[29] "He conceived of art as a means of deliverance and regeneration. The deliverance would be from the social constraints of morality and convention, and from the priorities of a western civilization—of which Russia was increasingly a part—dominated by a competitive and self-denying ethic. The regeneration would involve the recovery of a spontaneous emotional life.[30] For him, "primitivism" was a reversion to a time free of the moral and religious restraints of contemporary Europe.

Stravinsky worked diligently with Roerich to create a format for the ballet. They referred to the work in its early stages as *The Great Sacrifice*, in line with Stravinsky's avowed dream scene. In its final form, TROS has two parts, as follows:

> First Part: A Kiss of the Earth
> > Introduction
> > The Augurs of Spring (Dance of the Young Girls)
> > Ritual of Abduction
> > Spring Rounds
> > Ritual of the Two Rival Tribes
> > Procession of the Oldest and Wisest One
> > The Kiss of the Earth
> > The Dancing Out of the Earth
>
> Second Part: The Exalted Sacrifice
> > Introduction
> > Mystic Circle of the Young Girls

---

27. Modris Eksteins, *Rites of Spring*, 51.
28. André Levinson in Lederman, *Stravinsky in the Theater*, 27.
29. Eksteins, *Rites of Spring*, 32.
30. Ibid., 30.

"HOW PRIMITIVE!" 93

The Naming and Honoring of the Chosen One
Evocation of the Ancestors or Ancestral Spirits
Ritual Action of the Ancestors
Sacrificial Dance

The pervasive atmosphere of the ballet is religious. The mystical context is clear even from the names of the musical segments. "Augurs" are omens ritually danced. The Kiss (alternately translated as Adoration) of the Earth by the Oldest and Wisest in the village unleashes a wild display of primal energies. The elders evoke the ancestral spirits.The essence of Stravinsky's dream now comprises the Second Part, in which one young girl is chosen and honored to represent the group, and concludes the ballet by dancing to death in front of the elders.[31] The First Part appears to come from the imagination of Roerich, the amateur archaeologist, who had written on pagan rituals and done a series of paintings with remarkably similar titles: *Ritual Dance, The Elders Gather, The Prophet Stone, Holy Place, Idols, The Stone Age*. The ballet is not so much a coherent story, but a series of scenes. One might even say that the performance of the TROS is not so much the portrayal of certain ancient rituals, but a ritual itself in its enactment.

I have noted the primitive or crude nature of the scenery, costumes, and choreography of the ballet.[32] Stravinsky's music is a brilliant integration of extremely sophisticated versions of traditional Russian folk music and what sounds at first to be primitively raw percussive power. Pierre Monteux, who would conduct the infamous premiere performance in 1913, recalled his first hearing in 1912: "With only Diaghilev and myself as audience, Stravinsky sat down to play a piano reduction of the entire score. Before he got very far I was convinced that he was raving mad. Heard this way, without the color of the orchestra ... the crudity of the rhythm was emphasized, its stark primitiveness underlined."[33]

Stravinsky achieves the impression of pagan primitiveness in a variety of ways, many of which would carry us deeper into technical musical terminology than is called for here, but I must mention a few. First, he uses the extreme registers for woodwinds and strings to conjure in the mind a strange and mysterious scene. The first notes, for example, are played by a solo bassoon in a register so high that story has it that renowned composer Camille Saint-Saëns did not even recognize the instrument.[34] He avoids

---

31. It is noteworthy that there is no evidence of human sacrifice in ancient Slavic practice; at least for Stravinsky, primitivism need not be authentic.
32. Or at least the perception thereof.
33. Pierre Monteux in Lederman, *Stravinsky in the Theatre*, 128.
34. He is supposed to have said, "If that is a bassoon, I am a baboon." If he actually

the solo strings with their warmer, more human connotation. Second, he utilizes a very large orchestra—120 instruments—allowing for what is at times overwhelmingly powerful sound. Third, and most important, Stravinsky uses rhythm in such fundamentally pervasive and innovative ways that twentieth century music would dramatically be changed as a result.[35]

Roerich, then, yearned for the primitive Russia (or even the primeval, Stone Age world), Nijinsky for a more primitive form of dance unencumbered by traditional standards, and Diaghilev for primitively liberated mores. But Stravinsky "was attracted by the idea of 'reconstructing the mysterious past' chiefly because it gave him free scope in his search for unusual rhythms and sounds. Naturally nothing was known of the music of those remote days and Stravinsky felt himself free from all constraint and all rules."[36]

Though TROS may appear to be "primitive," "the means to this end were sophisticated in the extreme."[37] In an insightful monogram, Peter Hill argues that TROS is a "supreme manifestation of *stikhiya*," the elemental nature in contrast to shifting, artificial *kultura* of modern society and the intelligentsia. It is a "drama beyond good and evil, beyond the strivings of free will, a drama of life lived in instinctive acceptance, whether of the forces of nature or of the spirits;" Stravinsky made both his music and the figures on stage behave like machines and thus "what purported to be a stone-age ballet [was also] prophetic of the modern world—of war, destruction, of life dehumanised."[38]

In contrast to the limited, private inaugural presentation of LDD, the premiere of TROS in Paris on May 29, 1913 is one of the outstanding legends of twentieth century culture. According to Eksteins, "[t]o have been in the audience that evening was to have participated not simply in another exhibition but in the very creation of modern art, in that the response of the audience was and is as important to the meaning of this art as the intentions of those who introduced it."[39] As with any legend, evaluating how much of the legend is based on actual events is difficult.[40]

---

said this or not, it has entered the lore of *The Rite*. Another attendee that night wrote that the sounds of the bassoons were "as if perforated skulls were beaten by the agile fingers of a cannibal" (Levinson, in Lederman, 26).

35. Claude Debussy referred to TROS as "*une musique nègre*" (Stravinsky and Craft, *Memories*, 90).

36. Benois, *Reminiscences*, 347.

37. Hill, *Stravinsky*, 142.

38. Ibid., 143–44.

39. Eksteins, *Rites of Spring*, 15.

40. In 2005, the BBC made a film of *Riot at the Rite* directed by Andy Wilson.

Take, for example, this firsthand account: "The young man seated behind me in the box stood up during the course of the ballet to enable himself to see more clearly. The intense excitement under which he was labouring betrayed itself presently when he began to beat rhythmically on top of my head with his fists. My emotion was so great I did not feel the blows for some time."[41] It is hard to reconcile such an account with the common testimony that there was so much noise in the hall that the music could hardly be heard. Stravinsky himself was so exasperated at the tumult that he went backstage and "for the rest of the performance [he] stood in the wings behind Nijinsky holding the tails of his *frac*, while he stood on a chair shouting numbers to the dancers, like a coxswain."[42]

It was only by the astounding calm and determination of Pierre Monteux, the conductor, that the performance was actually completed. Although some of the noise came from vocal supporters of the work, much of the disruption was caused by opponents with boos and catcalls. "Neighbors began to hit each other with fists, canes, or whatever came to hand. Soon this anger was concentrated against the dancers, and then, more particularly, against the orchestra, the direct perpetrator of the musical crime. Everything available was tossed in our direction."[43] For most Parisians, TROS was cultural blasphemy. "With its violence, dissonance, and apparent cacophony, the music was as energetic and primitive as the theme."[44] Its assault was parallel to that of LDD:

> The ballet contains and illustrates many of the essential features of the modern revolt: the overt hostility to inherited form; the fascination with primitivism and indeed with anything that contradicts the notion of civilization; the emphasis on vitalism as opposed to rationalism; the perception of existence as continual flux and a series of relations, not as constants and absolutes; the psychological introspection accompanying the rebellion against social convention.[45]

This is what Jacques Barzun notes was characteristic of the turn of the twentieth century; as Picasso sought emancipation from the straightjacket of

---

41. Carl van Vechten, quoted in Eric Walter White, *Stravinsky*, 214.
42. Stravinsky and Craft, *Memories*, 91.
43. Monteux, in Lederman, *Stravinsky in the Theatre*, 148.
44. Eksteins, *Rites of Spring*, 50.
45. Many in the Paris press joked about *Le Massacre du printemps* (Ibid., 52). After the near riot at the premiere, Diaghilev reflected how much ahead of his cultural time he was with his comment: "Exactly what I wanted." (Stravinsky and Craft, *Memories*, 91).

lifeless European cultural traditions, so the collaborators involved in TROS sought in their individual ways emancipation from the perceived deficiencies of their cultural contexts. Both Picasso and Stravinsky created a new language by integrating traditional Western forms with what seemed to be an audaciously revolutionary treatment of those forms.[46] Each reflects a spent Western culture at a loss to address the challenges of the new century. Each finds inspiration in an earlier time and place, purer and free of "civilized" restraints.

The Azusa Street Revival

What remains is to demonstrate how the modern Pentecostal movement has a connection to all this. While it is true that the first General Council of the Assemblies of God occurred in an opera house, its participants probably were inclined to exorcize the place beforehand! What, indeed, does Azusa Street have to do with the Champs-Élysées? Besides the fact that the Azusa Street revival, the explosion of modern Pentecostalism, occurs in the same Cubist Decade as the iconic works of Picasso and Stravinsky, what other common factors are there?

Humans throughout history have pined for a time, a "golden age," when things were much better. Sometimes the nostalgia is motivated by a deterioration in social behavior, corruption or ineffectiveness in government, or the lamentable state of the arts. The object of our desires may be as remote as the beginnings of the earth or as recent as the day before.[47] The idealization of a pristine time has been particularly marked in the United States, since the "recovery of primal norms has been a fundamental preoccupation of the American people."[48] One of the most important writers in American history, Thomas Paine, wrote of the American opportunity, free of centuries of corrupting European institutions: "We are brought at once to the point of seeing government begin, as if we had lived in the beginning of time."[49] We could start fresh, untarnished by millennia of "the errors of tradition."[50]

---

46. Many scholars refer to the creation of a new "language" or "vocabulary" by Picasso, Warncke, *Pablo Picasso,* 151–53; Rosenblum, *Cubism,* 25–26; and Stravinsky, Yarustovsky, "Foreword," vii.

47. For many contemporary Caucasian Americans, at least, the 1950s was a golden age.

48. Richard Hughes and C. Leonard Allen, *Illusions of Innocence,* 3.

49. Thomas Paine, *Rights of Man,* 282.

50. Ibid.

The desire to recover the characteristics of an earlier form of the faith can be traced throughout Christian history, as well. Of special relevance is the fact that all Protestants descend from a movement in the sixteenth century to restore the faith to a purer, biblical form. The Reformation can only be understood as part of a Christian humanism that placed highest value on the manuscripts of Scripture and the earliest church in much the same way that the artists of the Renaissance placed highest value on Greco-Roman culture. The early primitivist colonial Puritans "held tenaciously to the notion of human depravity, but not so tenaciously as to preclude their conviction that they could, through determined and concerted effort, launch a millennial age born ultimately of first times;"[51] Puritan settlement in America was nothing less than a "restorationist crusade."[52]

The Second Great Awakening (1790–1840) spurred a renewed interest in primitive Christianity. What is known as the Restoration Movement of the nineteenth century gave birth to an array of groups: Mormons (The Latter Day Saint Movement), the Churches of Christ, Adventists, and Jehovah's Witnesses. Though these groups demonstrate a breathtaking diversity on the continuum of Christianity they share an intense restorationist impulse.

Picasso and Stravinsky reflect a primitivism that came to the fore around the turn of the twentieth century that more broadly has been characterized as a "retreat from the industrialized world."[53] Industrialization and urbanization were taking their toll on society. Labor unrest was high. Anarchistic violence threatened the stability of government and social institutions. An anarchist had assassinated the United States President in 1901. Theodore Roosevelt, on April 14, 1906—the same weekend of the opening of the Azusa Street Mission—stated in a major speech that the country was passing through a period of "social, political, and industrial unrest."[54] Population was exploding, creating a new, mass society. This was particularly frightening to many Americans because of the unprecedented number of immigrants entering the country. Immigration reached its all-time zenith between 1905 and 1914; the absolute peak came in 1907, with the most immigrants in any one year in American history: 1,285,349.[55] Resultant social tensions, not surprisingly, led to violence; the first decade of the century was marked by race riots and lynchings.[56]

51. Richard Hughes, *American Quest*, 13.
52. Hughes and Allen, *Illusions of Innocence*, 25–33.
53. Barzun, *From Dawn to Decadence*, 617.
54. Cited in Edmund Morris, *Theodore Rex*, 443.
55. Sean Dennis Cashman, *America Ascendant*, 88.
56. The Atlanta race riots, with dozens of blacks killed, occurred over a few days in

These social realities had a major impact on the eschatology of religious groups in America. Earlier in the nineteenth century, postmillennialism[57] had been predominant. But as the turn of the century drew near, civilization seemed to be deteriorating rather than progressing; the optimism of postmillennialism no longer appeared to align with the times.[58] "Owing to a nostalgic sense of the pristine purity of early Christian experience, restorationists often remember selectively and yearn for the return of 'the good old days.' In the closing decades of the nineteenth century, some restorationists sought to restore the apostolic faith; others anticipated a divine restoration."[59]

This looking forward to the past was reflected in different ways. The French, in a mild form of this condition, nostalgically feared the results of the ebbing of their culture. The Russian version was more eschatological or even apocalyptic.[60] In the United States, evangelicals, on whom early Pentecostals often relied for doctrinal guidance, increasingly saw the approach of the new century as significant.[61] Signs indicated that biblical prophecies would soon be fulfilled and influential writers like Dwight Moody and A. T. Pierson foresaw some great event at the turn of the century.[62]

What Pentecostals added to the scenario was the conviction that the divine outpouring of the Holy Spirit with the gifts described in the New Testament was evidence that God was empowering the church for a final evangelistic thrust before the Second Coming of Christ. Charles Parham, among others, believed this meant in particular that the ability to speak in unlearned languages would be the means by which the world would be converted,[63] and he so instructed William Seymour, pastor-to-be of the Azusa Street Mission. The early editions of the newspaper of The Azusa

---

September, 1906.

57. The belief that God would enable the church to so transform the world that Jesus would return *after* a millennium of peace on the earth.

58. Marsden, *Fundamentalism*, 66–67.

59. Blumhofer, *Restoring the Faith*, 13.

60. TROS has been deemed a reflection of violent "Scythianism" in prerevolutionary Russia, since the ancient Scyths, a mythical half-human ancestor race, were associated at the time "with the form of the coming giant, of the full elemental force that would bring with it a new, unusual, but frightening and perhaps dangerous beginning." (Yarustovsky, "Foreword," vii). Also Tarushkin, *Stravinsky*, 437, 856–58, Bowlt, *Moscow*, 347–48.

61. Grant Wacker states that the "dry rot of mainstream conservatism . . . " contributed to the "religious ferment of the late nineteenth century." Wacker, "Holy Spirit," 62.

62. Blumhofer, *Restoring the Faith*, 15; Marsden, *Fundamentalism*, 102.

63. He probably got this idea from his visit to Frank Sandford and his The Holy Ghost and Us community in 1900. See Robeck, *Azusa Street Mission*, 41–42.

Street Mission, *The Apostolic Faith*,[64] highlighted the expectation that missionaries called to fields around the world would be enabled to preach the gospel in the language of the native lands without having studied it.[65]

Early Pentecostals were not uniformly distinguished by a belief in "missionary tongues," however, but by the more general conviction that God's bestowment of the gifts of the Spirit proved that the church had only a short time for an empowered ministry before the end of time. If anyone needed any clearer sign that the apocalypse was near, within days of the opening of the mission on Azusa Street in Los Angeles, San Francisco was rocked by the now famous earthquake of April 18, 1906. For those at the mission, it was no coincidence that the *Los Angeles Times* first published reports of the Azusa revival on that same day, and that minor quakes hit Los Angeles itself the next day.[66]

Early Pentecostal primitivism thus was apocalyptic. Adherents did not expect a progressive restoration of the New Testament church and thereby the larger culture as did the postmillennialists a century earlier. Rather, the very fact that God was empowering the church to its original character was proof that the time was very short. Prophecies and interpretations of tongues in those early days of the Pentecostal revival emphasized that Jesus was coming soon, and that there was little time to bring in the final harvest of souls.

One of the most popular metaphors used by Pentecostals was the biblical description of the "early and latter rain" of Palestine.[67] The "early rain," it was proclaimed, was that rain that came early in the Palestinian growing year to give the seed initial growth, while the "latter rain" was rain that came late in the agricultural year before harvest.[68] In Pentecostal eyes, the early rains were the blessings of God described in the Book of Acts to get the church going, the latter rains the "new Pentecost" to finish the work of the church in this age. In one fell swoop, then, the movement linked directly to the Book of Acts; it "leaps the intervening years crying, 'Back to Pentecost.'"[69]

---

64. Presumably edited or approved by Seymour.

65. Although an early disciple of Parham, Seymour broke alliance with his former teacher over issues of doctrine and race relations.

66. Robeck, *Azusa Street Mission*, 6, 76–80.

67. The latter rain concept "hung thick in the sectarian air pentecostals breathed." Grant Wacker, *Heaven Below*, 256.

68. See passages such as Deut 11:14 and Joel 2:23. It is surely not insignificant that the Joel passage is followed by verses important to Pentecostals since they are cited in Acts 2.

69. Lawrence, "Apostolic Faith Restored," in Dayton's *Three Early Pentecostal Tracts*, 12.

G. F. Taylor in 1907 worked out the analogy to allow for some divine work over 1900 years, but not its fullness:

> This early rain continued for more than a hundred years, during which time the church was kept inundated with mighty floods of salvation. But when the church became popular and was formed into a great hierarchy, the long drought began, interspersed with a local shower of gracious revival now and then through the middle ages. Under the reformation, the latter rain began to be foreshadowed. The holiness revivals which have been going on in our land for the last few years are the preliminary showers of this rain. . . . The Scriptures seem to teach that the latter rain is to be far greater than the former.[70]

The primitivism of these Pentecostals reflects, "in accord with its Latin root *primus*, a determination to return to first things, original things, fundamental things."[71] "It denotes believers' yearning to be guided solely by God's Spirit in every aspect of their lives, however great or small. . . . They yearned physically to enter the apostolic world, to breathe its air, feel its life, see its signs and wonders with their own eyes."[72] As B. F. Lawrence put it in 1916: "And now perhaps you are asking, 'In what particulars are you so earnestly striving to revert to primitive Christianity?' The answer, of course, 'In every way.'"[73]

Those at the Azusa Street Mission believed that God was doing this eschatological work in their midst. Frank Bartleman provides an important first hand perspective: "Los Angeles seems to be the place and this the time, in the mind of God, for the restoration of the Church to her former place, favor, and power. The fullness of time seems to have come for the Church's complete restoration. . . . The base of operations has been shifted, from the old Jerusalem to Los Angeles for the latter 'Pentecost.'"[74] Seymour, in *The Apostolic Faith*, thinks in the same way, choosing telling language in the headlines of the first issues: "PENTECOST HAS COME: Los Angeles Being

---

70. Taylor, "Spirit and the Bride" in Dayton's *Three Apostolic Tracts*, 90–91.

71. Wacker, *Heaven Below*, 12; Prior to his treatment of Pentecostal primitivism in this work, Wacker had earlier written "Playing for Keeps: The Primitivist Impulse in Early Pentecostalism," in Hughes, *American Quest*.

72. Wacker, *Heaven Below*, 72.

73. Lawrence, "Apostolic Faith Restored," in Dayton's *Three Early Pentecostal Tracts*, 13. Of course, all restorationists are selective in what features of "biblical Christianity" they seek to reinstitute. It has been said that primitivism works like a kind of two-way mirror in which one sees more of oneself than of the object supposedly on the other side of the glass.

74. Bartleman, *Another Wave of Revival*, 100.

Visited by a Revival of Bible Salvation and Pentecost as Recorded in the Book of Acts," and "The Pentecostal Baptism Restored: The Promised Latter Rain Now Being Poured Out on God's Humble People."[75] This vision of "primitive Christianity" looks like a mixture of the New Testament and recent Americana when he elaborates that "the apostolic faith movement" "[s]tands for the restoration of the faith once delivered unto the saints—the old time religion, camp meetings, revivals, missions, street and prison work and Christian Unity everywhere."[76]

The press first begins to react to what was happening in the run-down building on Azusa Street within days of the opening of the mission; the initial headline was "Weird Babel of Tongues."[77] In July 1906 one newspaper announced, "'Religious Fanaticism Creates Wild Scenes.' Accompanying this headline were such delectable subtitles as, 'Holy Kickers Carry on Mad Orgies,' and 'At All Night Meetings in Azusa Street Church, Negroes and Whites Give Themselves Over to Strange Outbursts of Zeal.' Not to be outdone, another newspaper excitedly cried out, 'Women with Men Embrace.' Others joined in: 'Whites and Blacks Mix in a Religious Frenzy.'"[78]

Pastors of local churches considered what was happening as dangerous. One ridiculed the Azusa Mission this way:

> they come with the blare of trumpets out of tune and harmony, but lustily blown with all the power of human or inhuman lungs; they shine with phosphorescent gleam, strangely like that of brimstone, and with odor more or less tainted; they distract the affrighted atmosphere with a bewildering jargon of babbling tongues of all grades—dried, boiled, and smoked; they rant and dance and roll in a disgusting amalgamation of African voudou superstition and Caucasian insanity, and will pass away like the hysterical nightmares that they are.[79]

---

75. Seymour, *Apostolic Faith*, 1.1 (September 1906); 1.2 (October 1906). Of course, the name of the paper itself is significant, having been taken from Parham's name for his own ministry. As noted above, the editorial work in *The Apostolic Faith* is either done or approved by Seymour.

76. Seymour, *Apostolic Faith*, 1.1:2.

77. *Los Angeles Times*, April 18, 1906, cited in Robeck, *Azusa Street Mission*, 75.

78. Robeck, *Azusa Street Mission*, 125–26; At a similar meeting nearby, a *Los Angeles Daily Times* journalist wrote that although a young woman claimed to be speaking Arabic, she "sounded like the rapid chattering of a frightened simian." Wacker, *Heaven Below*, 100.

79. Cited in Robeck, *Azusa Street Mission*, 9.

Proposals

The term *fin de siècle*, literally "end of century," originated in a play in 1888, and came to be applied to a "cultural malaise" in late-nineteenth-century Europe. With the failure of liberalism, anarchism became by the end of the century an organized movement promoting violence to overthrow governments in Italy, Spain, France, Russia, and the United States. By the early twentieth century, there was throughout Europe an awareness that a "major war was inevitable and would be disastrous, but many observers also felt that a cataclysm was needed to wipe out the clinging remnants of a 'decadent' civilization."[80]

One can find in the first years of the twentieth century a spirit of anarchistic emancipation from the cultural powers. The three main figures in this paper, respectively, find the art, the music, and the church of the time totally inadequate for the demands of the new era. It is nothing new to find parallels between Picasso and Stravinsky; *Les Demoiselles D'Avignon* and *The Rite of Spring* are considered by many to be the birth pangs of modern art and music, even "modernism."[81] The forces that had held Western culture together were at the breaking point, the same forces that would inevitably lead to the catastrophe of World War I. Picasso and Stravinsky had to create "a new language" because the language into which they were born no longer held "true." What makes Picasso and Stravinsky geniuses is that they were able to express the principles that were in the air, that were "twitching in everybody's fingers."[82]

What I have attempted to demonstrate is that the "modern Pentecostal movement" is actually more "modernist" than it is "modern."[83] Pentecostals responded to the same cultural forces that influenced Picasso and Stravinsky; they were born in the same air of unrest—social, economic, political, artistic. For example, early Pentecostals were well aware of and disturbed by the economic tensions of the time. Charles Parham wrote:

> United States, with her I.W.W.'s, radical socialists and anarchist element, afford a more fertile soil for the propagation of Bolshevism than Russia herself. The gulf between capital and labor

---

80. Shearer West, *Fin de Siècle*, 15.

81. In *Dawn to Decadence*, Barzun calls 1905–1914 the Cubist Decade (643–79). The fifteen years prior to World War I have often been called *la belle époque*, no doubt the case compared to the horror of the War, but also an interesting example of a nostalgic primitivism, 651, 684–98. See, e.g., Hunter et al., *Modern Art*, 136.

82. Mitchell, *Language of Modern Music*, 63, 78.

83. That is, it reflects the twentieth-century "modernist" rebellion against long-established norms in the modern West.

is so wide and deep that it can never be filled or salved by any government or capitalistic propaganda. The death struggle is on, and the working classes are determined to rule in the future, not only in Europe but in the United States.[84]

And in the second issue of *The Apostolic Faith* (October 1906) there is an intriguing prophecy by a Sister Mary Galmon of Pasadena. The Lord revealed to her an earthquake coming to Los Angeles in which there will be (in God's words): "mangling and tangling of wires, and street car rails will bend and twist, and the telegraph poles will come down." This describes nothing less than a divine attack on modern transportation and communication! The revelation continues. In a section entitled "Labor Against Capital," the Lord tells of a time when the rich will horde goods and the poor will then break in to get something to eat. Then "the rich man will come out with his gun to make war with the laboring man." The blood will be ankle deep, like rain pouring on the streets. The Lord is also quoted as saying that "all these unions are bringing the sword to their own head, to cut off their own heads off." Sister Galmon then clarifies: "I had never heard of unions before the Lord showed me this and I asked my husband what 'labor against capital' meant."[85] Anxiety about economic unrest is evident among Pentecostals of the time, who, it turns out, were demographically much like Americans[86] and very much like other evangelicals of the time.[87]

As far removed from the Paris of Picasso and Stravinsky as they were, Pentecostals like William Seymour struggled, in a time of social unrest, with similar cultural restraints that kept them from realizing their mission. The church was dead, wholly unequipped to fulfill its function. In the words of Frank Bartleman in 1906:

> We are to drop out the centuries of the Church's failure, the long, dismal "dark ages," and telescoping time, be now fully restored to pristine power, victory, and glory. We seek to pull ourselves by the grace of God, out of a corrupt, backslidden, spurious Christianity... The precious ore of truth, the Church's emancipation from the bondage of man's rule, has been brought about in a necessarily crude form at first, as rough ore. . . . A great

---

84. Parham, *Everlasting Gospel*, 26.
85. Seymour, *Apostolic Faith*, 1.2:2.
86. Wacker, *Heaven Below*, 216.
87. "Pentecostals, like other radical evangelicals, were often people who experienced a deep sense of cultural loss, even betrayal. They perceived encroaching modernity as a sinister enemy eroding social values, bankrupting theology, and displacing individuals" (Blumhofer, *Restoring the Faith*, 12).

truth is struggling in the bowels of the earth, entombed by the landslide of retrograding evil in the Church's history. But it is bursting forth, soon to shake itself free from the objectionable matter yet clinging to it.[88]

Drop the reference to God (and the word "backslidden") and replace "Church" and "Christianity" with "Western culture," and you have a statement that either Picasso or Stravinsky might have written.

We can now return to our bar scene. "You fellas look pretty primitive to me," said the barkeep. "What'll you have?" Seymour, glancing at the collection of bottles behind the bar, said, "Give me a shot of Early Times." Stravinsky, spying what he had in mind, roared, "I'll have some of that Ancient Age!" But Picasso could find nothing to meet his primitive intentions. Finally, he declared, "Well, since I'm the most interesting man in the world, I'll have a Dos Equis." *Les Demoiselles D'Avignon*, *The Rite of Spring*, and the Azusa Street Revival were all prison breaks; each was an "emancipation" from the shackles of the cultural powers at the turn of the twentieth century. Picasso and Stravinsky found liberation from a dying culture in the life of African and Iberian objects, and the life of pagan Russia, respectively. Seymour and the Pentecostals found liberation from such a dying culture in the life of the Book of Acts. In each case, the general observer considered the "liberation" a radically new language, but each of these cultural primitivists believed that a primal tongue was being restored.

BIBLIOGRAPHY

Bartleman, Frank. *Another Wave of Revival*, edited by John G. Myers. Springdale, AR: Whitaker, 1962.

Barzun, Jacque. *From Dawn to Decadence. 500 Years of Western Cultural Life: 1500 to the Present*. New York: Harper, 2000.

Benois, Alexander. *Reminiscences of the Russian Ballet*. Translated by Mary Britnieva. New York: Da Capo, 1977.

Blumhofer, Edith L. *Restoring the Faith. The Assemblies of God, Pentecostalism, and American Culture*. Urbana, IL: University of Illinois Press, 1993.

Bowlt, John E. *Moscow and St. Petersburg 1900–1920*. New York: Vendome, 2008.

Cashman, Sean Dennis. *America Ascendant*. New York: New York University Press, 1998.

Chekhov, Anton. "Peasants." In *The Oxford Chekhov*. Vol. VIII. Translated by Ronald Hingley, 193–222. New York: Oxford University Press, 1965.

Dayton, Donald, ed. *Three Early Pentecostal Tracts*. New York: Garland, 1985.

Diepeveen, Leonard, and Timothy Van Laar. *Art with a Difference*. Mountain View, CA: Mayfield, 2001.

---

88. Bartleman, *Another Wave of Revival*, 100–2.

Eksteins, Modris. *Rites of Spring. The Great War and the Birth of the Modern Age.* New York: Doubleday, 1989.
Flam, Jack, and Miriam Deutch, eds. *Primitivism and Twentieth-Century Art.* Berkeley, CA: University of California Press, 2003.
Hill, Peter. *Stravinsky: The Rite of Spring.* New York: Cambridge University Press, 2000.
Hughes, Richard, and C. Leonard Allen. *Illusions of Innocence. Protestant Primitivism in America 1630–1875.* Chicago: University of Chicago Press, 1988.
Hughes, Richard, ed. *The American Quest for the Primitive Church.* Urbana: University of Illinois Press, 1988.
Hunter, Sam, John Jacobus, and Daniel Wheeler. *Modern Art. Painting, Sculpture, Architecture, Photography.* 3rd ed. New York: Prentice-Hall, 2004.
Joachimides, Christos M. and Norman Rosenthal, eds. *The Age of Modernism and Art in the 20th Century.* Stuttgart: Verlag Gerd Hatge, 1997.
Lederman, Minna, ed. *Stravinsky in the Theater.* New York: Da Capo, 1975.
Leighten, Patricia. "The White Peril and L'Art nègre: Picasso, Primitivism, and Anticolonialism." *The Art Bulletin* 72 (1990) 621–30.
Marsden, George M. *Fundamentalism and American Culture.* New York: Oxford University Press, 1980.
Mitchell, Donald. *The Language of Modern Music.* London: Faber & Faber, 1976.
Morris, Edmund. *Theodore Rex.* New York: Random, 2002.
Paine, Thomas. *The Rights of Man* in *The Life and Works of Thomas Paine.* Vol. 6. Edited by William M. Van der Weyde. New Rochelle, NY: Thomas Paine National Historical Association, 1925.
Parham, Charles F. *The Everlasting Gospel.* Baxter Springs, KS: Apostolic Faith Church, 1911.
Perry, Gill. *Primitivism, Cubism, Abstraction. The Early Twentieth Century.* New Haven, CT: Yale University Press, 1993.
Picasso, Pablo. *Les Demoiselles D'Avignon.* New York: Museum of Modern Art, 1907.
———, *Portrait of Gertrude Stein.* New York. Metropolitan Museum of Art, 1906.
Richardson, John. *A Life of Picasso.* Vol. 2, 1907–1917. New York: Random, 1996.
Robeck, Cecil M. *The Azusa Street Mission and Revival.* Nashville: Thomas Nelson, 2006.
Rosenblum, Robert. *Cubism and Twentieth-Century Art.* New York: Harry N. Abrams, 1960.
Rubin, William, ed. *Primitivism in 20th Century Art.* Vol. 1. New York: The Museum of Modern Art, 1984.
Salmon, André. *André Salmon on French Art.* Translated by Beth S. Gersh-Nesic. New York: Cambridge University Press, 2005.
Seymour, William. *The Apostolic Faith Newsletter* 1.1 (September 1906).
———. *The Apostolic Faith Newsletter* 1.2 (October 1906).
Stravinsky, Igor, and Robert Craft. *Memories and Commentaries.* London: Faber & Faber, 2002.
Tarushkin, Richard. *Stravinsky and the Russian Traditions,* Vol. 1. Berkeley, CA: University of California Press, 1996.
Wacker, Grant. *Heaven Below. Early Pentecostals and American Culture.* Cambridge: Harvard University Press, 2001.
———. "The Holy Spirit and the Spirit of the Age in American Protestantism, 1880–1910." *The Journal of American History* 72.1 (1985) 45–62.

———. "Playing for Keeps: The Primitivist Impulse in Early Pentecostalism." In *The American Quest for the Primitive Church*, edited by Richard Hughes, 196–219. Urbana: University of Illinois Press, 1988.

Warncke, Carsten-Peter. *Pablo Picasso 1881–1973*, edited by Ingo F. Walther. Hong Kong: Taschen, 2006.

West, Shearer. *Fin de Siècle*. Woodstock, NY: Overlook, 1994.

White, Eric Walter. *Stravinsky. The Composer and his Works*. Berkeley, CA: University of California Press, 1979.

Wilson, Andy, dir. *Riot at the Rite*. BBC. 2005.

Yarustovsky, Boris Mikhailovich. "Foreword." In *Igor Stravinsky's The Rite of Spring in Full Score*, vii–xi. New York: Dover, 1989.

6

"Teach me to curse mine enemies": Unexplored Female Power in Shakespeare's *Richard III*

Diane Awbrey

Introduction: Renaissance and Restoration Roles for Women

FEMALE ROLES IN SHAKESPEARE's plays have stimulated discussion of the choices available to women in the Renaissance and the treatment of women in a male dominated society. Some critics have suggested that Shakespeare's plays slight women because of the limited number and types of parts depicting women, and because of the practice of using young boys to perform women's roles.[1] The Restoration, on the other hand, appears to be much kinder to women both in text and performance. This period ushered in the era of female actors on the English stage, cultivated the first female dramatists of note, and attracted increasing numbers of women to the audiences. Many of the minor female roles of Shakespeare's plays were expanded or adapted on the Restoration stage, and resulted in increased stage time and dialogue for women: for example, Lady Macduff in William Davenant's *Macbeth* (1664), Andromache in Dryden's *Truth Found Too Late* (1678), and a proliferation of women characters in the Restoration versions of *The Tempest* (1670 and 1674). Myra Reynolds cites John Genest's record for Drury Lane and Lincoln Inns Fields that lists seven plays by six women in

---

1. For a discussion of the limited roles for women, see Roberts, "Making a Woman," 366–69. For a discussion of the male actors in female roles, see Taylor, *Reinventing Shakespeare*.

1696.² According to Reynolds, actresses such as Mrs. Betterton and Anne Bracegirdle "broke... conventions, [and] defied the feminine ideal... completely" by "appearing in public at all."³

The appearance of women in the Restoration theater world illustrates a seemingly expanded freedom among women whose options in life earlier had been limited. A comparative reading of the changes made in the Restoration, however, reveals that while the number and size of roles for women were often expanded in adaptations of Shakespeare, the types of characters and representations of women's social or political importance were significantly reduced. Very little scholarship to date has focused on this reduction. Jean I. Marsden claims that the Restoration maintained and even expanded women's parts primarily to provide a love interest for the central male role.⁴ Many female characters, however, were already objects of romantic love in Shakespeare's originals, such as Kate in *Taming of the Shrew* and Cressida in *Troilus and Cressida*. The flattened female characters in Restoration adaptations occupy a more complex position than simple romantic interest. The originally well-drawn personalities of these women did not need to be changed to help them function as an object of romantic devotion; still, Restoration dramatists altered them substantially.

The questions remain: Why were changes made? What do the changes signify concerning male perceptions of women in the Restoration? What purpose did they serve? Whom did they affect? Changes in the female characters of Restoration adaptations of Shakespeare's plays illustrate the intricate relationship between history and literature. On the one hand, the plays reflect a change in attitudes toward and positions available for women in society. On the other hand, the plays serve as a means of educating women who attend the plays in appropriate behavior within newly emerging social codes. The historical changes in attitude toward women drive the playwrights' textual choices. In turn, performances reinforced those attitudes by consciously and subconsciously "teaching" audiences acceptable behavior for women.

Lawrence Stone's theory of a late-seventeenth-century change in family structure provides a potential motive behind many of these alterations. As Stone argues, the Restoration saw the rise of the closed domesticated nuclear family, meaning that the nuclear family took precedence over the extended family, that marriage alliances were more often based on ties of

2. Reynolds, *Learned Lady in English*, 131. For a more modern treatment of women on the English stage, see Howe, *First English Actresses*.

3. Reynolds, *Learned Lady in English*, 83.

4. Marsden, "Rewritten Women," 43–56. See also Marsden's book, *Re-Imagined Text*.

affection and personal choice than on political and economic alliances, and that the roles of men and women within the domesticated family became more clearly defined.[5] Although Stone implies that these changes had a positive effect on the role and status of women in society, the evidence available in the adaptations of Shakespeare's plays reveals the attitude created a narrowing and confining effect on women. Choices for most women in society were limited to the roles of wife and mother. As the lives of women such as Mary Astell show, the worlds of politics, economics and ideology were increasingly closed to women, particularly to those who were unattached to male-dominated households. This tendency toward domestication, toward the idealization of women in domestic roles, eventually culminates in the nineteenth-century concept of the "angel in the house."

Some scholars have already noted the connection between historical attitudes toward women and literary representations of women in adaptations of Shakespeare. In "Pathos and Passivity: D'Urfey's *The Injured Princess* and Shakespeare's *Cymbeline*"[6], Marsden illustrates convincingly the sociohistorical sources of passive female traits in the "she-tragedies." Many of these sociological traits, such as domesticity, passivity, and submission, parallel Stone's thesis. Although Stone's description of the domesticated family is useful for understanding general trends, the "positive" implications of this domestication cited by Stone fall far short of the reality for women of the era. Ellen Pollak argues in the introduction to *The Poetics of Sexual Myth* that women were increasingly socialized for passive domestic roles:

> A woman's "duties" were identified exclusively with such qualities, or passive states, of soul as meekness, modesty, affability, compassion, and piety, her "calling" with the dependency of marriage. Education, when advocated at all, was to serve a woman not as a means of acquiring worldly competence, but rather ... as a way of cultivating techniques for bearing domestic solitude, idleness, economic dependence, and subservient social and conjugal status happily, without ennui, expense, or recourse to pedantry.[7]

---

5. Stone, *Family, Sex and Marriage*. See especially pt. 4, chaps. 6–8.

6. Marsden, "Pathos and Passivity," 71–81. See this article for a thorough and convincing discussion of the connection between the behavior advocated in Restoration conduct books and the behavior of the heroines of "She-tragedies." This connection between contemporary didactic literature and theatrical representation parallels the changes made in many of the Restoration adaptations of Shakespeare's women. Marsden's comparison of *Cymbeline* and D'Urfey's *The Injured Princess* is similar to the comparisons in this text of other Restoration plays to their Shakespearean counterparts.

7. Pollak, *Poetics of Sexual Myth*, 2–3.

The confining nature of domestication contradicts Stone's position that the increase in companionate marriages resulted in an increase in power for women within such relationships. About Stone, Marsden says that, "in stressing the importance of companionship in marriage he overlooks the sometimes negative impact this idealization of the domestic has on women. One such ramification is the creation of the passive wife."[8] Critics who explore the education of women through contemporary conduct books reveal the differences between the potentially active role of a Renaissance wife and the primarily passive role of the Restoration wife.[9] The change is reflected, Marsden says, in the emphasis of the conduct books on meekness, compliance, and marital obedience. Renaissance handbooks, she claims, "compared the husband/wife relationship to the relationship between Christ and the Church, an image which indicates the [potentially] active powers of the wife within the hierarchy of marriage,"[10] while Restoration marriage manuals described the marital relation using the master/slave metaphor. The wife's compensation for such slavish devotion, according to Richard Allestree in *The Ladies Calling* (1674), is the reward of her husband's love. His love is that which "makes the yoke fit so lightly, that it rather pleases than galls."[11] In exploring notions of the "ideal" woman in the seventeenth century, Jan de Bruyn exposes the essentialist arguments in contemporary handbooks that claim that women are "naturally" deficient and therefore in need of male protection.[12]

It is important to note that the social change described through the study of conduct books is based primarily on women in the Renaissance aristocracy. Throughout the Renaissance, women of all social categories were restricted in their choices, but women of the upper classes experienced some flexibility in behavior as long as they fulfilled the requirements of marital alliance for the sake of maintaining property or power. As the need for kinship alliances waned, increased domestication of women of all classes became more evident.

---

8. Marsden, "Pathos and Passivity," 72. See also Brown, "Defenseless Woman," 429–43.

9. See also Armstrong's *Desire and Domestic Fiction* and "Rise of the Domestic Woman," 96–141 for close analyses of the conduct books available to Restoration women. Although Armstrong applies her findings to female characters in the eighteenth-century novel, they are similarly applicable to Restoration drama.

10. Marsden, "Pathos and Passivity," 73.

11. Ibid., 74.

12. De Bruyn, "Ideal Lady," 19–28. de Bruyn includes counter-arguments made later in the seventeenth and eighteenth centuries by Mary Astell, Edward Fleetwood, Daniel Defoe, and Anna Maria van Schurman in favor of female education (23–26).

The female passivity described by Marsden and Pollak is an extreme result of the domesticating tendencies Stone praises. Although not all revised Shakespearean female characters fall into the category of pathetic heroines, many have been altered to become, at the least, domesticated, "wifely" women or at the most, virtuously passive sufferers.[13] The result of this more strictly defined role for women is that the options for variety, ambiguity, and human complexity are removed. Thus, a woman either fits the pattern of domesticity and virtue or she fails as a woman, and becomes a threat to masculine privilege and power. For example, the most powerful Renaissance female villain, Lady Macbeth, is rewritten in the Restoration version so that the audience identifies her evil as "unwifely" behavior and blames it on her husband's lack of leadership.[14]

Three specific changes in the Restoration adaptations of Shakespeare's women characters are apparent. First, the characters themselves were flattened and weakened, in spite of the seemingly perfect opportunity for expanding the roles of women in correspondence with the presence of women on the stage. Second, the reduction of the female roles assumed an emerging societal direction, in that the women are consistently removed from the public arena and placed specifically in the private sphere. Their "education" in the plays promotes the passive, submissive, "wifely" virtues which were increasingly valued by Restoration audiences. Finally, the plays self-consciously teach and reinforce the emerging ideology concerning the ideal woman. The plays both produce and reinforce a patriarchal agenda, resulting in the containment of female power, both textual and social on the Restoration stage.

Colley Cibber's *Richard III*, published in 1700, provides an example of the reduction of female roles in the Restoration while at the same time it exhibits a self-conscious awareness of the interaction between the stage and the audience, clearly delineating the playwright's awareness of the influence of plays on social behavior. Like Cibber, playwrights in the Restoration limit women to domestic roles by means of an essentialist argument. They assume that the nature of women is not only to desire domesticity but also to need assistance from men to avoid the potential dangers of coquetry.

The comparisons of Restoration adaptations with their Shakespearean counterparts result in convincing literary evidence that the historical role of women in the Restoration was increasingly limited to the private sphere

13. See Cordelia in Nahum Tate's *King Lear*, Cressida in Dryden's *Truth Found Too Late*, Cleopatra in Dryden's *All for Love*, Peg in Lacy's *Sauny, the Scot*, and Dorinda in Dryden and D'Avenant's *The Tempest or, The Enchanted Island* for some examples.

14. Marsden also notes this twist of interpretation in the Restoration in her article on "Rewritten Women," 47.

and linked to male domination. Although this thesis has been argued using evidence from conduct books and other socio-historical sources, similar changes can be found on the stage. With Shakespeare's plays as the historical record of dramatic treatment of female roles in an earlier age, we can clearly see the changes made—often most significantly and nearly exclusively—in the representations of women in a later age.

Shakespeare's Richard III: A Case Study

Of the many choices for study, *Richard III* offers a strong example of losses on many levels when Shakespeare's version was adapted by Cibber in 1700. At the textual level, many of the female roles were cut altogether, reducing the number of women on the stage and strongly suggesting that women had very little to do with the events of the royal household in turmoil (see below). Their place was in domestic chambers, not political ones. The changes also eliminate an important source of spiritual power in the construction of the plot. Although Cibber kept elements of the ghostly procession in Richard's pre-battlefield dream, the source of those powerful images was lost when Margaret and her curses were excised. Finally, some of Cibber's changes heighten the message from the Restoration stage that women's natural weaknesses and ignorance of political realities fit them for domestic rather than political or historic roles. This message deviates far from Shakespeare's treatment of women in the same play.

Early in Shakespeare's *Richard III*, Margaret, the ousted queen, enters the chambers of the reigning queen during a family council and prophesies the downfall of the family. She utters the following series of curses, covering everyone from the present king to the future king and all their allies:

> Can curses pierce the clouds and enter heaven?
> Why then give way, dull clouds, to my quick curses!
> Though not by war, by surfeit die your king,
> As ours by murther, to make him a king!
> Edward thy son, that now is Prince of Wales,
> For Edward our son, that was Prince of Wales,
> Die in his youth by like untimely violence!
> Thyself a queen, for me that was a queen,
> Outlive thy glory like my wretched self!
> Long mayst thou live to wail thy children's death,
> And see another, as I see thee now,

> Deck'd in thy rights, as thou art [in]stall'd in mine!
> Long die thy happy days before thy death,
> And after many length'ned hours of grief,
> Die neither mother, wife, nor England's queen!
> Rivers and Dorset, you were standers by,
> And so wast thou, Lord Hastings, when my son
> Was stabb'd with bloody daggers: God, I pray him,
> That none of you may live his natural age,
> But by some unlook'd accident cut off!
> (*Sh.* I.iii.194–213)[15]

Each of these literary prophecies looks backward and forward. Each threat is based on Margaret's past experience, and each looks forward to what befalls the threatened characters. Although those being addressed dismiss Margaret's curses as the Greeks dismissed Cassandra's prophecies, the curses come true one by one: the king *does* die of excess (surfeit), Edward *does* "die in his youth" as Margaret's Edward did, Elizabeth *does* outlive her glory as England's queen, and Rivers, Dorset, and Hastings *do* meet untimely deaths. For Richard, Margaret reserves this grotesque and spiteful curse:

> The worm of conscience still begnaw thy soul!
> Thy friends suspect for traitors while thou liv'st,
> And take deep traitors for thy dearest friends!
> No sleep close up that deadly eye of thine,
> Unless it be while some tormenting dream
> Affrights thee with a hell of ugly devils!
> (*Sh.* I.iii.221–26)

These prophecies also come true as Richard is plagued by doubts about his kingship and about Buckingham's friendship—doubts which eventually drive Buckingham away. The curses foretell his insomnia, reported later by Anne, and illustrated in the dream sequence before the battle of Bosworth. Finally, Margaret predicts a time when Elizabeth will not scoff at her. Instead, she says, "the day will come that thou shalt wish for me / To help thee curse this poisonous bunch-back'd toad" (*Sh.* I.iii.244–45).

This entire scene of Margaret's cursing and prophesying sets up an underlying series of insights in the progression of the plot. Each hearer initially

---

15. This and subsequent quotations of Shakespeare's texts come from Shakespeare, *The Riverside Shakespeare*. References are to act, scene, and line of this edition of Richard III.

discounts Margaret's words, yet as each encounters his or her own moment of fulfillment of the prophecy, each remembers Margaret's imprecations and reminds the audience of the warning. Hastings is the first to recall Margaret's voice. As he is about to be beheaded, he says, "O Margaret, Margaret, now thy heavy curse / Is lighted on poor Hastings' wretched head!" (*Sh.* III.iv.92–93). Elizabeth also remembers Margaret's prophetic threats as she speeds Dorset on his way to France. She says, "Go hie thee, hie thee from the slaughter-house, / Lest thou increase the number of the dead, / And make me die the thrall of Margaret's curse" (*Sh.* IV.i.43–45). Elizabeth also remarks on the fulfillment of the prophecy in her own life when she and the Duchess are commiserating and Margaret joins them. Elizabeth remembers that "thou didst prophesy the time would come / That I should wish for thee to help me curse / That bottled spider, that foul bunch-back'd toad. . . . teach me how to curse mine enemies" (*Sh.* IV.iv.79–81, 117). Later, the audience observes how well Elizabeth learns from Margaret.

Anne, another female Shakespeare empowers with the gift of prophecy, curses Richard's wife, unconsciously pronouncing a prophetic word against herself. Anne begins the wooing scene in Act I by cursing Gloucester for killing her husband and her father-in-law. She speaks the oath to the body of King Henry VI:

> O, cursed be the hand that made these holes!
> Cursed the heart that had the heart to do it!
> Cursed the blood that let this blood from hence!
> ....
> If ever he have child, abortive be it,
> ....
> If ever he have wife, let her be made
> More miserable by the [life] of him
> Than I am made by my young lord and thee!
>   (*Sh.* I.ii.14–28)

Her curses revisit her by means of her marriage to Richard. She brings them to the remembrance of the audience when she says to Elizabeth:

> O, when . . . I look'd on Richard's face,
> This was my wish: 'Be thou,' quoth I, 'accurs'd
> For making me, so young, so old a widow!
> And when thou wed'st, let sorrow haunt they bed;
> And be thy wife—if any be so mad—
> More miserable by the life of thee

Than thou hast made me by my dear lord's death!'
Lo, ere I can repeat this curse again,
Within so small a time, my woman's heart
Grossly grew captive to his honey words,
And prov'd the subject of mine own soul's curse,
Which hitherto hath held [my] eyes from rest.
   (*Sh.* IV.i.70–81)

Anne's nearly verbatim repetition of her curse serves to remind the audience of her response in Richard's wooing of her in Act I. That original curse occurs so early in the play that the audience may not have taken note of it, so this reiteration serves as a reminder for the audience and reinforces the validity of women's curses throughout the play.

All of the curses and prophecies spoken by Shakespeare's female characters indicate that women in the play have insight into the results of the behavior of others. These prophecies work as the artistic device of foreshadowing, but the fact that they are spoken by women emphasizes a gendered relationship between the women and the spiritual world of the play. The women are attuned to the consequences of the choices being made primarily by men in the play. Buckingham is the only male character who comes close to predicting the consequences of his own behavior, but his cynicism counteracts the persuasive power of his insights. Buckingham falsely reassures King Edward of his allegiance:

Whenever Buckingham doth turn his hate
Upon your Grace [*to the Queen*], but with all duteous love
Doth cherish you and yours, God punish me
With hate in those where I expect most love!
When I have most need to employ a friend,
And most assured that he is a friend,
Deep, hollow, treacherous, and full of guile
Be he unto me! This do I beg of [God]
When I am cold in love to you or yours.
   (*Sh.* II.i.32–40)

His oath is uttered insincerely and in ignorance of its potential power. He seems confident that his words will not come back to haunt him because of his political power and relationship with Richard. In his mind, his position outweighs any prophetic power his oath may carry. Indeed, he exposes his disbelief in the power of prophecy by saying, "curses never pass / the lips of those that breathe them in the air" (I.3.285–86). These utterances accent the gendered distinction between the "masculine" world of politics and the "feminine" world of prophecy. Buckingham undermines his prophesied demise by minimizing the power of prophetic insight; however, Margaret's curse befalls him anyway. Later in the play, he leaves England when he senses Richard's displeasure. However, he returns in the Sheriff's hands, and remembers both his empty oath and Margaret's curse. At that point, he becomes a believer and admits her to be a "prophetess" (*Sh.* V.i.27). With the exception of Buckingham's hypocritical swearing of an allegiance he does not mean to keep, Margaret and Anne provide all the instances of prophesying and cursing. The fact that these predictions are spoken by women confers on the women of the play a power that stands outside the political realm of men.

The culminating illustration of women's spiritual power in Shakespeare's *Richard III* occurs when old Queen Margaret, old Queen Elizabeth, and the Duchess of York meet. Margaret is about to flee to France. She has seen all she needs to see of the fulfillment of her curses, but the Duchess and Queen Elizabeth enter the stage as she ends her reverie. Margaret decides to stay and watch them. Both the dialogue and the stage directions work together to produce a camaraderie among the women through which they identify with each other's pain. They have successfully bridged their differences and function as a unit of female solidarity against the evil force of Richard's cunning. They have no physical means to stop him, but they find mutual consolation in their joint hatred of him. Female bonding is powerfully portrayed in their slowly joining forces. Not only are their speeches entwined but their actions as well. First the Duchess sits down and expresses her sorrow. Then Elizabeth sits down, and four lines later, Margaret joins them. One can imagine these three women, formerly enemies, now seated together, chins in hands, mourning their losses. At first, they try to outdo each other by cataloging their injuries, but soon they lapse into mutual consolation, until finally, they end with a lesson from Margaret in cursing one's enemies. The scene portrays not only the way in which women bond, but also the way in which they teach successive generations "womanly" and "spiritual" things—in this case, cursing and prophesying—which men do not learn in their formal education.

After this scene of commiseration, Elizabeth has successfully learned her lessons from Margaret. In a key plot reversal that determines the outcome of the play and, ultimately, the direction of the English crown, she parleys with Richard over marriage to her daughter, Elizabeth of York. Richard, determined to marry his niece to secure his throne, confronts Elizabeth with his plan. In a scene that echoes the wooing scene with Anne, Richard tries to win the young Elizabeth through her mother. He uses the same sort of sophisticated rhetoric that worked with Anne, but Elizabeth, unlike Anne, sidesteps his conclusions, even though she seems to comply during their dialogue. In fact, Richard ends their conversation with a derisive comment: "Relenting fool, and shallow, changing woman!" (*Sh.* IV.iv.431). He speaks as if he believes he has convinced her to marry her daughter to him. Instead, we learn from Stanley that Elizabeth has consented to espouse her daughter to Richmond, in defiance of Richard (see V.v). She has derived power from Margaret's lesson on cursing her enemies that has enabled her to resist Richard's advances and to choose a different path from the hapless Anne.

The subplot among the politically marginalized but dramatically powerful women of the ruling class in Richard III lies at the heart of the play. Without Margaret's and Anne's demonstration of the effects of curses, Elizabeth's courage and motivation for defying Richard in his bid for her daughter's hand in marriage goes unsupported. Shakespeare connects the women to the spiritual realms of prophesies and curses as aspects of human power untapped by—and therefore unavailable to—the politically powerful males of the play.

Reductions and Losses in Colley Cibber's Adaption of *Richard III*

In contrast to the original, Cibber's version of *Richard III*, 1700, omits the curses of Margaret and her prophetic role in the play. In fact, Cibber excises the character of Margaret altogether. On the artistic level this omission may seem merely to diminish foreshadowing; on a thematic level, however, it eliminates the dynamic movement of the women from enmity to female unity and lessens the impact of spiritual progression in the play, both individually and collectively. Cibber's revision collapses the layers of meaning in the play to only the physical/material world, cutting off access for the audience and characters to the spiritual/intuitive. As for the depiction of women, Cibber's version preserves Anne's weakness in the early wooing scene with Richard. It also maintains Elizabeth's strength in resisting his advances late in the play. However, without the unifying element of their shared lessons in cursing, these extremes (Anne's weakness contrasted with Elizabeth's strength) effectively cancel out the representations of women in the play, leading the audience with the conclusion that the female roles are included merely to fulfill necessary historical functions as wives and queens.

With the omission of Margaret and the women's sections comes the omission of the supernatural in the Cibber version. There is some attempt to include a prophetic element when the Duchess of York, Queen Elizabeth, and Anne hear the news of the Queen's brothers' deaths. They lament, and then Elizabeth exclaims, "O! I foresaw this ruin of our House" (*Cib.* IV.i.36),[16] but no previous textual evidence supports her prophetic tendency, so the comment is essentially unfounded.

Cibber's *Richard III* provides more than simply the example of how female roles were reduced. It also exhibits a heightened awareness of how a play may be changed to redefine and reinforce social values and behavior. In one aside and two self-referential soliloquies, characters in Cibber's *Richard III* draw attention to the fact that the story may be replayed before future generations. The speakers speculate either on what those "future generations" will think of this story or on what they ought to learn from it. The first such passage occurs when Tressel and Lord Stanley observe and comment upon Richard's wooing of Anne in II.i. Their running commentary in itself is Cibber's innovation and provides a distraction from the intense exchange between Richard and Anne. In Shakespeare's version, Anne is accompanied by Tressel and Berkeley, but they do not comment upon the action. Cibber's Tressel and Stanley are not so restrained. When Richard challenges Anne to speak the word and he will kill himself, Tressel starts the following conversation:

> *Tress.* By Heaven she wants the heart to bid him do't.
> *Ld. Stan.* What think you now, Sir?
> *Tress.* I'm struck! I scarce can credit what I see.
> *Ld. Stan.* Why, you see—A Woman.
> *Tress.* When future Chronicles shall speak of this
> They will be thought Romance, not History.
>   (*Cib.* II.i.199–204)

Lord Stanley explains Anne's lack of vengeful action by means of her gender. His tone implies that one could expect nothing more of a woman. The tension between the sexes in Tressel's mind turns this story from history to romance. Stanley sees with incredulity the coming marriage between Anne and Richard and credits the possibility for such an alliance to woman's weakness. Tressel's comment on how future generations will see such a change of heart, however, underscores the consciousness of the playwright that his play could shape an audience's view of history or social order.

---

16. This and subsequent quotations of Colley Cibber's *Richard III* are taken from Spencer, *Five Restoration Adaptations of Shakespeare*. References are to act, scene, and line of this edition of Cibber's rendition.

A second reference to coming generations emerges at the end of Anne and Richard's "romance" in II.ii, when Lady Anne laments her marriage. Richard enters and in an aside informs the audience of his need for her death. He tells Anne she has outlived his liking, so she begs him to kill her, but he refuses, citing the displeasure of the world as his excuse. He tells her she must kill herself because her husband hates her and loves another. She replies

> Forgive me Heaven, that I forgave this Man.
> O may my story told in after Ages,
> Give warning to our easier Sexes ears:
> May it Unveil the hearts of Men, and strike
> Them deaf to their dissimulated Love.
> (*Cib.* III.ii.63–67)

Since, in this domesticated society, a woman's fate depends on her husband's, her salvation lies in choosing that husband wisely. Anne falls victim to vanity in allowing herself to be wooed by Richard. Her repentance of this decision stands as a warning to all women who view this play. She is aware that her story may be told again and again. In this speech, as in the previous one, Cibber has included a reference to the weakness or frailty of the "easie Sex." Cibber clearly perceives that the "weak-heartedness" of women should be reiterated for the benefit of "future generations."

A final moment in which the speaker associates women, weakness and future audiences occurs when Cibber chooses to present Richard with a bit of conscience, a moment of seeming repentance, just as he is having the young princes killed in IV.iii:

> Wou'd it were done: There is a busie something here,
> That foolish Custom has made terrible,
> To the intent of evil Deeds; And Nature too,
> As if she knew me Womanish, and Weak,
> Tugs at my Heart-Strings with complaining Cries,
> To talk me from my Purpose—
> And then the thought of what Mens Tongues will say,
> Of what their Hearts must think; To have no Creature
> Love me Living, nor my Memory when Dead.
> Shall future Ages, when these Childrens Tale
> Is told, drop Tears in pity of their hapless Fate,
> And read with Detestation the Misdeeds of Richard,

> The crook-back Tyrant, Cruel, Barbarous,
> And Bloody—will they not say too,
> That to possess the Crown, nor Laws Divine
> No Human stopt my way—Why let 'em say it;
> They can't but say I had the Crown;
> I was not Fool as well as Villain.
> (*Cib*. IV.iii.19–36)

For the third time in the play, Cibber has reinforced the notion of woman's weakness with the consciousness that this story is to be repeated from generation to generation. He is teaching the audience what to think—about the plot of the story itself, about the political intrigue within the story, but also about women and their "weaknesses."

Most significantly, the relationship of these adaptations to their Shakespearean originals provides a link in the audience's mind to a tradition of behavior. With more than twenty years since the Shakespearean versions had been seen on the stage, the audience would not be aware of, nor recognize, the changes the adaptor made. Many of the adaptations of Shakespeare's plays were taken for their originals for many years. Adaptations of *Richard III*, *Macbeth*, and *King Lear* were all billed as Shakespeare's well into the nineteenth century. For example, Davenant's version of Macbeth became so well known that, according to Christopher Spencer, "when it was announced that Garrick would restore much of Shakespeare in his version, Quin [who acted the part at Lincoln's Inn Fields, Covent Garden, and Drury Lane for over thirty years] is reported to have asked, 'what does that mean? Don't I play Macbeth as written by Shakespeare?'" Although the Cibber Version of *Richard III* was not immediately successful, it developed popularity through the eighteenth century, gaining momentum that culminated in the Garrick debut of this role on October 19, 1741.[17] Using Shakespeare's name as an authority, these plays and other adaptations effectively establish an essentialist argument for the emerging priority society placed on domesticated female behavior.

Conclusion

Colley Cibber's adaptation of Shakespeare's *Richard III*, interferes with female characterization through a process of reduction. By eliminating one female character, Margaret of Anjou, wife of the murdered King Henry VI,

---

17. Spencer, *Five Restoration Adaptations*, 15.

Cibber substantially revises the roles of and relationships between women throughout the rest of the play. A greater loss from Margaret's absence, however, is the diminution of the spiritual aspect of human interaction that the male characters ignore or marginalize by their focus on political power. In addition, Margaret's presence in Shakespeare's version establishes a focal point to which the other female characters eventually gravitate and from which they ultimately learn to derive a power that foils Richard's political plots. Shakespeare's play reaches a climax in the final gathering of the women in a shared chorus of lament. Because Cibber eliminates Margaret's role, he also destroys the powerful subplot that moves the women from hatred to reconciliation. Without this movement, the audience is left with a mostly material and political plot devoid of the expansive spiritual and intuitive motivations offered by female characters in Shakespeare's originals.

Of course, it is easy for modern readers to praise the immortal Bard at the expense of his later imitators, but this criticism moves well beyond such simplistic purposes. The long-standing use of Cibber's edits over Shakespeare's originals has under-educated generations of audiences, including those watching modern film versions that continue to take their cues from Cibber's cuts.[18] It is time to restore a play that explores the complex relationships among women, that demonstrates the consequences of failing to see the truth that lies beyond the political or material realm, and that presents a more accurate depiction of the subtlety and complexity of Shakespeare's vision of women's roles in the shaping of English history.

BIBLIOGRAPHY

Armstrong, Nancy. *Desire and Domestic Fiction: A Political History of the Novel.* New York: Oxford University Press, 1987.

———. "The Rise of the Domestic Woman." In *The Ideology of Conduct: Essays on Literature and the History of Sexuality*, edited by Nancy Armstrong and Leonard Tennenhouse, 96–141. New York: Methuen, 1989.

Brown, Laura. "The Defenseless Woman and the Development of English Tragedy." *Studies in English Literature* 22 (1982) 429–43.

de Bruyn, Jan. "The Ideal Lady and the Rise of Feminism in Seventeenth-Century England." *Mosaic* 17 (1984) 19–28.

Howe, Elizabeth. *The First English Actresses: Women and Drama, 1660–1700.* Cambridge: Cambridge University Press, 1992.

---

18. Sir Laurence Olivier's 1955 version and Richard Loncraine's more recent 1995 version of Richard III both eliminate much of Shakespeare's original text discussed here. Certainly, neither highlights the powerful movement of the women's insights that Shakespeare makes possible.

Marsden, Jean I. "Pathos and Passivity: D'Urfey's *The Injured Princess* and Shakespeare's *Cymbeline*." *Restoration* 14 (1990) 71–81.

———. *The Re-Imagined Text: Shakespeare, Adaptation, and Theory in the Restoration and Eighteenth Century*. Lexington: Kentucky University Press, 1995.

———. "Rewritten Women: Shakespearean Heroines in the Restoration." In *The Appropriation of Shakespeare: Post-Renaissance Reconstructions of the Works and the Myth*, edited by Jean I Marsden, 43–56. New York: St. Martin's, 1991.

Pollak, Ellen. *The Poetics of Sexual Myth*. Chicago: University of Chicago Press, 1985.

Reynolds, Myra. *The Learned Lady in English, 1650–1760*. Boston: Houghton Mifflin, 1920.

Richard III. Directed by Richard Loncraine. United Artists, 1995.

Richard III. Directed by Laurence Olivier. London Films, 1955.

Roberts, Jeanne Addison "Making a Woman and Other Institutionalized Diversions." *Shakespeare Quarterly* 37 (1986) 366–69.

Shakespeare, William. *The Riverside Shakespeare*. Edited by G. Blakemore Evans. Boston: Houghton Mifflin, 1974.

Spencer, Christopher, ed. *Five Restoration Adaptations of Shakespeare*. Urbana: University of Illinois Press, 1965.

Stone, Lawrence. *The Family, Sex and Marriage in England 1500–1800*. New York: Harper and Row, 1977.

Taylor, Gary. *Reinventing Shakespeare: A Cultural History from the Restoration to the Present*. Oxford: Oxford University Press, 1989.

7

Pioneering Missionary Women in Asia and the Pacific Rim[1]

Barbara Cavaness Parks

WOMEN LEADERS, PREACHERS, MISSIONARIES, and evangelists are God's idea! After the Samaritan woman at the well met Jesus, she became the first woman evangelist. In the garden Jesus commissioned Mary Magdalene to go and announce to the disciples the news of the Resurrection. She was the first woman missionary—an apostle to the apostles. Women such as Lydia, Priscilla, Phoebe, and Junia worked in partnership with men, as well as independently, to lead the early church (Acts 16:14–16, 18:18–26, Rom 16:1–5). Other leaders of house churches included Mary, the mother of John Mark

---

1. Twila Edwards is remembered and respected as a pioneering woman in the Biblical Studies and Philosophy Department at Evangel University. For a number of years she served as the only female faculty member in the department; her male peers so esteemed her that they selected her as the Department Chair.
  One of Twila's signature course offerings was "The Role of Women." I was privileged to sit in her class, offered jointly with the Assemblies of God Theological Seminary. The course attracted both male and female students. In the middle of my doctoral research, I discovered that she was probably the most knowledgeable person in the Assemblies of God when it came to the literature on the topic. Her passion fueled my passion. I have taught basically the same course material as "The Theology of Women in Ministry" in American schools and colleges overseas for the past two decades. In 2004, Deborah Gill and I added our experiences and coauthored the book, *God's Women—Then and Now*, with Twila's blessings. She opined that it was the book she would have loved to write. Debbie and I could not have done it without her trail blazing inspiration.
  Part of Twila's call was to mentor young women who were sensing God's call to ministry. She did this by providing them a strong biblical foundation and by encouraging them to follow the leading of the Holy Spirit in their lives. As God enables, I am following her footsteps and those of the pioneering women below.

in Jerusalem (Acts 12:12–17); Apphia in Colossae (Phlm 2); and Nympha in Laodicea (Col 4:15). Though such leadership must not have been easy in these patriarchal contexts, God placed His hand on them, anointed their voices for ministry, and directed their steps. God chooses whom He will.

In recent days, Spirit-filled women have expanded the Kingdom as church planters, prophets, evangelists, and apostolic leaders in their home countries and in mission settings. At times they obeyed God's voice rather than human beings (Acts 5:29) and persevered through trying circumstances, despite losing children and husbands to illness and difficult conditions. Evidence points to the fact that revival movements and missionary expansion most often begin with people on the fringe of church structure, and that includes women.[2] God empowers people, sometimes unlikely ones, and delights in such choices.

As churches write their histories, it becomes clear that God has used women in apostolic roles to plow, plant, and harvest in many locations, both urban and rural. For instance, "more than one thousand women, both single and married, had served as evangelists in the Assemblies of God before 1950," including "women like Blanche Brittain—known as the 'sod buster' for having planted over forty churches."[3] From the churches she planted in the Midwestern United States came dozens of pastors, evangelists, and missionaries, including General Superintendent G. Raymond Carlson and his wife Mae.[4]

My doctoral research focused on 656 single/widowed women who served as appointed missionaries with the Assemblies of God (AG) from 1914 to 1994.[5] Data was taken from the lists of credentialed ministers published by the General Secretary's office, as submitted to them by the Foreign Missions Department.[6] I examined the overall percentage of women to serve in foreign missions specifically single female workers,[7] and discovered a marked decline.[8] More than three hundred of these single women served

---

2. Pierson, Syllabus.
3. McGee, *People of the Spirit*, 346.
4. Ibid.
5. Cavaness, "Factors Influencing the Decrease."
6. The name has changed over time: Foreign Missions Department, 1919–73; Division of Foreign Missions, 1973–2001; Assemblies of God World Missions, 2001 to the present.
7. The highest overall percentage of single women was in 1928 with 43.3 percent, but some individual countries were even higher: India 53 percent, Japan 50 percent, and Palestine 63 percent.
8. Cavaness, Appendix A: From 1921 to 1935, the percentage of appointed active missionaries made up of single, divorced, or widowed women averaged 40.5 percent of

in the Asia Pacific Region. Of the sixty single women who served in the first five years (1914-1919), thirty-four worked in Asia. Of the seventy serving in 1996, thirty percent were working in Asia.[9] These resilient entrepreneurial women played significant roles as pioneers and in at least ten countries, single women were first to plant the church for the AG or to play significant partner roles in that process.

Why were single females so effective in establishing strong indigenous works? It seems to me that they were quick to start schools and perhaps less of a threat to nationals than male teachers. They were often very relational, worked to achieve facility in the local language (and were attuned to nonverbal communication as well), lived on a simple level where they mentored converts in everyday situations, and involved themselves in feeding and caring for orphans, teaching children, and offering medical care. Such women earned the right to be heard because of their compassionate and nurturing ministries. They were often quick to indigenize by placing the work in the hands of those they had trained, and able to move on to other challenges because of their singleness.

CHINA

Second to India, narratives of the exploits of pioneering women are most numerous from China. The AG had eighty-two single women who served there for various lengths of time in the years 1914 to 1950. After being forced to leave China, many continued to minister to the Chinese people in other countries or in the USA.

Maria Stephany was ordained and arrived in China in 1916. She took only one furlough in twenty years and spent her ministry holding tent meetings, operating a home for orphans, and planting more than twenty

---

the total, with the number of all women averaging 66 percent. By the years 1991-2000, the percentage of these single women dropped to an average of 4.8 percent and the number of all women among active missionaries to 52 percent.

Certainly many women without credentials and those without official appointment also served in various functions. In the early years, independent missionaries who had served several terms overseas before accepting the Pentecostal message were required to visit Springfield MO to meet the Missions Committee if they wanted to affiliate with the AG. Many could not come due to lack of finances or the difficulties of travel. In addition the myriad ministries of missionary wives have not been well documented or preserved. In fact sometimes wives were not even listed. My experience and the available data, however, led me to focus my research on single women.

9. For many years India and Ceylon were grouped with the countries that now make up the Asia Pacific region. As late as 1959 the Far East and Southern Asia were supervised together under Maynard Ketcham. In the 1960s the regions were reconfigured.

churches in regions untouched by the gospel. Much of her ministry reached out to opium addicts and their families. She also opened a Bible school to prepare Chinese workers. She suffered at the hands of Japanese soldiers and Communist bandits. When the outbreak of war in 1942 forced her to return home, she left behind many converted workers, called to full-time service, and trained under her ministry.[10]

During her years of ministry in China (1911–1940), Blanche Appleby was responsible for many converts—some of whom became Bible school teachers and future AG leaders.[11] She is perhaps remembered by many, however, for her internment and suffering in the Philippines (1941–1945). She and Rena Baldwin had gone to Baguio to help establish a Bible school. Seven months later they were captured and held in the Los Banos camp with 2000 others on starvation rations. The evening she and the other prisoners were to be shot, American parachutists began to land and saved their lives.[12]

Grace Agar had already spent twenty years along the Tibetan border in Southwest China before her affiliation with the AG in 1922. She had been baptized in the Holy Spirit in 1912 and ordained in 1914, but felt she should return to the field on faith alone, not with any organized group. She served nearly twenty more years in remote mountain villages, winning Buddhists, Muslims, and Tibetans to Christ. Agar even wrote a book to help missionaries with language study: *Mandarin Tones Made Easy*.[13]

Ada Buchwalter ventured to China as a single missionary from 1918 to 1928 when she married Leonard Bolton. They served together and pioneered at least sixteen churches, until his death in 1961. As a widow she went to Taiwan to minister until 1965—a total of forty-seven years given to missions.[14] Her sister Mary Buchwalter also went as a single after joining the AG in 1914. She was one of the first missionaries in southwest China, Yunnan Province. In December 1917 she married Alfred Lewer, an independent missionary and together they continued to work with the Lisu people. They had two daughters and a son (who died in infancy). Alfred drowned in 1924 on the way to meet a new missionary couple. Mary received AG appointment in 1926 and actively engaged in pioneer and evangelistic work—despite the loss of her husband, son, and daughter Katherine—until forced to

---

10. Dalton, "Mother Peace," 3–5, 17.
11. Appleby, "I Remember," 5. She remained in ministry until 1953.
12. Appleby, "Our Remarkable Deliverance," 1, 4–5.
13. Spence, *Dark Is this Land*.
14. News release from Bolton's AGWM Archives file, dated just after her death on 6 Feb 1984 at age ninety.

flee in 1949 from the Communists. She resigned from missions in 1952 after nearly forty years.[15]

Anna Zeise went to China in 1920, lost touch with the Missions Department during the war and was not heard from for years. A German by birth (in an area of East Germany in the post-war division), she was able to stay at her post in Taiyuan, Shanxi, where she ministered especially to prisoners.[16] Word came in 1965 that she was still alive, but she went on to her reward from the land of her calling in 1969. She lived and worked among the Chinese she loved.[17]

What fascinating adventures; what courage and vision! The millions of Christians in China today can be attributed largely to the accounts of thousands of "Bible women", who were first trained by women missionaries, and planted house churches the length and breadth of the country while no foreign missionaries and few male Christians were able to work there. If only every story could be detailed, but space does not permit and many will be known only in heaven.

FIJI

Alma Starkenberg and Agnes Jacobson, the first known Pentecostal missionaries to Fiji, came to the islands in 1911.[18] Pearl Hewitt, ordained as an AG evangelist in 1916, was the first AG missionary to pioneer in Fiji, beginning in January 1917. With her fellow evangelist Eva Mae Caton, she studied the language and preached in the city of Suva and the surrounding area. Caton wrote that "there are many rocks thrown at the house and scoffing on the outside," but those who heard the message marveled at the power of Pentecost. "They recognize the difference between the work of the Holy Spirit and that of the natural mind."[19] A couple of months later she wrote about Starkenberg's sound Bible teaching and a service in which Caton saw "a crowd of young men on their knees crying to God" in response to her own message.[20] Hewitt and Caton transferred to ministry in Hawaii in

15. "Retired Missionary." She was ninety-one when she died.

16. "Eighty-six Prisoners Baptized," 10, and "Letter from Anna Zeise," 11. Seventeen female and 129 male prisoners were reported as being baptized.

17. Bundy, "Anna Zeise," 12–19.

18. Starkenberg, "From the South Sea Islands," 13–14. They were not appointed because the Assemblies of God was not organized until 1914.

19. Caton, Letter in *Weekly Evangel*, 10. Caton was ordained by Stanley Frodsham in 1916. A couple, the Albert Pages, had come to Fiji earlier, but were not AG until late 1917. They both died of Spanish influenza, the husband in 1918 and the wife in 1919.

20. Caton, Letter in *Christian Evangel*, 10.

1920, but Starkenberg and Jacobson worked in Fiji until 1924. When Adrian and Charlotte Heetabry came as AG missionaries in 1926, the Pentecostal message had already been proclaimed there for fifteen years. The first great Pentecostal outpouring their converts experienced came in three weeks of meetings led by missionaries Alice E. Luce and Dr. Florence Murcutt in 1931. They had stopped in Suva on their way back to the United States from services in Australia.[21] Luce had ministered in India from 1896 to 1914, and had been baptized in the Spirit in 1910.[22]

HONG KONG

Twenty-one-year-old Willa Lowther was ordained with the AG in 1914 and went back to Hong Kong (HK), where she had already been ministering. She received appointment in 1918 and thus became the first AG missionary there, but had to leave the field in 1929 due to illness.[23]

Mattie Ledbetter, formerly an invalid, was saved and healed under the ministry of M. M. Pinson in 1905, and received a call to China. In 1911 she began her work in Sam Shui, South China, and subsequently reported 300–400 converts in four years. She affiliated with the AG in April of 1917, and moved to HK in 1928.[24] First Assembly in Kowloon had its beginnings in a small street corner mission she started that year. Many Chinese accepted Christ in tent meetings she organized in 1929–32 with well over one thousand in attendance at times. For months she led prayer meetings every other day for the converts.[25] She died in HK at age sixty-seven (1938).[26]

Evangelist Lula Bell Hough was ordained by the AG and came to South China in 1929, working there and in HK forty-six years.[27] After learning the language she engaged in village evangelism and prepared Sunday school literature. She was the first missionary to work in the Pearl River hamlet. After two years she had planted a church with a significant number of Buddhist

21. *Fiji*.

22. McGee, "Alice E. Luce." She was ordained by the AG in 1915, worked in Mexico until 1933, and then as an evangelist/teacher and writer until her death in Mexico City in 1955 at age 73.

23. Ledbetter, Personnel Card.

24. Carmichael, "Beginning of Our Work," 19.

25. "Hong Kong Church," 30. The church had more than one thousand members by 1954.

26. "A Good Fight Finished," 7.

27. Hong Kong and its New Territories were a part of the South China District, so it is not always clear now which of the villages may have been just inside or just outside that area. Names have changed.

converts. She later taught in Bible schools in Fat Shaan and HK, and held District offices. Hough planted a church in the New Territories with nearly two hundred attendees before World War II. Captured in the church, she was interned by the Japanese for six months and returned to the United States as an exchange prisoner in 1942. After the war she came back and baptized fifty-five more converts at that church.[28] Her witness subsequently reached many British soldiers with the gospel. Hough reported that eight or ten of them went on to Bible school and entered the ministry. Hough retired in 1975.[29]

Annie Bailie, who came to China in 1928, was also interned by the Japanese in 1941. She later supervised churches in the New Territories, close to the China border. She established four preschools, administered a primary school with several hundred students, and pastored several local congregations. She exemplified the heart of a servant and pioneer for fifty-eight years in missions before her death in HK 1986.[30]

INDIA

Candidates for Pentecostal "sainthood" are numerous among the 143 single AG women who served India's millions from 1914–1994. Some established outposts, treated lepers, took in orphans, evangelized, and distributed literature in local festivals. Others taught Sunday school, opened Bible schools, witnessed in remote areas despite disease and hardships, and planted churches that remain open today.

One of the first was Susan Easton, who went to India in 1886, served on the Foreign Missions Committee (1917), and then back to India until her death in 1925.[31] Hattie Hacker arrived in 1908, was appointed by the AG in 1919, and went on to establish the Girls' Industrial School in Basti. She worked in India until 1939, and then in the Missionary Home in New York until 1948.[32] Mary Chapman came in 1910, joined the AG in 1914, and died on the field in 1927.[33] Margaret Felch went to India in 1913 (until 1951);

28. Her weekly schedule included Sunday school, four services in Cantonese, choir, open air services in villages, home prayer meetings and one at the church, Friday night Bible studies, and two Saturday English services for soldiers and English-speaking neighbors. The church had been self-supporting from the beginning.

29. Schwarze, "China Fertile Land." Hough died in 2002 at age ninety-five.

30. Bailie, news release. Supported by the Chinese people, she worked twenty-eight years without a furlough.

31. Easton, Personnel Card.

32. "Missionary News Notes," 15.

33. Chapman, Personnel Card.

Anna Marie Helmbrecht from 1913 to 1946; and Esther Bragg also in 1913 (until 1961, being widowed twice). Marguerite Flint was one of the next to come (1915–1960) after God called her by an audible voice. Flint worked in evangelism and eventually established a girls' orphanage and school in Bettiah, ministering to over 200 girls. In her third term she founded a Pentecostal Bible Training School first started for women in Hardoi. After twenty-four years the school had graduated two hundred women and forty men, most of whom were active in preaching and teaching. She served on AG District executive committees for extended periods of time, esteemed by both nationals and missionary colleagues.[34] Anna Tomaseck worked in India from 1926 until 1976 and is best known for her children's home on the Nepali border, though she considered that secondary to her work of evangelism in the area.[35]

I am more familiar with the ministry of Doris Edwards nee Koeppe, from my home state of Wisconsin. During her fifty-plus years in India, she evangelized and discipled many converts, established a large vocational-training school and nine other schools, planted the Schencottah Memorial Church (from which has come more than two hundred other churches), and toward the end maintained a feeding program for over three thousand children. Shortly after ten members of her family were baptized in the Holy Spirit on the same night, Jesus appeared to Doris and spoke one word to her, "India." She and her husband Clarence Maloney arrived in India in June 1937. When World War II broke out in 1942, Clarence stayed in India but Doris and Clarence Jr. returned to the United States. Her husband rejoined them but passed away with a brain hemorrhage before they could go back to India (1944). Doris' burden for India did not wane, despite her grief. As she traveled to raise her funds, God brought Robert Edwards into her life. They arrived in India in 1946 and studied Tamil for a year. Robert Jr. was born in the village of Schencottah. They built First Assembly in Tamil-Nadu, started a Bible school in Madari, and held services, clinics, and performed baptisms in some sixty-two nearby villages. They founded the Industrial School for boys—teaching masonry, carpentry, tailoring, blacksmith fitting, and eventually printing. By 1958 they had eight churches, many outstations, and three other schools besides the Industrial School. They took their first furlough in mid-1960, but Doris' second husband passed away in July of 1961. At the graveside a beautiful presence surrounded her and a voice spoke, "There is still an unfinished task!" After finishing her itinerary, she and Robert Jr. arrived back in India that December. Missionaries Coleen Guinn and Fern Ogle joined them to take charge of the Girls' School, Sunday school,

---

34. Loomis, *With All My Love*.
35. Tomaseck, "Last House in India," 20–22.

and first aid for the thirty-three young pastors and their families then in Tamil-Nadu. The next five years Doris saw 110 students baptized in the Spirit and twelve new churches established. The work continued to grow, even as Doris' strength waned.[36] She died in 1991 at age eighty-five and was buried in India.

INDONESIA

During the 1920s a nurse from Holland, Margaretha Alt, was baptized in the Holy Spirit while ministering in Indonesia. For fifty years she pioneered churches and developed an organization known as the Pentecostal Mission. Sumardi Stefanus, a Javanese man, accepted Christ under her ministry and became the editor of her publication, *Gandum Mas*.[37] Then in the 1930s a Dutch missionary visited Seattle's Bethel Tabernacle, and several couples in the service responded, subsequently going to Indonesia as missionaries: Ken and Gladys Short to Borneo, Ralph and Edna Devin to Ambon (1938), and Ray and Beryl Busby to Java (1939). Alt was imprisoned by the Japanese in 1941, but the Americans went back to the United States. Before returning to Indonesia, they affiliated with the AG. Miss Alt and her group became AG when a General Council was formed in Indonesia just after the war. In 1959 her convert Sumardi Stefanus became the first Indonesian General Superintendent of the AG, a post which he held for twenty-two years.[38]

Margaret Brown went to Indonesia in 1945 and Marcella Dorff in 1952. They were the first AG missionaries in the East Java region.[39] Marcella pastored the struggling church in Malang and started two others.[40] Together they pioneered the Bible school in Malang, East Java, and later a second school in Salatiga, Central Java. They served forty-four and thirty-five years, respectively.[41]

---

36. Kruger, *To Light a Candle*, 1–68.

37. "Assemblies of God Beginnings," *Field Focus: Indonesia*. Alt was born in 1883, died in 1962.

38. "July Emphasis: Indonesia," 19.

39. "Called to Indonesia," 19–21.

40. Dorff, news releases, 1957 and 1977.

41. *Celebrating the Years of Missions*.

JAPAN

Several female heroines of the faith were called to plant churches in Japan. One of the most fascinating stories recounts how God baptized businessman Carl Juergensen with the Holy Spirit and called him to Japan. He was 50 years old, and when he prayed about the seemingly impossible task ahead, especially the difficult language, God spoke clearly: "When I called Moses, he also said he could not speak, and I gave him Aaron to be his mouthpiece. Your mouthpiece will be your daughter Marie."[42] So they went to Japan in July 1913, not having friends or provision ahead of them, only a family of four with all their possessions in two trunks.[43]

After two years of study, fourteen-year-old Marie became the interpreter for nightly meetings. She also began ministries in her own right, teaching Sunday classes and a weekly class of Japanese women, as well as evangelizing in the area.[44] For the next twenty years she worked by her father's side, seeing hundreds of Japanese come to know the Lord. Her sister Agnes also interpreted for many early missionaries. Marie lived and ministered there for a total of seventy-eight years, until her death at age eighty-nine. The Juergensens founded Central Bible Institute in Tokyo in 1931. The family remains greatly revered by the Japanese church.[45]

Missionary Jessie Wengler came to Japan in 1919 and served thirty-nine years. She pioneered a church in a city thirty miles west of Tokyo that later planted two more congregations in nearby towns. At the time of attack on Pearl Harbor, Wengler was the only AG missionary remaining in Japan. She had no communication with the US for four years, living under house arrest and experiencing bombing raids every day. Since food was scarce, her weight dropped to only eighty-five pounds. After the American troops arrived late in 1945, she returned to the US. When Wengler returned to Japan in 1947, she served as the AG representative to General MacArthur's occupation headquarters. She was able to assist the entrance of many missionaries to Japan and help them acquire property. She was also principal of a school of 450 students and served on the council of fifteen advisors that guided the formative years of the Japanese General Council of the AG from

---

42. "Assemblies of God Beginnings," *Field Focus: Japan*.
43. Juergensen, "Veteran Missionaries Honored," 6.
44. Juergensen, "A Young Missionary Writes from Japan," 12,
45. Jones, "Called Home," 19. After WWII, at age eighty-one, Friderike (Marie's mother) returned to Japan and gave seven more years of service there (1949–56). Five family members are buried there.

1949–1956. She planted another church at age sixty-six and taught in the Bible school before her death on the field at the age of seventy-one (1958).⁴⁶

Florence Byers also worked in Japan from 1928 until 1977—nearly fifty years. At age nine she received a vision of Japan and felt called to go there. After Bible School she went to Japan, learned the language, and opened a mission station. Her ministry included directing an orphanage before the war (building a center with her own funds), working with three thousand Japanese prisoners of war and two churches in Hawaii during the war, then restarting the orphanage after receiving a re-entry permit from General MacArthur, and conducting tent meetings and outstation services. In 1954 she reported that many were saved and 300 had been filled with the Spirit. In 1968 Byers received a citation from the Emperor for her welfare services to orphans. During her last term she established a church and children's home in Kobe as well as engaging in evangelistic work in Osaka.⁴⁷

KOREA

Four Korean students accepted Christ when they heard John Juergensen preach at an open-air meeting in Tokyo (he had a burden for Korea, but no finances to open the field; at that time Korea was under Japanese occupation). At his invitation they attended Bible school in Tokyo and then returned to Korea. The AG had no appointed missionary in Korea, but Mary Rumsey of Cortland, New York, had ministered there since 1926 as an unofficial AG representative.⁴⁸ God had called her from a teaching ministry in Japan to work with the Korean Mission of the Pentecostal Church in Seoul.⁴⁹ She worked with these four men and encouraged them in the faith, until the war forced her to leave in 1941.⁵⁰ When evangelist Arthur Chesnut arrived in 1952, he found the men serving God and pastoring churches. In 1953 one of them, Pak Song San, became the first Korean superintendent of the AG at the organization of the South Korea General Council. The first appointed

---

46. Carlow, *Jessie Wengler*.

47. Clemenson, "Long-time Missionary." Byers' orphanage continued to function after her retirement, having been recognized by the Japanese government.

48. Rumsey, "Japan," 22. Rumsey had first studied Japanese and worked with Elim missionary Harriett Dithridge, who had a Bible Training School for Women, the only Pentecostal school in Japan. They ministered at three other preaching points and taught an English Bible class for college men in a nearby town. In one letter Rumsey writes that 50 young people, mostly men, had been saved and many baptized in the Holy Spirit.

49. Rumsey, Letter to Noel Perkin.

50. "Assemblies of God Beginnings," *Field Focus: Korea*.

AG missionaries to Korea, John and Edith Stetz, came in 1954 and built on the foundation laid by Mary Rumsey.

MALAYSIA

In 1932 Katherine Clause opened an AG work in Ipoh, Malaysia, after working as a missionary to China (beginning in 1923).[51] Carrie Anderson, who had also ministered in China and HK since 1914, started the first AG work in Kuala Lumpur in 1933 and worked there until 1942. The David Nyiens became the pastors in 1950 and found the nucleus of the original congregation still together.[52]

Missionary Evelyn Hatchett was instrumental in bringing the Pentecostal message to Penang. She had received appointment to Malaya in 1940,[53] but the war, Chinese language studies in Canton, and interludes of teaching and evangelizing elsewhere kept her from realizing her dream. She ministered to Chinese populations in Cuba, HK, and the Philippines before arriving in Penang in 1953.[54] She conducted services in nearby Georgetown as well as in a number of fishing villages. In one year she had 150 students in Sunday school, baptized forty people in water, witnessed twelve people baptized in the Holy Spirit, sent six individuals to Bible school, and oversaw 600 students complete a short Bible course by mail. Feeling a great burden for young people, Hatchett mentored many and sent others to Bible school in HK. When the Bible Institute of Malaysia was established in Kuala Lumpur in 1960, she began to send students there. One student, Prince Guneratnam (who became General Superintendent), testified:

> Although I was brought up hearing about Christ, I did not find Him to be a reality in my life. It was in Penang (now Pinang) that I attended an AG church pastored by a single lady missionary, Evelyn Hatchett. Under her ministry I found Christ a reality in my life, accepted the Lord, was baptized in the Holy Spirit, and later, at the age of 12 received a call to the ministry. Her life was a tremendous inspiration to me. Her dedication, her vision for the lost, became a great foundation to my response to the ministry

---

51. "New Work in the Malay States," 8–9.
52. Baird, "Malay and Singapore History."
53. What is now the Assemblies of God of Malaysia and the Assemblies of God of Singapore were one General Council of Malaya and Singapore at that pre-war time, both countries being part of the British Commonwealth.
54. Ketcham, "Evelyn Hatchett Called Home," 11. Hatchett taught in Bible schools in Hong Kong and Canton, 1947–49; Bethel Bible Institute in the Philippines, 1949–51; and in Penang, 1953–62.

when God began to call me. At about 15 or 16 years of age I had a tremendous experience with God; I had a vision of the Lord Jesus Christ.

As I was growing up I was impressed by what I saw. My [professors] not only taught, they also set a beautiful example. Even today I am greatly challenged by Evelyn Hatchett, a missionary who died very suddenly in Pinang. She had a tremendous burden and vision for the lost. She was not satisfied with pastoring the church in which she labored in Pinang. She would drive 50 miles to Taiping to start another church. As I saw this example it spoke to me. It is no wonder that Calvary Church which I pastor, has become a missionary church in giving, because I saw her example.[55]

After Hatchett died on the field in 1961, the missionary who followed her wrote of a Chinese choir at a youth camp made up of Bible school graduates now active in Malaysia as pastors and evangelists:

This is the result of Evelyn's dedicated ministry. Through them and through those still in Bible school, her life has reached and continues to reach out to those in need of the gospel all over Malaya—real multiplication. She ministered alone . . . in a difficult place [Buddhist center, snake temple, temple of 10,000 Buddhas]. We can appreciate, after six months in Penang, what we never before realized—the great battle she waged here.[56]

MYANMAR (BURMA)

Clifford and Levada Morrison sent Lisu workers from China to Burma in the early 1930s.[57] After WWII they and their daughter Geraldine settled there in Burma. Geraldine could preach in Lisu and two other local languages.[58] She taught a roving Bible school in three or four locations each year. AG Field Secretary Maynard Ketcham wrote of her:

Geraldine is carrying on a great work and is doing as much as three or four ordinary couples would do! The men have nothing

---

55. Guneratnam, Testimony.
56. Baker, Letter from Baker.
57. Morrison, "Breaking Virgin Soil," 10–11; and Morrison, "Four Hundred and Fifty Lisu Families," 14. Levada Leonard had gone to China in 1917 and married Morrison in 1923. They served until 1960.
58. Morrison, Application.

but praise for the efficiency of her ministry.... This young lady is one of the greatest missionaries that we have in our ranks today. It is also true that the work in Northern Burma is probably one of the most remarkable, best organized, best carried on, and most truly indigenous work that we have in any country in the world.[59]

For some years (1955–65) she worked alone in Northern Burma with over ten thousand AG members, two Bible schools, and a tremendous amount of responsibility. Missionary Ray Trask says hers was a "great work ... in very good shape with no divisions or false doctrines, and this is a testimony that Geraldine has worked very hard."[60]

SINGAPORE

After pioneering churches in Kentucky and Texas, Lula Ashmore went to China in 1937 and began working in Singapore in 1939. Feeling called to the Chinese of Singapore she started a gospel mission and taught Bible classes with missionary Lawrence McKinney. Before World War II, she also pastored the church in Kuala Lumpur, Malaya, until forced to evacuate. During the war she and Evelyn Hatchett ministered to a large Chinese population in Cuba for three years.

After the war, Ashmore returned (April 1947) with a Jeep and supplies, to pastor Elim Church—the only AG church in Singapore. By the end of the year the congregation had grown to forty members plus twenty young people and dozens of children. She added a service at another location to reach the Malay-speaking Chinese community. In November 1948 she married Vallence Baird and they pioneered two Chinese missions in a lower income Cantonese-speaking neighborhood. These missions later became Faith Assembly and Grace Assembly—thriving churches to this day. The Bairds' work was continued on after they went on furlough by widow Lau To Chan from HK (1952–62), and Americans Sarah Johnson (1953–54), and Jean Wagner (1954–62).[61] From 1957 to 1962 the Bairds established a work in their home in Ipoh, Malaysia, and in two nearby towns. The Ipoh church dedicated a building seating two hundred in 1962. When Vallence's health

---

59. Ketcham, Letter to Geraldine Morrison.

60. Trask, Letter to Maynard Ketcham.

61. Abeysekera, *History of the AG of Singapore*, 178–79, 206–13. Grace AG numbered over 1,700 in 1992.

failed, they returned to the San Francisco area to direct Chinese ministries there.[62]

A number of other single women have labored in Singapore—the latest being Naomi Dowdy. She became pastor of Trinity Christian Centre (TCC) in 1976 with about 250 people. Attendance grew to about four thousand with three properties and a strong missions program by the time Singaporean Dominic Yeo was appointed as senior pastor in 2005. Today the congregation of more than seven thousand crowds out two buildings in five weekend services. Over one thousand TCC members serve as lay leaders in their home-cells, both in counseling and community-care programs. TCC has daughter churches in India, Indonesia, Canada, and Australia, as well as a strong college with four schools.[63] Now Superintendent of the Singapore General Council, Dominic Yeo continues as pastor and Dowdy travels to many countries in an evangelistic role. The teaching of her Global Leadership Network has inspired and equipped church planters and evangelists in many countries.[64]

CONCLUSION

Besides these ten countries in the Asia Pacific region, women pioneered and planted churches in many other countries around the world. Elsewhere in Asia Pacific, I have not mentioned the work of Naomi Dowdy with Sam and Florence Sasser who first opened the work in Micronesia or the ministries of Rosa Reinecker in Ceylon from 1936–85, Alice Stewart in China and Taiwan (1926–76), and Josephine Spina in Ceylon and Bangladesh (1948–83). More recently Jean Johnson pioneered in Cambodia[65] and other singles are again breaking new ground in Myanmar and China. The stories are just too many to tell. At the end of her biographical history of Christian missions, Ruth Tucker concluded that women missionaries were neither supernatural saints nor zealous misfits, but they were "called by God, and their rate of success was phenomenal."[66]

God continues to call and anoint women for service, though subtle forces in church and society still negatively affect the roles filled by women. Today the number of pioneering women has seriously declined within the

---

62. "Missionary Lula M. Baird Honored," 29. She died at age 100 in 2008.
63. Trinity Christian Centre. See www.Trinity.net for details.
64. See Naomi Dowdy Ministries for more information at http://www.naomidowdy.com/.
65. Gill and Cavaness, *God's Women*, 207–9.
66. Tucker, *From Jerusalem to Irian Jaya*, 488.

AG; older women have retired or gone on to their eternal reward and fewer women are being accepted in leadership roles. Female ministry role models for young women are dwindling. Both male and female mentors are needed if the church is to continue to grow as God intended. Though the AG officially holds no restrictions on the ministry of women and still offers full credentials to those who qualify, many women continue to receive mixed signals.[67]

My sentiments might be best expressed as a paraphrase of John the Evangelist of the Fourth Gospel: "Women apostles, prophets, evangelists, and pastor-teachers are doing many other exploits as well. If every one of them were written down, I suppose that even the whole world would not have room for the books that would be written." It will take eternity to tell them all.

BIBLIOGRAPHY

Abeysekera, Fred. *The History of the AG of Singapore*. Singapore: Abundant, 1992.
Appleby, Blanche. "I Remember." *Pentecostal Evangel* (May 24, 1964) 5.
———. "Our Remarkable Deliverance from Los Banos Internment Camp." *Pentecostal Evangel* (June 16, 1945) 1, 4–5.
"Assemblies of God Beginnings." *Field Focus: Indonesia*. Springfield, MO: Division of Foreign Missions, 1981.
"Assemblies of God Beginnings." *Field Focus: Japan*. Springfield, MO: Division of Foreign Missions, 1979.
"Assemblies of God Beginnings." *Field Focus: Korea*. Springfield, MO: Division of Foreign Missions, 1978.
Bailie, Annie. News Release, 1985, AGWM Archives, Springfield, MO.
Baird, Lula Ashmore. "Malay and Singapore History." Unpublished manuscript in Carrie Anderson file, July 1951, AGWM Archives, Springfield, MO.
Baker, D. Hugh. Letter from Baker (Superintendent of Malaya and Singapore) to Elva Johnson, 16 Sept 1962. In Evelyn Hatchett file, AGWM Archives, Springfield, MO.
Bundy, David. "Anna Zeise, For God and China." *Assemblies of God Heritage* (Fall 2000) 12–19.
"Called to Indonesia." *Missionette Memoes* (July 1963) 19–21.

---

67. General Council, "Role of Women," 7–8. The official position paper of the denomination concludes:
> After examining the various translations and interpretations of biblical passages relating to the role of women in the first-century church, and desiring to apply biblical principles to contemporary church practice, we conclude that we cannot find convincing evidence that the ministry of women is restricted according to some sacred or immutable principle.... A believer's gifts and anointing should still today make a way for his or her ministry.... The Bible repeatedly affirms that God pours out His Spirit upon both men and women and gifts both sexes for ministry in His Church. Therefore, we must continue to affirm the gifts of women in ministry and spiritual leadership.

Carlow, Margaret. *Jessie Wengler: The King's Daughter.* Heroes of the Conquest Series No. 19 Springfield, MO: Foreign Missions Department, 1966.
Carmichael, Christine. "Beginning of Our Work." *Pentecostal Evangel* (Feb 28, 1960) 19.
Caton, Eva M. Letter published in *Christian Evangel* (June 29, 1918) 11.
———. Letter published in *Weekly Evangel* (April 20, 1918) 10.
Cavaness, Barbara. "Factors Influencing the Decrease in the Number of Single Women in Assemblies of God World Missions." PhD diss., Fuller Theological Seminary, 2002.
Celebrating the Years of Missions. Springfield, MO: AGWM, 2006.
Chapman, Mary. Personnel card in file. AGWM Archives, Springfield, MO.
Clemenson, Pamela. "Long-time Missionary 'Converted' at Age 9." *The Tribune-Democrat* (Oct 21, 1976) n. p.
Dalton, Adele Flower. "Mother Peace." *Assemblies of God Heritage* (Winter 1987–88) 3–5, 17.
Dorff, Marcella. News releases dated 1957 and 1977, in Marcella Dorff file, AGWM Archives, Springfield, MO.
Easton, Susan. Personnel card in file. AGWM Archives, Springfield, MO.
"Eighty-six Prisoners Baptized." *Pentecostal Evangel* (Jan 12, 1935) 10.
Fiji (field pamphlet). Springfield, MO: Foreign Missions Department, 1960–61.
General Council of the Assemblies of God. "The Role of Women in Ministry as Described in Holy Scripture." Adopted by the General Presbytery of the General Council of the Assemblies of God in Session, August 9–11, 2010. Online: http://ag.org/top/beliefs/position_papers/pp_downloads/pp_4191_women_ministry.pdf.
Gill, Deborah, and Barbara Cavaness. *God's Women—Then and Now.* Rev. ed. Colorado Springs, CO: Authentic, 2009.
"Good Fight Finished." *Pentecostal Evangel* (Mar 26, 1938) 7.
Guneratnam, Prince. Testimony in Evelyn Hatchett file, AGWM Archives, Springfield, MO.
"Hong Kong Church Begins 42nd Year." *Pentecostal Evangel* (Nov 15, 1970) 30.
Jones. Wilma. "Called Home." *Pentecostal Evangel* (Feb 18, 1962) 19.
Juergensen, Marie. "A Young Missionary Writes from Japan." *Weekly Evangel* (Dec 23, 1916) 12.
———. "Veteran Missionaries Honored." *Pentecostal Evangel* (Oct 29, 1938) 6.
"July Emphasis: Indonesia." *Call to Prayer* (June 1997) 19.
Ketcham, M. L. "Evelyn Hatchett Called Home." *Pentecostal Evangel* (Feb 4, 1962) 11.
———. Letter to Geraldine Morrison, 16 Jul 1963. In Geraldine Morrison file, AGWM Archives, Springfield, MO.
Kruger, Joan. *To Light a Candle.* B. & J., 1987.
Ledbetter, Mattie. Personnel card in file. AGWM Archives, Springfield, MO.
"A Letter from Anna Zeise of Taiyuan-fu, China." *Pentecostal Evangel* (Dec 19, 1931) 11.
Loomis, Majorie. *With All My Love . . . the Story of Margaret Flint.* Springfield, MO: Gospel, 1963.
McGee, Gary. "Alice E. Luce." Unpublished manuscript in Alice E. Luce's file, AGWM Archives, Springfield, MO.
———. *People of the Spirit.* Springfield, MO: Gospel, 2004.
"Missionary Lula M. Baird Honored for 50 Years of Planting Chinese Churches." *Pentecostal Evangel* (Feb 12, 1989) 29.

"Missionary News Notes." *Pentecostal Evangel* (Mar 1956) 15.

Morrison, Geraldine. Application to Foreign Missions Department, Mar 28, 1957. In Geraldine Morrison file, AGWM Archives, Springfield, MO.

Morrison, J. C. "Four Hundred and Fifty Lisu Families Turn to God." *Pentecostal Evangel* (Nov 19, 1932) 14.

———. "Breaking Virgin Soil in Yunnan, S. W. China." *Pentecostal Evangel* (Jan 30, 1932) 10–11.

"The New Work in the Malay States." *Pentecostal Evangel* (May 27, 1933) 8–9.

Pierson, Paul. Syllabus for "The Historical Development of the Christian Movement." Fuller Theological Seminary, 1990.

"Retired Missionary at Home with the Lord." *Pentecostal Evangel* (Mar 25, 1979) 29.

Rumsey, Mary. "Japan." *Trust* (Nov–Dec 1928) 22.

———. Correspondence to Noel Perkin, in Mary Rumsey file, April 18, 1939, AGWM Archives, Springfield, MO.

Schwarze, Richard. "China Fertile Land for Woman's Zeal." *Journal Herald* (1969).

Spence, Inez. *Dark Is this Land: Grace Agar*. Springfield, MO: Foreign Missions Department, 1962.

Starkenberg, Alma. "From the South Sea Islands." *Latter Rain Evangel* (Feb 1917) 13–14.

Tomaseck, Anna. "The Last House in India." *Pentecostal Evangel* (June 10, 1979) 20–22.

Trask, Ray. Letter to Maynard Ketcham, Sept 12, 1963. In Geraldine Morrison file, AGWM Archives, Springfield, MO.

Tucker, Ruth. *From Jerusalem to Irian Jaya*. Grand Rapids: Zondervan, 1983.

8

Herbert's Ratios of Psalmic Intertextuality in *The Temple*: A Prospectus for Further Study

NATHAN H. NELSON

GEORGE HERBERT'S LITERARY-CRITICAL STATURE as a poet in our day has not been established primarily by his echoes and emulations of the Hebrew Psalms, but they have certainly contributed to a consensus that the Old Scriptures were near his mind's eye and ear.[1] The resonances range from overt paraphrases to the merest suggestion raised by intense figuration. In *The Temple*, for instance, "The 23rd Psalm" begins with the obvious shadow-lines "The God of love my shepherd is, / And he that doth me feed"; but "Grief," which does not emulate an entire psalm, does deal in Old Scripture-style hyperbole about the physical effects of emotional torment: "Let ev'ry vein / Suck up a river to supply mine eyes, / My weary weeping eyes. . ." The lines are clearly in the same registers of sorrow and verbal extravagance as Ps 6:6, "Every night I make my bed swim, / I dissolve my couch with my tears" (NASB) and Jer 9:1, "Oh that my head were waters / And my eyes a fountain of tears, / That I might weep day and night / For the slain of the daughter of my people!" (NASB). Much attention has been given to Herbert's biblical intertextuality, and in Helen Wilcox's recent (2007) edition of Herbert's poems, she finds so many psalmic borrowings and emu-

---

1. In his introduction to *Music for a King*, Coburn Freer remarks that "[a] poet and parson like Herbert, who recommended metrical psalms to his parish, who sang metrical songs, and could write perhaps the best single psalm of his age, invites a reading with the context of psalmody" (2).

lations that they warrant a thick index of resonant psalms split out from her larger Index of Biblical References.[2] C. A. Patrides remarks that "almost every aspect of Herbert's poetry is traceable to the Bible," particularly to the "palpable influence of wisdom literature, of the Psalter, and of the parables embedded in the Gospels."[3]

On the other hand, *The Temple* cannot be seen as a competitor for the laurels in the period's vogue of psalm-emulations, metrical or otherwise. Beth Quitslund has shown that the mixed reception of the literarily adventurous Sidney Psalter of 1599 (more suitable for "chamber" devotional use than congregational singing in church) provided a cautionary example for later poets such as John Milton and Herbert, both of whom for the most part eschewed writing metrical psalm paraphrases suitable for corporate singing.[4] Milton, she claims, came to use classical epic and tragedy as the "vehicle[s] of divine poetry," and Herbert "chose to write the 'original' lyric corpus of 'The Church' instead of a metrical psalter."[5] Quitslund sees *The Temple* as a literary—but not fully psalmic—descendant of the Sidney psalter; it is great "devotional verse" better seen as a major step in the development of the English lyric. Just as the heightened poetic sophistication of the Sidney Psalms reduced their usefulness for public, corporate worship,[6] Herbert's daring flights of what we now call "metaphysical" fancy seem to disqualify most of the poems included in *The Temple* for the same purpose. Quitslund's point is well taken, but in this paper I want to use the word *psalter* in the qualified sense of "a book of songs written in the *spirit* of the Hebrew psalter with some emulation of its varying moods and topics on something like the same scale."[7] The usage is not entirely figurative. Such

---

2. Herbert, *English Poems of George Herbert*, 727. Wilcox uses the Authorized Version for all biblical references except those to the Psalms, for which she uses the Book of Common Prayer translation that would have been in Herbert's hands. In this essay, I generally use the Authorized Version for its resonances with Herbert's language and time as well as for easy articulation with Wilcox's findings.

3. Patrides, *Figures in a Renaissance Context*, 120.

4. The reception was limited, of course, by the fact that the Sidney Psalms, a gift in manuscript to Queen Elizabeth in 1599, were circulated only in hand-copied manuscripts, sixteen of which are known to have been made between 1590 and 1630, see Brennan, "Licensing the Sidney Psalms," 304. The complete collection was not published as a book until 1823 (the Chiswick Press edition). Psalms 1–43 were composed by Sir Philip and Psalms 44–150 after his death by his sister, Mary Sidney Herbert, Countess of Pembroke.

5. Quitslund, "Teaching Us How to Sing?," 109–10.

6. See ibid., 103–4. She takes considerable pains to show that the Sidney Psalter is difficult to sing and seems to suggest that its language is at times a bit too difficult for a common congregant to understand readily.

7. Wilcox admits that "Herbert's biblical inspiration is often what we might call

a book would admittedly be far enough from the liturgical ideal of careful translation or paraphrase to make the term *psalter* seem metaphoric to Hebrew scholars—but I am interested in Herbert's refractions of biblical psalmody for his own sensitive soul and, by Nicholas Ferrar's fortunate preservation, for that of any reader.

Wilcox, citing work by John N. Wall, notes that "the parallels between Herbert's poems and the psalms even include the numerical, in that the number of poems in *The Church* [sic; the longest section of *The Temple*] is the same as that of the psalms as divided up for liturgical use in the Church of England calendar."[8] Furthermore, we can see that, having 163 poems, "The Church" is of the same order of magnitude as the number of poems in the canonic Book of Psalms: 150. These signs of Herbert's motivated imitation are sufficient to make us wonder how deeply his conscious or unconscious emulation ran. Wilcox's careful tracking and indexing of psalmic allusions in *The Temple* encourage further scrutiny of the poems' intertextuality. If "The Church" is his psalter, we might look beyond lexical similarity into the complexities of collection-structure, thematic poem-grouping, rhetorical-liturgical modalities, and postures of supplication. Much scholarship has recognized *The Temple*'s high ratio of concern about personal spiritual rectitude, and it is commonly understood that the Psalms themselves have a high ratio of individual concern—that is, concern for the well-being of the psalms' personae, spiritual or otherwise.[9] Somewhat less attention has been given to Herbert's concern over personal and corporate *social* rectitude exclusive of his own court experiences and hopes. This essay will investigate the degree to which Herbert addresses matters of social concern like those found in the Book of Psalms.

Biblical scholars have long attempted to categorize the Hebrew psalms in order to understand their topical and generic contributions to cultic worship in ancient Israel. Many systems ranging from the simple to the complex have been suggested, but the overlaps from system to system are significant

---

subterranean" (*English Poems of George Herbert*, xvii), but the occasional direct allusion and narrative or topical structure keep suggesting at least passing intertextuality with the Psalms.

8. Ibid., xxviii. Wilcox cites Wall, *Transformations of the Word*, 170. Note: Wilcox uses italics for all titles; I will use them for the title of the entire collection, *The Temple*, but I will use quotation marks for the sub-collection called "The Church."

9. Old Testament scholar Hermann Gunkel in *The Psalms* resists an ancient tendency to allegorize the psalmic speaking voices (the *personae*) that refer to themselves as "I." In many psalms, he says, "an allegorical interpretation of the 'I' would result in a very unnatural understanding of the psalm. Thus we maintain that, apart from a few isolated cases, the 'I' almost invariably refers to the individual, and that therefore we have in the Psalms a rich collection of the poetry of the individual" (16).

enough to allow some reasonable hybridization to be done. Following the work of Hermann Gunkel and Claus Westermann, W. H. Bellinger Jr., suggests the following classification of the Hebrew psalms:[10]

- Praise Psalms
- Lament Psalms
- Royal Psalms
- Wisdom Psalms

Bellinger subdivides the "Praise" category into eight subclasses and the "Lament" category into two. For each category and subclass, he supplies a list of psalms that seem to fit. Our interest in Herbert's "psalter" can lead us to consider whether or not "The Church" has anything like the ratios between categories that Bellinger sees in the biblical collection.

According to Bellinger's analysis, sixty-one of the Hebrew psalms (40.67 percent) are of the "Praise" variety; sixty-seven (44.66 percent) are "Lament" poems; eleven (7.33 percent) are "Royal" psalms; and eleven (7.33 percent) are "Wisdom" psalms.[11] Although Bellinger's classification of individual psalms undoubtedly has some idiosyncratic bias, it is nevertheless striking to find that the largest category of Hebrew psalms appears to be that of lament.[12] Claus Westermann argues, in fact, that the lament is the psalmic *ur*-form underlying virtually all of the Hebrew psalms and their variety of secondary forms,[13] and Walter Brueggemann has observed "a close correspondence between *the anatomy of the lament psalm . . .* and *the anatomy of the soul*."[14] This latter phrase clearly describes a great number of Herbert's poems in "The Church."

Much like Brueggemann, Norman Gottwald understands the lament psalms to be commentaries on issues of social concern and justice.[15] In other words, both scholars would encourage us not to spiritualize the psalms (or to select only the most spiritually "uplifting") to the point at which the concrete, historical differentials of power and privilege in the ancient Hebrew world become invisible. Given that Herbert's collection called "The Church"

---

10. Bellinger, *Psalms*, 23. See Gunkel, *Introduction to Psalms*, and *The Psalms*.

11. All numbers in the sentence are mine. Bellinger simply lists the psalms in each category by their canonic numbers.

12. Other scholars may differ about the numbers of psalms in each category, and they may "cross-list" some psalms in more than one category. Gunkel, for example, places Psalm 82 in his list of "Psalm Liturgies" and in his list of "Miscellaneous" psalms.

13. Reported by Brueggemann in *Message of the Psalms*, 18.

14. Ibid., 18–19.

15. In his "Excursus: The Psalms and Sociology," from *Psalms*, Bellinger summarizes Gottwald's arguments at length, referring to Gottwald's *The Hebrew Bible*, 522–41.

may be considered his psalter, we may reasonably ask how much of the collection participates in the biblical mode of lamentation for a disoriented society. Here we must often distinguish poems of individual lament from poems of corporate lament.

Many of Herbert's poems begin in some condition of lamentable unrest; some end in rejoicing or at least satisfaction. They pose most of the same difficulties of classification that scholars have had with the Psalms, but it is not very difficult to see that most of the poems in "The Church" are about individual (rather than corporate or social) struggles, needs, complaints, or praises.

In dealing with the biblical psalms of lament (sixty-seven by his analysis), Bellinger further distinguishes "Individual Psalms" from "Community Psalms," supplying the following ratios: fifty "Individual" and seventeen "Community" psalms. Thus, 33.33 percent of the Psalmic lamentation is of the Individual sort, and 11.33 percent is of the "Community" sort. Of these groupings, the more obvious match with Herbert's poetry is the first. Most of Herbert's personae can, with reason, be described as proto-monastic, or (with a somewhat different timbre) at least puritan, for they fall easily into meditative melancholy lending itself to personal lamentation, which includes the whole range of topics about human discomfort and distress. Because both High Church and Low/Dissident Church traditions endorse versions of spiritual self-analysis, scholars have mightily exercised themselves in trying to determine where Herbert stood on the spectrum from Calvinism to Arminianism, but Herbert still seems to elude them all by exhibiting a practical ecumenism based on Scripture. As Christopher Hodgkins has observed, "[Herbert's] spirit was typical of neither" the more-Calvinist Jacobean church or the more-Arminian Caroline church (under Laud).

> James [I] led a church that was tolerant by default, which the Arminians made one that was unyieldingly and swiftly coercive. Neither had much use for conscience. In contrast, Herbert was a man of great inner spaces whose spiritual experience produced a mind at once highly principled, humbly practical, and deeply respectful of that region called the heart, near the conscience, where no one but God has the prerogative or the power to move.[16]

In short, it is not hard to find Herbert's model, if not directly allusive, emulations of the "Individual Lament" psalms, particularly those dealing with some perceived alienation from God or His righteousness.

16. Hodgkins, *Authority, Church, and Society*, 85.

On the other hand, we know that Herbert understood and acted upon Scriptures that, from a Christian perspective, are centered in the profundity of the Second Great Commandment: "Love thy neighbor as thyself."[17] His injunctions and examples in the long *Temple* poem "The Church-porch" and in the manual-like prose didacticism of *The Countrey Parson* are lengthy cases in point. In fact, the poet-priest's reputation as "Holy Mr. Herbert" has grown to such legendary status that it has recently been attacked as a debilitating influence upon today's Church of England ministers, who simply cannot do all that Herbert's reputation or his *Countrey Parson* require.[18] Judging by the social-concern standards set in "The Church-porch" and *The Countrey Parson*, and cognizant of Herbert's penchant for psalm-emulation throughout *The Temple*, we might expect to find a significant number of poems having social-concern topicality in the section called "The Church." By reference to Bellinger's accounting of the biblical model, we might use 11.3 percent as an informal criterion.

By collating Wilcox's index of Psalm-references in *The Temple* with Bellinger's psalm-categories, I have generated a provisional chart showing the relative frequencies and percentages of Herbert's Psalm-emulation per category—as far as Wilcox's analysis extends (see Table 1). The results should probably not be surprising, since Herbert's own devotional life as well as his pastoral life was saturated with the full range of Hebrew psalm-topicality prescribed for twice-daily reading by the 1559 *Book of Common Prayer*: "AT THE MORNING AND EVENING PRAYER THROUGHOUT THE YERE, [. . .] THE Psalter shalbe readde through, ones euery moneth [. . .]."[19]

---

17. Of course, this NT scriptural injunction (Matt 22:39, Mark 12:31, Luke 10:27, Rom 13:8, Gal 5:14, James 2:8, I John 3:17, 4:7) has its roots in many OT passages (Lev 19:18, Isa 58, Amos 5, and Mic 6:8 resonantly among them).

18. Lewis-Anthony, *If You Meet George Herbert*, e.g., 5–22, 215. At the time of his provocatively titled book's publication, Lewis-Anthony was Rector of St. Stephen's Church in Canterbury.

19. Wohlers, "Book of Common Prayer."

Herbert's Psalm References Per Bellinger Type*			
Bellinger's Classification of the Psalms	Herbert's References Per Type	Herbert's % of Total References	Bellinger's % of the Book of Psalms Per Type
I. Praise	98	40.00	40.66
General Hymn	30	12.24	12.67
Creation	15	6.12	3.33
Enthronement	8	3.27	4.67
Zion	4	1.63	4.00
Entrance	4	1.63	1.33
Hymn w/Prophetic Warnings	0	0.00	2.00
Trust	14	5.71	3.33
Indiv Thanks	19	7.76	5.33
Comm Thanks	4	1.63	4.00
II. Lament	101	41.23	44.66
Indiv Lament	84	34.29	33.33
Comm Lament	17	6.94	11.33
III. Royal Psalms	19	7.76	7.33
IV. Wisdom Psalms	27	11.02	7.33

*Table 1: This table represents my collation of Wilcox's "Index of Biblical References, Part 2: Psalms" with Bellinger's "Classification of the Psalms."

All calculations and figures are mine.

My analysis of Wilcox's Index also allows me to make the following observations: by her interpretation and accounting as well as her reporting of other scholars' findings, Herbert recognizably refers in some fashion to at least ninety-five of the 150 Psalms. Wilcox does not find and does not report others' finding *Temple* references to fifty-five of the Psalms (36.67 percent). Obviously, Wilcox's net may not have caught every allusion or parallel, but her careful work over all 163 poems in *The Temple* provides a heavily significant sample of likely references. Notice the striking similarity of percentages between (a) the biblical distribution of psalms in categories according to Bellinger's analysis and (b) Herbert's references to psalms in those categories. "Praise" poems in the Psalter are 40.66 percent of the total; Herbert's references to "Praise" psalms constitute 40 percent of his total allusiveness to the Psalms as recorded by Wilcox. Bellinger finds 44.66 percent of the Psalter composed of "Lament" poems; Herbert's references to "Lament" psalms make up 41.23 percent of his recognized psalmic allusiveness. "Royal" psalms constitute 7.3 percent of the Psalter; Herbert's references to "Royal" psalms compose 7.76 percent of his total references. The biblical "Wisdom" psalms compose 7.33 percent of the Psalter; Herbert's "Wisdom"-psalm references constitute 11.02 percent of his recognized psalmic references. These are remarkably similar figures that tempt one to suspect Herbert of matching by plan. It is probably not possible to determine whether or not Herbert had any intention of matching the volume or weight-distribution of topics or types in the Psalms, but perhaps his careful attention to the biblical texts by devotional rule simply gave him a more and more thorough "feel" for the particular balance of the Hebrew collection.

By my accounting of Wilcox's editorial scholarship, at least ninety-five of the 163 poems in "The Church" are demonstrably intertextual with biblical psalms.[20] My own analysis suggests that twenty-four make some reference to issues of social concern (a category that overlaps heavily with that of Community Lament), but most of the poems are not wholly or even largely about such issues.[21] While approximately 14.7 percent of the poems in "The Church" broach social-concern topics to any extent at all, only three—"Humilitie," "Constancy," and "Lent"—seem to qualify as whole-poem treatments of social concern as Bellinger defines them. Another seven poems provide fairly substantial treatments of social concern

---

20. In Norman Fairclough's terms, many of the intertextualities are *manifest*; others are *constitutive*. See *Discourse and Social Change*, 117.

21. My working criterion for a poem's inclusion is extremely low—on the order of lines 13–14 in "The H. Scriptures. I.," which say of the Bible "Thou art joys handsell: heav'n lies flat in thee, / Subject to ev'ry mounters bended knee"; or lines 9–10 in "Repentance," which say "we are all / To sorrows old." Both are extremely brief nods to egalitarian verities; neither conceit is developed further in the poem. In "Trinitie Sunday," the penitential *telos* of the poem clearly makes its social-concern aspects subdominant: "And sancifi'd me to do good" is a moment's reference to good works during the earnest prayer for purgation of sins, and "Enrich my heart, mouth, hands [. . .] / With [. . .] charitie" is another, slightly less direct.

issues. All together, the prominently social-concern poems in "The Church" number only around ten to fourteen by my analysis, so the ratio of social-concern poems in the collection is approximately 6.13–8.58 percent. The biblical psalms of "Community Lament" are not all about social justice or probity, but those topics do fit the category. Herbert's "community" psalms are few, and they are almost exclusively about those topics. Comparing his figures to Bellinger's listing and percentage of "Community Lament" psalms in the Psalter (11.33 percent), I find that Herbert appears to have produced only half to three-quarters (54-75 percent) as many "Community Lament" (or social-concern) poems as the number that appear in the Psalter. We can only speculate about reasons. Perhaps Herbert would have written more such poems if he had lived longer and seen more of the coming political storm. Perhaps he spent more time in the "Individual Lament" mode because of his own personal inclination toward monastic melancholy. Perhaps he consciously or unconsciously stayed on the fence between high-church and low-church spirituality by writing about personal holiness within a poetic tradition with immense and ancient liturgical credibility. This last speculation would, of course, add fuel to the fire of controversy over Herbert's "truest" ecclesial allegiance.

In making my analysis, I have considered a passage of Herbert's poetry to have a social-concern factor if it simply refers literally or figuratively for even the briefest period to any sort of interaction between human beings on earth. The range of topics runs from broken or lamentably unestablished relationship (what Brueggemann would call *disorientation*) to whole, proper, and salutary companionship (*orientation, re-orientation, new orientation*). The range of rhetorical treatments of the topics runs from (a) mere description of a problem through (b) didactic prescription for, and exemplification of, its solution to (c) description of a blessed state or condition of human relationship. Obviously, poems of the last sort may not qualify as *laments*, so they would be part of the "social concern" category that does not overlap with that of Community Laments or Individual Laments. Psalm 133:1–3, for example, is clearly a song about healthy (well-"oriented") human relationship:

> 1 Behold, how good and how pleasant it is for brethren to dwell together in unity!
>
> 2 It is like the precious ointment upon the head, that ran down upon the beard, even Aaron's beard: that went down to the skirts of his garments;
>
> 3 As the dew of Hermon, and as the dew that descended upon the mountains of Zion: for there the Lord commanded the blessing, even life for evermore. (KJV)

A Song of Ascent that Bellinger classifies among the "Wisdom Psalms," Psalm 133 extravagantly uses two concatenated similes and the expressed tenor of the overarching figure to recommend a condition of social bliss made possible by willing human agents. Herbert's poem most similarly indulgent in the good feelings of proper social *orientation* may be "Constancie," in which the character of "the honest man" is held up in seven stanzas as the "Mark-man" whose "goodnesse sets not" when the sun sets.

The further a poem may be situated toward the "disorientation" end of the social-concern spectrum, the more likely it is to be a lament or to refer to lamentable social (interpersonal) conditions. Thus, God, represented as speaking in Ps 50:19–21, descends to specifics of social injustice and issues a prophecy:

> 19 Thou givest thy mouth to evil, and thy tongue frameth deceit.
> 20 Thou sittest and speakest against thy brother; thou slanderest thine own mother's son.
> 21 These things hast thou done, and I kept silence; thou thoughtest that I was altogether such an one as thyself: but I will reprove thee, and set them in order before thine eyes. (KJV)

Such disorientation can only be humanly redressed by "him that ordereth his conversation aright" (v. 23b)—the one who lives among others with proper respect for them and with proper demonstration of compassion and good will. It is no wonder that Bellinger places Psalm 50 into the same small subcategory with Psalm 82—"Hymns with Prophetic Warnings"—for both have an "angry God" speaker and a prophetic pronouncement for the socially malfeasant.

No poem in Herbert's "The Church" quite strikes that pair of notes, but "Unkindnesse" presents one of the longest of Herbert's reflections upon social probity. Ironically, however, the poem is not primarily about "horizontal" relationships or social justice. Its persona refers to his appropriate social behavior in four situations in order to contrast his treatment of *Christ* as shockingly disoriented in a manner that would be unthinkable to the persona in regard to his merely human friends. The judgment quality of the poem comes in the final lines, where the persona admits to treating Christ ("My God upon a tree") as worse than a foe. The unspoken suggestion is that the persona has thus apparently jeopardized his hope of salvation.

Unkindnesse.

> LORD, make me coy and tender to offend:
> In friendship, first I think, if that agree,
>   Which I intend,
>   Unto my friends intent and end.
> I would not use a friend, as I use Thee.
>
> If any touch my friend, or his good name,
> It is my honour and my love to free
>   His blasted fame
>   From the least spot or thought of blame.
> I could not use a friend, as I use Thee.
>
> My friend may spit upon my curious floor:
> Would he have gold? I lend it instantly;
>   But let the poore,
>   And thou within them, starve at doore.
> I cannot use a friend, as I use Thee.
>
> When that my friend pretendeth to a place,
> I quit my interest, and leave it free:
>   But when thy grace
>   Sues for my heart, I thee displace,
> Nor would I use a friend, as I use Thee.
>
> Yet can a friend what thou hast done fulfill?
> O write in brasse, *My God upon a tree*
>   *His bloud did spill*
>   *Onely to purchase my good-will.*
> Yet use I not my foes, as I use Thee.

Although "Unkindnesse" is primarily an individual lament about relationship with God (i.e., a spiritual relationship), the examples of proper social behavior function as an extended simile of how Christ should be treated—but it is negated five times in order to figure the extent of the spiritual sin. In other words, the tenor of the figuration has to do with the spiritual problem;

the references to proper and improper social behavior (or justice) are just the vehicle of the figure. In stanza 3, lines 13–14, the two types of sin are conflated in the sense of Matt 25:31–46, wherein Jesus explains the malfeasance of the "goats" as opposed to the behaviors of the "sheep." In "Unkindnesse," the deadliest wrong is that of failing to recognize and help the suffering Christ by "let[ting] the poore, / And *thou within* them starve at door" (my italics to emphasize the reference to Christ as "one of the least of these"). By ending the poem on the note of his treating the dying Christ worse than a foe, Herbert's persona leaves us without explicit solution to the problem. The implicit solution is to act justly in every aspect of one's life, spiritually as well as socially. In this regard, Herbert mingles the two concerns, again making it difficult to pin him down as a Calvinist or an Arminian; however, it is difficult to call "Unkindnesse" truly a social-concern poem unless we say it is so "by indirection."

On the other hand, I do not mean to disparage the value of any indirect, sidelong, or tangential social-concern gesture in Herbert's work. The mixed case of "Unkindnesse" does alert us to ask whether or not the notes of communal lament or social concern are sounded in poems of generally other sort in *The Temple*. If we consider the many highly introspective expressions of a Puritan, or at least Reformed, concentration upon personal holiness, it is but a short step to recognize that such holiness was the molecular transformative element in society. In Puritan reasoning, social righteousness could theoretically come about by multiplying the number of righteous individuals and their salutary effects upon society. Thus a reader of even Herbert's most individualistic poems might legitimately stay alert for the irruption of some social concern triggered by a process or moment of introspection. That other discourse may not be long or loud, but if it is there, Herbert should certainly be given credit for allowing its voice to be heard.

Christopher Hodgkins remarks that "moments of explicit social awareness are rare in 'The Church,' but he suggests that, all together, its poems could have a "Tudor humanist" effect upon readers whose "transformed spiritual and intellectual li[ves]" may "overflow naturally in good works."[22] Tudor humanism is hardly the spirit that the Puritan reformers would have found sufficient in Christians of their day, so perhaps it was politic for Herbert to keep the casually perceived social-justice/personal-holiness ratio of his poetic output to a figure no greater than that of the Psalms themselves. In a following essay on this topic, however, I intend to demonstrate that Herbert's understanding of and poetic engagement with

---

22. Hodgkins, *Authority, Church, and Society*, 206–7.

biblical social justice goes somewhat further and deeper than the assumptions of Herbert scholarship to date.

BIBLIOGRAPHY

Bellinger, W. H. *Psalms: Reading and Studying the Book of Praises*. Peabody, MA: Hendrickson, 1990.
Brennan, Michael G. "Licensing the Sidney Psalms for the Press in the 1640s." *Notes & Queries* 31.3 (1984) 304.
Brueggemann, Walter. *The Message of the Psalms: A Theological Commentary*. Minneapolis: Augsburg, 1984.
Fairclough, Norman. *Discourse and Social Change*. Cambridge, UK: Polity, 1992.
Freer, Coburn. *Music for a King: George Herbert's Style and the Metrical Psalms*. Baltimore: Johns Hopkins University Press, 1972.
Gottwald, Norman K. *The Hebrew Bible: A Socio-Literary Introduction*. Philadelphia: Fortress, 1985.
Gunkel, Hermann. *Introduction to Psalms: The Genres of the Religious Lyric of Israel*. Edited by Joachim Begrich. Translated by James D. Nogalski. Macon, GA: Mercer University Press, 1998.
———. *The Psalms: Form-Critical Introduction*. Philadephia: Fortress, 1967.
Herbert, George. *The English Poems of George Herbert*. Edited by Helen Wilcox. Cambridge: Cambridge University Press, 2007.
Hodgkins, Christopher. *Authority, Church, and Society in George Herbert: Return to the Middle Way*. Columbia, MO: University of Missouri Press, 1993.
Lewis-Anthony, Justin. *If You Meet George Herbert on the Road, Kill Him: Radically Rethinking Priestly Ministry*. London: Mowbray, 2009.
Patrides, C. A. *Figures in a Renaissance Context*. Edited by Claude J. Summers and Ted-Larry Pebworth. Ann Arbor: University of Michigan Press, 1989.
Quitslund, Beth. "Teaching Us How to Sing?: The Peculiarity of the Sidney Psalter." *Sidney Journal* 23.1/2 (2005) 109–10.
Wall, John N. *Transformations of the Word: Spenser, Herbert, Vaughan*. Athens, GA: University of Georgia Press, 1988.
Wohlers, Charles. *Book of Common Prayer—1559*. Online: http://justus.anglican.org/resources/bcp/1559/BCP_1559.htm.

9

Eat, Drink, and Include: A Theology of Hospitality in Luke-Acts & Beyond[1]

Martin William Mittelstadt

Les hivers de mon enfance étaient des saisons longues, longues. Nous vivions en trois lieux: l'école, l'église et la patinoire; mais la vraie vie était sur la patinoire.[2]

The winters of my childhood were long, long seasons. We lived in three places—the school, the church and the skating rink—but our real life was on the skating rink.[3]

---

1. An earlier version of this essay was published in the spring of 2014 in *Word and World*. I first found inspiration for this topic through my dear friends, Jim and Twila Edwards. They epitomized hospitality. Upon my arrival to Evangel University as a new professor, they took me under their wing, fed me, and mentored me. They led a Sunday School class fittingly named "Life Together" that continues to shape my life and calling. Jim has since moved to Chicago and I have the wonderful opportunity and responsibility to facilitate their dream as the new co-facilitator of the class they founded. Finally, when Evangel University received a gracious grant from the Lilly Foundation for "Theological Exploration of Vocation," he invited me to co-teach a course on the "theology and literature of hospitality." I am indebted to Jim and Twila for their ability to model, mentor, and share in God's gracious hospitality.

2. Carrier, "Une abominable feuille d'érable sur la glace," 1.

3. The citation above translates as "An Abominable Maple Leaf on the Ice." The story was translated by Sheila Fischman and published as *The Hockey Sweater*.

IN THE SUMMER OF 2004, during my annual summer vacation to my native Canada, I took great delight in my discovery of a newly issued five dollar note. Finally, my American friends would understand Canadian passion for hockey. Whereas American currency portrays presidents and stately commentary, this new Canadian note expresses the heart of Canadian identity. I was filled with pride as I could now show my southern friends that "our real life was on the skating rink." I had not heard of this adage or its author, Roch Carrier, so I searched for its origin. I soon discovered that Carrier ranks among the more popular writers from Quebec enjoyed by English-speaking Canadians. Though a prolific novelist, many readers first encounter him through his iconic work entitled *The Hockey Sweater*. This story proved so popular that the National Film Board of Canada produced an animated short film now used widely in public schools across Canada.

Carrier, like most French-Canadian boys of the 1950s, grew up a fan of the Montreal Canadiens and the great Maurice "The Rocket" Richard. In *The Hockey Sweater*, Carrier describes how he and his friends would play "five Maurice Richards against five Maurice Richards", all of them with the famous number 9 on their jerseys. The young Carrier eventually grows too big for his tattered sweater, so his mother orders a new one via the English-Only catalogue through Eaton's Department Store in Toronto. Carrier's excitement is dashed when he opens the package and finds a Toronto Maple Leafs sweater. After he cannot persuade his mother to return the order, he must wear his new sweater to the rink. Beyond the personal humiliation of wearing an "enemy" sweater, Carrier is harassed by his friends, loses his playing position, and gets benched for the most of the game. When he finally enters the game, Carrier receives an immediate penalty and a tongue lashing by the referee, who also *happens* to be the parish priest: "just because you're wearing a Toronto Maple Leafs sweater . . . doesn't mean you're going to make the laws around here."[4] The priest sends Carrier to confession, where the young boy prays that God would "send me, right away, a hundred million moths that would eat my Toronto Maple Leafs sweater."[5]

A cursory reading of this story resonates well with the "winters of our childhood" spent on ice rinks, the playful yet often intense rivalry between the Leafs and the Canadiens, and humorous commentary mixing sports and religion. But Carrier's work demands more than a sentimental reading. Instead, the story is filled with failed hospitality. A common refrain among Canadians often includes a commentary of our celebration of ethnic diversity. Though we take pride in our mosaic culture, Carrier's story tempers

---

4. Carrier, *Hockey Sweater*, 5.
5. Ibid.

such enthusiasm; the tensions between English and French Canada pose a threat to hospitality. In his tale, not unlike the Jewish/Samaritan divisions, Carrier uses literature to readdress the need to deal head on with such tensions. The inhospitable acts of young hockey players and the priest point to larger issues. Unless addressed, such tensions persist individually and collectively, and cripple a society. What should be a Christian response to the other? What might the Gospel offer to such a situation?

In this essay, I propose that Luke provides such a model for hospitality embodied by Jesus and the new people of God.[6] I offer the following course: 1) a brief summary of the rise of hospitality in the ancient world and specifically in the New Testament; 2) the function of the hospitality motif in Luke-Acts; and 3) pastoral reflections. I argue that Luke employs this motif in order to extend a primary message of the gospel to the ends of the earth not only as geographic expansion, but as a barrier-breaking hospitality that brings healing between individuals and communities marred by histories of separation and conflict. I frame the entire essay by way of stories that call humans, particularly believers, to embody the need for and the transforming power of hospitality.

Hospitality in the Ancient World

Moralists of the ancient world consider the art or practice of hospitality a fundamental moral virtue.[7] Whereas current ethicists devote their primary attention to hot button moral questions like sexuality (e.g., abortion, marriage, LGBT, and bio-ethics), ancient moralists recognize hospitality as the basic practice central to all aspects of human activity from family and friends to strangers and enemies. By definition, hospitality facilitates the social process in which someone who is an outsider shifts from stranger to guest. S. C. Barton suggests three stages of hospitality employed in the ancient world. A host must first *evaluate* the stranger to determine if incorporation of this guest is possible without undue threat to the security and purity lines of the group for whom the host is responsible. If yes, the host will *incorporate* the stranger as a guest, and in accordance with culture-specific codes of hospitality, the host will extend obligations understood by both parties. Finally, the *departure* of the stranger now turned guest not only signals a healthy parting of ways between an honorable host and the

---

6. Though hospitality often includes food, I do not intend to restrict hospitality to the table. The table serves only as a metaphor for hospitable practices.

7. For an excellent explication and bibliography, see Pohl, *Making Room*.

refreshed traveler, but also serves to solidify future relations between the two parties and their respective communities.[8]

By the first century, moralists describe at least five broad categories of hospitality all attested in Jewish, Greek, and Roman sources. First, the materialization of the Roman Empire gives rise to the need for *public* hospitality. A growing infrastructure must provide accommodations for those who journey as representatives of the empire. The geographic expansion of the empire might best be paralleled to the recent burst of globalization felt in the late twentieth century. Second, developing propaganda concerning *Pax Romana* literally paves the way for increased travel. Promises of safety and better routes on land and sea lead to the emergence of *commercial* hospitality, the beginnings of a food and lodging industry targeted at traveling business folk. Third, the growth of the empire also proves critical for those involved in *temple* hospitality, designed to facilitate worshipers on pilgrimages to holy places. Luke gives no better example than Paul's evangelistic efforts in Ephesus where opponents appear not to be upset by his message, but rather the potential threat to businesses that profit from the Temple to Artemis (Acts 19). Fourth, *theoxenic* hospitality refers to human generosity to gods, heroes, and semi-divine guests. Indeed, the author of Hebrews calls upon his readers ". . . not [to] neglect to show hospitality to strangers, for by doing that some have entertained angels without knowing it" (Heb 13:2). Finally, *private* hospitality becomes increasingly esteemed and encouraged throughout the ancient world. Although more and more people travel for business, political, and personal reasons, "Holiday Inns" free of filth, insects, drunkenness, and orgies remain in the distant future. To address such conditions, moralists describe a system to secure private accommodations. Travelers begin to solicit and carry letters of recommendation in order to commend or request hospitality for friends and acquaintances (3 John). It is therefore no surprise that early Christians similarly reflect upon and practice hospitality.[9]

The New Testament and Hospitality

Although theologians and pastors of spiritual formation typically (and rightly) seek biblical support for spiritual disciplines and practices such as prayer, study, simplicity, and worship, many ignore the discipline of hospitality.[10] Preachers of Paul's letter to the Romans often emphasize his

8. Barton, "Hospitality," 501–7.
9. Fitzgerald, "Hospitality," 522–25.
10. Rieger's *Traveling* serves as a rare exception. Globalization and (im)migration

exhortations for readers to offer their bodies as living sacrifices, endure persecution, submit to governing authorities, and a host of other Old Testament commandments (Rom 12–15), only to bypass Paul's refrain to "extend hospitality to strangers" (Rom 12:13). As an itinerant apostle, Paul not only implores the people of God to live hospitable lives, but also depends upon their hospitality (cf. 1 Cor 9:4–14; Acts 21:4, 7, 16–17; 28:7). For example, Paul appeals to Philemon in anticipation of release from prison: "prepare a guest room for me, for I am hoping through your prayers to be restored to you" (Phlm 22). Paul also instructs the Colossians to receive Mark, a traveling itinerate and Paul's delegate for the gospel (Col 4:10). When Paul rehearses the many hardships of his apostolic ministry, he includes the frequent absence of hospitality and even severe experiences of inhospitality from his enemies (1 Cor 4:11–13; 2 Cor 6:4–10; 11:21–33).

In the Pastoral Epistles, Paul shifts from general instructions and his personal travel to obligations for church leaders. Paul lists the essential qualifications of overseers in the local church. Once again, it has been my observation that hospitality rarely plays a vital role in the selection of contemporary leaders. Instead, modern concerns for qualification typically (and legitimately) include marital status, character, teaching ability, sobriety, and general people skills (1 Tim 3:2–5; Titus 1:8). But what about Paul's exhortation that a leader "must be hospitable" (Titus 1:8)? For Paul, institutional hospitality falls under the category of patron/client relationships as part of a larger ancient concept of households. If God's household provides a metaphor for the church and if an overseer serves as God's household steward, the overseer must exhibit the best qualities of familial and institutional hospitality. The overseer must welcome traveling Christians, itinerant preachers, and other strangers into the church. The plethora of warnings throughout the New Testament about false teachers only heightens implications for the home of the overseer as a place of screening to avert threats to church life and order. Leaders must oversee charitable activity in the church, ensure fair administration with regard for the poor, secure internal unity, and uphold the reputation of the church. Make no mistake; even a cursory review demonstrates that hospitality is no small matter for early Christians.

Hospitality in Luke-Acts

Switching to Luke-Acts requires a methodological pause. While Paul writes letters with propositional instructions, Luke tells stories. Regrettably and all too often, readers limit Luke (and the other Gospel writers) to the role

---

should surely produce a resurgence of interest in the practice of hospitality.

of historian, or in the case of Acts, a narrative that helps readers understand Paul better. While the Third Gospel and Acts supply the facts, and Acts certainly provides excellent context for Paul's epistles, does Luke intend more? Length limitations do not give me the space to unpack this idea; suffice to say, the growing majority of scholars emphasize the didactic value of stories.[11] In other words, if "all Scripture is inspired by God" (2 Tim 3:16), and if letter writers exhort, poets and psalmists compose prose and song, prophets deliver oracles and visions, then writers of the Gospels and Acts tell stories valuable for faith and practice (see also 1 Cor 10:1–11).

A. Pentecost: Enlarging the Vision

No contributor to the New Testament pays more attention to the Holy Spirit than Luke, and since I write as one firmly planted within the Pentecostal tradition, readers should not be surprised that a Pentecostal begins with Pentecost. However, I intend to celebrate and interrogate the classical Pentecost(al) reading of Acts 2. The Pentecost narrative is the story of the transfer of the charismatic Spirit from Jesus to the disciples (Acts 2:33). The same Spirit who rests upon Jesus now rests upon the disciples so that they will "continue to do and teach those things which Jesus began to do and teach" (Acts 1:1). The events of Pentecost provide the first example of an expanding mission that fulfills Jesus' promise that the disciples would "receive power . . . to be witnesses . . . to the ends of the earth" (Acts 1:8). The new people of God extend the ministry of Jesus under the anointing of the Holy Spirit. Sadly, for many within my tradition, the meaning of Pentecost ends with power for evangelism.

A rehearsal of the Pentecost narrative proves telling. Most participants presumably come from a Jewish background and would enjoy Pentecost as an extended Jewish party, a community feast in celebration of God's goodness and faithfulness (Exod 23:16; 34:22). Many Jews would attempt in their lifetime a journey to Jerusalem in order to attend at least one Jewish feast (Pentecost, Booths, or Passover). The context for Luke's account consists of the new people of God, having recently encountered the resurrected Jesus, gathered before Pentecost to wait, pray, study, and eat. On the day of the feast, the experience of about one hundred and twenty disciples draws the attention of travelers "from every nation under heaven" (2:5), who hear tongues in diverse languages (2:7; many of them listed in 2:9–11). As these onlookers stand amazed, Peter (and the Eleven) provide clarity for the confused crowd, and watch more than three thousand come to the resurrected

---

11. Marshall, *Luke*, and Johnson, *Prophetic Jesus Prophetic Church*.

Jesus. Luke employs Peter's emphasis on the fulfillment of the prophecy of Joel (Joel 2:28–32 > Acts 2:17–21) as a declaration of the potential universality of God's Spirit upon all people regardless of or, better stated, inclusive of male and female, young and old, clergy and laity, and not only Jews, but Samaritans, Gentiles, and beyond. Here lies the importance of tongues; no event speaks to the hospitality of God and the call upon God's people to embrace an open-ended vision like Pentecost. For Luke, Pentecost launches not only the geographic expansion of the gospel "to the ends of the earth" (Acts 1:8; cf. 2:39), but a barrier-breaking inclusivity (Acts 2:39). The Holy Spirit given by Jesus serves as God's eschatological envoy, extending the divine invitation of hospitality to Israel and the nations.

B. Jesus on the Margins: Guest and Host

At this point, I must tender another methodological pause concerning the relationship between Acts and the Third Gospel. In short, recent scholarship has seen a significant return to emphasis upon Luke-Acts as a two volume work. Although separated in the canon by John's Gospel, Luke intended for the Third Gospel and Acts to be read together. So why begin with Acts only to backtrack to the Third Gospel? If Luke's story of the new people of God supplies a sequel to the life of Jesus (Acts 1:1) and if the Spirit of Pentecost at the center of Luke-Acts serves as the driving force for the new mission, Luke must lay a foundation for his theology of hospitality. He does so through the pneumatic ministry of Jesus.

Whenever I read the Third Gospel, I cannot help but picture Jesus as a "party animal" (give me a break, I teach undergrads!). Luke's Jesus seems just as comfortable in ministry "behind the pulpit" as "wining and dining." In fact, unlike some other movements of his day, which sought to restrict table fellowship (Pharisees and the Qumran community), Jesus gets labeled "a glutton and a drunkard, a friend of tax collectors and sinners" (Luke 7:34). Though meant to be a pejorative comment, Jesus not only embraces the label, but displays his openness and vulnerability at table fellowship as a platform for transformational ministry.

Luke's Jesus accomplishes this by way of a great reversal. Typically and according to customs outlined above, Jesus enters a home as a guest and receives the hospitality of his host(s). But Jesus "spins the table"; he turns his hosts into guests so that they might receive his hospitality. Two beloved portraits unique to Luke demonstrate this reversal. According to hospitality custom, Mary and Martha open their home to the traveling Jesus and, as honorable hosts, take care of Jesus their guest (Luke 10:38–42). As Martha works hard (and justifiably so), she implores Jesus to insist that her sister Mary participate in the service of hospitality. In an affectionate manner, Jesus not only praises Mary for choosing to be nurtured by him, but invites Martha to settle down and receive his hospitality. Later on in the Third Gospel, Luke tells of Zacchaeus, the tax collector (Luke 19:1-10). When Jesus invites himself to the house of a corrupt government worker, the crowd begins to mutter: "He has gone to be the *guest* of a 'sinner'" (19:7; emphasis mine). Luke tells little of the dining between Jesus and Zacchaeus except for the remarkable economic reparation that Zacchaeus offers to those he had exploited. Ironically, the statement of the crowd fails to anticipate Luke's reversal. Zacchaeus may have entertained and nourished Jesus, but Zacchaeus becomes the guest of Jesus' hospitality: "Today salvation has come to this *house* . . . for the Son of Man came to seek and save what was lost" (Luke 19:9-10; emphasis mine). In both stories, Jesus the guest becomes Jesus the host and the agent of transformation. Furthermore, the transformation of both Martha, a woman, and Zacchaeus, a tax collector, foreshadows the barrier-breaking Pentecost symbolic of Jesus' extension to the margins of society and God's hospitality toward every outcast, whether sick, poor, disenfranchised, women, children, gentiles, and beyond.

C. The Church at the Margins: Jesus to the World

Turning to Acts, Jesus' hospitality to the socially marginalized continues through the ministries of the early church. The exuberant table fellowship of Jesus finds traction through various practices of the Jerusalem church; believers "had all things in common . . . [broke] bread at home and ate their food with glad and generous hearts" (Acts 2:44-47; cf. 4:32-37). Explicit expressions of hospitality overturn centuries of marginalization and separation toward the likes of an outcast Ethiopian eunuch and the hated Samaritans (Acts 8; see also Luke 10:25-42), and break the barrier for unfit Gentiles to enter into full communion with the new people of God (Acts 10-11). The Acts of the Apostles reveals the stories of a growing community that embodies the hospitality of Jesus and extends a welcome to all people without partiality (Acts 10:34). Not surprisingly, the Jerusalem Council addresses hospitality concerns and adopts less-restrictive regulations for table fellowship in order to integrate Gentile converts into the new people of God (Acts 15:1-29). Such liberties provide the opportunity for future household conversions in Acts. Thus, when the Philippian jailer and Lydia open their homes, Paul not only accepts their hospitality, but like Jesus turns the table and offers them the barrier-breaking hospitality of God.

D. Sacred Meals and Beyond...

Luke's passion for hospitality finds importance not only as a practice to facilitate inclusion, but also to propel early Christian embrace of a sacramental banquet. Luke alone produces the memorable account of Jesus' resurrection appearance to the disciples on the road to Emmaus (Luke 24:12–31). Jesus appears out of nowhere to his downcast disciples who were lamenting the death of their would-be messiah. The disciples, unable to recognize Jesus, mock their fellow traveler for his lack of information about the events of the previous days. As the unidentified traveler narrates the story of Israel's messiah through the Law and the Prophets, the disciples remain unable to identify him. As darkness draws near, the disciples display customary hospitality, for they open their home and feed the traveler. In dramatic fashion, Jesus not only reverses the role of host and guest but also provides what would become an early model for eucharistic fellowship; "when he was at the table with them, he took bread, blessed and broke it, and gave it to them. Then their eyes were opened, and they recognized him" (Luke 24:30–31).

A similar sacramental encounter occurs in Acts 8 when Luke tells of the doubly marginalized Ethiopian eunuch reading from Isaiah but not able to understand the implications. Philip appears out of nowhere, shares the good news, baptizes the eunuch, and disappears. Luke certainly intends to parallel these two stories; Philip continues the life and ministry of Jesus (Acts 1:1). Through their hospitality, Jesus and Philip provide revelation to wanderers and bring transformation through the respective sacraments of the "Eucharist" and baptism.[12]

E. The Banquet As The Taste of Heaven

Not only does Luke emphasize the hospitality of God and his people in the here and now, but he also builds upon Old Testament eschatological hopes: "On this mountain the Lord Almighty will prepare a feast of rich food for all peoples, a banquet of aged wine—the best of meats and the finest of wines ... [for] all peoples" (Isa 25:6–8). On one hand, the hospitality of the Lukan Jesus inaugurates the partially realized kingdom. On the other hand, Jesus anticipates an eschatological banquet that God insists must be well attended: "Blessed is he who shall eat bread in the kingdom of God" (Luke 14:15). Luke expresses Jesus' desire that people from every corner of the earth "take their places at the feast in the kingdom of God" (Luke 13:29). And those who share in the trials of Jesus will be invited to "eat and drink

---

12. I am indebted to Pervo, *The Mystery of Acts,* for this parallel.

at my table in my kingdom" (Luke 22:18–30). Luke undoubtedly intends for his readers not only to imagine a future eschatological feast, but also to use current table opportunities to extend a foretaste of heavenly celebrations.

F. No Room for an F in Hospitality

By now it is clear that Luke pays close attention to the need for and benefits of hospitality. However, all is not glamorous; he also takes great pains to emphasize the dire implications of failed hospitality. For Luke, failure in hospitality leads to a fractured community and, if left unattended, hinders kingdom exploits. I turn to two stories straddled between the growing persecution of the first followers. First, in a disturbing story, Ananias and Sapphira pay the ultimate penalty for their lack of integrity. Though they demonstrate concern for the needy among the new people of God, they lie about the percentage of money given from the sale of a property. Peter, under the direction of the Spirit, makes it clear that acts of generous hospitality without integrity carry grave consequences. Similarly, Luke tells of an averted schism due to a conflict over food distribution between Hebraic and Hellenistic widows (Acts 6:1–7). If left unattended, the table needs of the Hellenistic widows might have caused the first split of God's people. These stories stand between the respective arrests of Peter and John, the Twelve, and the subsequent martyrdom of Stephen. While it seems obvious that persecution might hinder the mission, Luke makes clear that God's people must serve with internal integrity and full regard for the marginalized. Luke uses this sobering interchange to remind readers that the church must remain fervent in the midst of pressures and be careful not to self-destruct.

A final example concerns the dramatic conversion of Peter (Acts 10–11). Ironically, while typically proclaimed as the conversion of Cornelius and his household, the story requires a closer look. While Luke describes Cornelius as ready for the message Peter brings, Peter must receive a triple vision from God in order to overcome his restrictive views on table fellowship in a Gentile home. Upon entry into Cornelius' home, Peter confesses: "I now realize how true it is that God does not show favoritism, but accepts men from every nation" (Acts 10:34). Though Peter's earlier Pentecost declaration that this "promise is for you, for your children, and for all who are far away" (Acts 2:39) expresses God's hospitality, Peter did not yet realize what he was saying. Based upon the quantity of detail and the content of Acts 10–11, Luke may be less interested in the addition of Cornelius than Peter's exclusivity. Although God's hospitality knows no limits, his people often struggle to embrace such inclusivity. Failure in hospitality, whether due to dishonesty, ethnocentrism, or exclusion, results in fractured community and a botched mission.

FINAL REFLECTION

Whereas Paul simply states "practice hospitality," Luke uses stories to encourage this practice. So what might Pastor Luke say to us? I offer a few possibilities. First, Christians would do well to consider the everyday opportunities afforded through loving table fellowship. Luke demonstrates that the table creates space for openness and vulnerability, and postures us to be recipients and agents of God's renovation. Second, if familial and private hospitality proves transformational, how much more the gathered people of God. What if our churches would provide space not only to hear Jesus' voice in a sermon, but also enlarge our theology of the table? Given the value upon relationships in our culture, creative hospitality will be critical to church unity and evangelism. Third, what if our church-related ministers, whether teachers, preachers, counselors, or administrators, would reflect anew upon their vocations? Beyond our regular sermons, lectures, and various talks, how might all servants of the gospel seek creative ways to model and enable the people of God to live hospitable lives in a fractured world? What if we would be encouraged to live our routines as an extension of God's hospitality? Fourth, what if we would more carefully read our lives, the church, and our world in order to better discern both beautiful and disappointing expressions of (in)hospitality. Thoughtful appropriation of literature, film, art, or social media should propel us to think more carefully about successful or failed hospitality in our broken world. And what if our understanding of the gospel would include not only individual hospitality, but also the barrier-breaking potential of collective hospitality.

In Flannery O'Connor's *Parker's Back*, the transformation of O. E. Parker stands in stark contrast to the rigid and unalterable fundamentalism of his wife, Sarah Ruth.[13] Parker leads a troubled life filled with failure and pain only to find periodic pleasure though his love of tattoos. In a bizarre series of events, he marries a stubborn Sarah and continues his destructive patterns. Parker continues to reject the gospel whether at revival meetings or through the "witness" of his wife and finds relief from his pain only through more tattoos. When Parker makes a final visit to a tattoo parlor, it is the piercing eyes of the Byzantine Christ (a work of *Christ the Pantocrator*) that lead Parker to get a tattoo on his back, the only remaining unmarked part of his body. Symbolic of a conversion, Parker receives mocking treatment

---

13. O'Connor, "Parker's Back."

from his friends at the bar. However, the reader is saddened by the response of Sarah Ruth who is incapable of understanding Parker's transformation and accuses him of idolatry. In vintage form, O'Connor, a devout Roman Catholic, interrogates believers for their destructive inhospitality.

May we pray that God would enliven our individual and collective imaginations to extend the hand of Jesus to our next door neighbor and those around the world. I am convinced that as we listen to God's heart through the stories of Scripture and great literature, the liberating possibilities for hospitality are endless. Cheers!

BIBLIOGRAPHY

Barton, S. C. "Hospitality." In *Dictionary of Later New Testament and Its Developments*, edited by Ralph Martin and Peter H. Davids, 501–7. Downers Grove, IL: InterVarsity, 1997.

Carrier, Roch. *The Hockey Sweater*. National Film Board of Canada, 1980.

———. *The Hockey Sweater*. Translated by Sheila Fischman. Illustrated by Sheldon Cohen. Toronto: House of Anansi, 1979.

———. "Une abominable feuille d'érable sur la glace." In *Enfants du bonhomme dans la lune*. Montreal: Stanké, 1979.

Fitzgerald, J. T. "Hospitality." In *Dictionary of New Testament Background*, edited by Craig Evans and Stanley Porter, 522–25. Downers Grove, IL: InterVarsity, 2000.

Johnson, Luke Timothy. *Prophetic Jesus Prophetic Church: The Challenge of Luke-Acts to Contemporary Christians*. Grand Rapids: Eerdmans, 2011.

Marshall, I. Howard. *Luke: Historian and Theologian*. Exeter, UK: Paternoster, 1970.

Mittelstadt, Martin W. "Eat, Drink, and Be Merry: A Theology of Hospitality in Luke-Acts." *Word & World* 34.2 (2014) 31–39.

O' Connor, Flannery. *Everything that Rises Must Converge*. New York: Farrar, Strauss and Giroux, 1965.

Pervo, Richard. *The Mystery of Acts: Unraveling Its Story*. Santa Rosa, CA: Polebridge, 2008.

Pohl, Christine D. *Making Room: Recovering Hospitality as a Christian Tradition*. Grand Rapids: Eerdmans, 1999.

Reiger, Joerg. *Traveling*. Fortress: Minneapolis, 2011.

10

"The Truest, Least Selfish Heart": God's Childlikeness in George MacDonald's Fairy Tales

LaDonna Friesen

Once upon a time, a selfish Giant repaired a breach in his wall to silence the voices of children who had found a hole into his garden, only to find that Snow and Frost wintered for long months in the children's absence. At last the children crept Spring into the garden again, and a little boy longing to be lifted into a tree melted selfishness into love. The Giant lifted the boy into the branches, which instantly blossomed while the boy "stretched out his two arms and flung them round the Giant's neck, and kissed him." When the Giant saw the boy again in the white-blossomed branches, he noticed nail scars on the boy's hands and feet. "Who hath dared to wound thee?" cried the Giant. The boy replied, "These are the wounds of love."[1]

Once upon a time, a dragon singed a kingdom. The king and queen of this land sent their only daughter Una to find a knight virtuous enough to defeat their fiery adversary. She found the Red Cross Knight in another land and on their return, the knight, having been strengthened in humility, wisdom, and affirmation of his true identity as Saint George, slew the dragon, and the kingdom knew peace again.[2]

Once upon a time a swamp fairy cursed a princess to sleep all day and wake with the moon, her beauty and age waxing and waning with the moon's form. A prince fleeing rebellion in his country paused in his journey,

---

1. Wilde, *Selfish Giant*, 1–28.
2. Hodges, *Saint George and the Dragon*, 7–32.

entranced by her dance in the moonlight. One night he found her when she was old and weak in the darkness of the new moon. He did not know this old woman was the princess, but seeing she was on the fringe of death, he kissed her, and his compassion transformed her into her true self, Princess Daylight.[3]

Fairy tales like these—"The Selfish Giant" by Oscar Wilde, *The Faerie Queene* by Edmund Spenser, and "Little Daylight" by George MacDonald—enflesh the cosmic-redemptive narrative assuring humanity that a situation darkened by evil and chaos can be transformed by the light and order of virtue. They are a few of many tales that circle around the world the voices of artists whose characters suffer the world's fallenness. Those refined in the purging fire of suffering forge a self-sacrifice powerful enough to conquer evil and restore life. In *The Lord of the Rings* series by J. R. R. Tolkien, the hobbits Sam and Frodo exemplify this victory through self-denial—Sam by seeing that Frodo's needs are met before his own, and Frodo by denying the call of a powerful ring which he could easily slide onto his hand and use for his own glory, but must instead destroy it in order to save Middle Earth. Fantastical tales like Tolkien's remind us that a microscopic redemption of the self can influence a macroscopic redemption of the world. Although this story and other fairy tales journey with readers into the darkness of humanity so familiar to us, they also help us envision T. S. Eliot's words, quoting medieval anchoress Julian of Norwich, "And all shall be well and / All manner of thing shall be well."[4]

The presence of this wellness exists in the conclusion of all three tales described at the beginning of this essay. It seems no coincidence that two of the tales—"The Selfish Giant" and "Little Daylight"—were intended for children and that St. George's story was eventually adapted for children into a picture book by Margaret Hodges. Although many of the early fairy tale creators and compilers, such as Charles Perrault in France and Jacob and Wilhelm Grimm in Germany, did not intend for children to be the primary audience of their published stories, the tales, because they were enjoyed by children as well as adults, were eventually made more suitable for young family members. Today most fairy tales are a common narrative influence in children's lives, whether through film or written language. Fairy tales are enjoyed by every age, but the especial association of this genre with children, either because these tales were written for children or eventually inherited

---

3. MacDonald, *At the Back*, 230–52. MacDonald will refer to George MacDonald unless specified otherwise.

4. Eliot, "Little Gidding," 1497.

by them, suggests humanity finds *childlikeness* embedded in the nature of fairy stories.

George MacDonald, author of "Little Daylight" and a Victorian writer of fairy tales, defines childlikeness in his sermon "The Child in the Midst" based on the passages where Jesus sets a child among his disciples as an example of humility (Mark 9:33–37; Matt 18:1–5).[5] In this sermon, MacDonald does not mention the writings of others, but his explanation would affirm the self-sacrifice of Saint George, the boy who loved the selfish Giant, and Sam and Frodo. Childlikeness, like the fairy story, is associated with the child, but is for every person, no matter the age, and is essential to knowing God. The person who understands pure childhood has also experienced the essence of God—"grace and truth—in a word, childlikeness."[6] In his sermons and novels, MacDonald emphasized oneness with God through self-abandonment and sacramental love, expressions of the grace and truth at the heart of childlikeness.

In 1872, when George MacDonald gave a seven month lecture tour in America where he drew large crowds to hear his talks on literary greats such as Robert Burns and William Shakespeare, as well as preached sermons, one reporter said of MacDonald's audience, "They feel that in him they have a true man, with the brain of a poet and *heart of a child*."[7] MacDonald could not have been more pleased that he, middle-aged at this time with eleven children, was described as childlike.

In his collection of unspoken sermons, George MacDonald explains childlikeness is natural to the image of God indwelling humanity because "the *childlike* is divine."[8] Even though MacDonald names God as friend, father, and mother, God is also childlike,[9] and this harmony of the entire family present in God is an embodiment of God's all-encompassing love.

Each member of the family is an essential perception of God's love, but the divine mother and child love were unconventional for George MacDonald's Victorian audience and may still be unique to some contemporary readers. For a fuller understanding of the child in God, and how it relates to the childlike in fairy stories, an introduction to MacDonald's illustrations of God as mother and father is helpful.

The love between the Father and the Son provided a model for George MacDonald's own understanding of love between humanity and God.

---

5. MacDonald, *Creation in Christ*, 29–36.
6. Ibid., 32.
7. Quoted in Hein, *George MacDonald*, 264 (italics mine).
8. MacDonald, *Creation in Christ*, 30.
9. Ibid., 33.

Creation is born out of God's love, and just as Christ lovingly gave "Himself with perfect will to God, choosing to die to Himself and live to God," the created also returns self-abnegating devotion—"the drowning of self in the life of God, where it lives only as love."[10] MacDonald's close relationship with his earthly father nurtured his insight into the nature of the divine Father-Son oneness in love. As a father himself, MacDonald practiced this grace with his children. In a letter to his daughter Mary, whom he affectionately called "Elfie," he tenderly responded to her confession that she could not adequately love God. He reminded her that God is the root of all loves, and as she knows Him more, He will teach her how to love Him. He ended by saying "So you need not be troubled about it darling Elfie . . . I am very very glad you asked me my child. Ask me anything you like, and I will try to answer you if I know the answer. For this is one of the most important things I have to do in the world."[11] MacDonald also acted in dramatic productions of Shakespeare's plays and Bunyan's *Pilgrim's Progress* with his wife and children, and he wrote them letters for their birthdays. In writing a birthday letter to his oldest son Greville, MacDonald does not assume fatherly authority but humbly points his son to his eternal Father: "More and more I see and feel that what the Father is thinking is my whole treasure and well being. To be one with him seems the only common sense, as well as the only peace. Let him do with you, my beloved son, as he wills."[12] While his children's obedience to himself as their earthly father was a natural communion of order and love, MacDonald ultimately desired for his children union with their heavenly Father as the highest way to live.

In his sermon on childlikeness, George MacDonald not only names God "father" but also "mother."[13] Since God is the source of all loves, and His image also abides in women, "The deepest, purest love of a woman has its well-spring in Him."[14] This love is present in many of MacDonald's works, and particularly in his fantasy writing, the physical beauty of women who are associated with the supernatural is a visual of love's beauty within them. One of these beautiful women is a spiritual mentor in his children's story, *At the Back of the North Wind*, which, like all of MacDonald's writing, is not an allegory but does have strong themes of spiritual truth. North Wind has long flowing black hair and flies coldly through the night personifying God's providence, which may at times seem cruel but can be the impetus for

10. Ibid., 18.
11. Quoted in Hein, *George MacDonald*, 228.
12. McDonald, *George MacDonald and His Wife*, 535.
13. MacDonald, *Creation in Christ*, 33.
14. Ibid., 34.

good born from adversity. She says, "I can do nothing cruel, although I often do what looks like cruel to those who do not know what I really am doing."[15] She is mysterious and powerful enough to sink ships, but she swoops low to talk with Diamond, the son of coachman, through a little hole in his wall, and in a nurturing image of love, she creates a nest in her hair for Diamond so that he can keep hold of her while she sweeps her wind through the city streets. She allows Diamond to visit a utopian natural paradise that exists behind her back, and when he dies, he is taken there permanently—evidence that life's difficulties have not defeated him, but Diamond has learned to love others in their need, helping goodness emerge from distress. Diamond likens North Wind's voice to this mother's, and when she is carrying him, he nestles close to her bosom and says, "You don't know how nice it is to feel your arms about me."[16] North Wind's mother-love, although comforting, is not pampering. Like MacDonald's perception of God's love, it is all-consuming and fosters spiritual maturity through suffering. Louisa Powell, MacDonald's wife for over fifty years, understood North Wind's nature when she wrote a concerned letter to her traveling and ill husband (asthma and coughing blood were intermittent afflictions for MacDonald throughout his life), hoping that "North Wind might after all comfort you in that long hair."[17] Love and adversity meet in the same experience. Louisa referenced MacDonald's books in more than one letter—a measure of the harmony shared by the couple. Unlike traditional Victorian family models, MacDonald did not practice authoritative control over his wife because she was his "partner in receiving the grace of life."[18] In his intimate love for Louisa as well as in strong friendships with family friends like Lady Byron, the poet Lord Byron's wife, and Lady Georgiana Mount-Temple, a spiritual mentor, MacDonald's language was ever respectful and admitted to being indebted to them for God's provision of grace and support in his life.

It is no wonder, then, that many of the women in MacDonald's fairy tales are powerful spiritual figures who encourage transforming faith experiences in men as well as women and children. In *Phantastes*, for example, it is a selfless, beautiful woman whose song delivers Anodos from the tower where he is trapped with his own shadow. He recognizes her as the girl whose precious glass globe he selfishly broke earlier in the story. The breaking caused the girl to visit the Fairy Queen's palace where she received healing and was given the gift of singing her own songs without the globe.

---

15. MacDonald, *At the Back*, 49.
16. Ibid., 57.
17. Quoted in Hein, *George MacDonald*, 215.
18. Hein, *George MacDonald*, 71.

The brokenness led to songs of deliverance, and she was able to free Anodos. As she walked into the forest, Anodos "watched her departure, as one watches a sunset. She went like a radiance through the dark wood, which was henceforth bright to me, from simply knowing that such a creature was in it. She was bearing the sun to the unsunned spots."[19] Her brilliance contrasts the shadow that has been following him through the story; her song redeems him from that darkness. MacDonald understood that God's love for humanity is too great to be confined to any particular role—father, mother, child, friend—of the human life. Scripture describes God as Abba father and as the mother hen who covers her children with her wings. To know the comprehensive love of God, one must experience it through the natures of both genders.

And one must also experience it through the childlikeness of God. When we open our lives to Christ, George MacDonald says, "he comes in, and dwells with us, and we are transformed to the same image of truth and purity and heavenly childhood."[20] "Heavenly childhood" is reminiscent of William Wordsworth's "Intimations of Immortality":

> Our birth is but a sleep and a forgetting:
> The Soul that rises with us, our life's Star,
>   Hath had elsewhere its setting,
>   And commeth from affar:
>   Not in entire forgetfulness,
>   And not in utter nakedness,
> But trailing clouds of glory do we come
>   From God, who is our home:
>   Heaven lies about us in our infancy!"[21]

The young child retains this lighted joy for a time until it fades with adulthood, and nature becomes the great comforter with its own intrinsic divine qualities.

An admirer of Romantic poets like William Blake, William Wordsworth, and Samuel Taylor Coleridge, George MacDonald and other Victorian writers were influenced by the child as divine in Romantic verse. One MacDonald biographer, Rolland Hein, believes MacDonald likely lectured on Wordsworth and Coleridge in his English literary addresses and asserts that "The presence in MacDonald's writings of ideas very similar to Blake's is

---

19. MacDonald, *Phantastes*, 165.
20. MacDonald, *Creation in Christ*, 28.
21. Wordsworth, "Ode: Intimations of Immortality," 1541.

so noticeable that MacDonald must have had some early acquaintance with his work."[22] In his biography of his father, Greville MacDonald compares a likeness between Mr. Raven in MacDonald's final fantasy *Lilith* and Blake's winged flight imagery from *Milton*, Book II.[23] MacDonald also had a bookplate made that featured an engraving by William Blake with a stooped, full-clothed elderly man entering a doorway into a dark cavern while a young man gazes upward, unclothed and surrounded by light. This elevation of the young is not uncommon in Blake's works, both in his illuminations and in his poetry. In the frontispiece for Blake's *Songs of Innocence* a child in cherub form with its golden hair and innocently naked body flies above a man who looks up to it. Blake's frontispiece for *Songs of Experience* illustrates a young man balancing a winged child on his head while holding the child's hands, and the adult hand linked with the child's is an ideal visual of the eternity of the child through adult life and beyond death.[24]

Before and during the period the Romantic poets were writing, literature for children was primarily instructional, and if a fairy tale was written for this audience, its moral was clear and often the author took special care to insure that the children's imaginations were not damaged by the appearance of fantastical creatures. The eighteenth century British writer Sarah Fielding, for example, used a character named Mrs. Teachum to warn her pupils about the dangers of fairy tales: "I have no objection, Miss Jenny, to your reading any Stories to amuse you, provided you read them with the Disposition of a Mind not to be hurt by them. A very good Moral may indeed be drawn from the Whole . . . But here let me observe to you that Giants, Magic, Fairies, and all sorts of supernatural Assistances in a Story, are introduced only to amuse and divert."[25] Mrs. Teachum then explains the allegorical meaning of the supernatural characters in Fielding's fairy tale and concludes, "Therefore by no means let the Notion of Giants or Magic dwell upon your Minds."[26] Fantastical elements are reduced to mere moral tools that a child's imagination should handle delicately. Fielding, like other authors writing at this time for children, assumed the child's mind was easily corrupted and needed overt spiritual and literary guidance.

The Romantic poets' notion of children entering our world while still bearing the radiance of a heavenly realm contrasted the Reformed doctrine that children were corrupt from birth. Rather than the adult standing tall in

22. Hein, *George MacDonald*, 119.
23. Greville MacDonald, *George MacDonald and His Wife*, 555.
24. Blake, *Songs of Innocence and Experience*, 2.
25. Zipes, "Introduction to Sarah Fielding," 189–90.
26. Ibid., 190.

an intimidating pose while pointing a finger of moral direction for the child, the grownup, like Blake's frontispieces, may look up to the heaven-like nature of children and be awed by their naked innocence, a trace of the glory from which they came. The child's imagination is sovereign, and childhood is a precious time of life. This vision of children's imaginative capabilities ushered in the Victorian Golden Age of children's literature with titles such as *The Secret Garden* by Frances Hodgsen Burnett, *Alice in Wonderland* by Lewis Carroll, and *The Princess and the Goblin* by George MacDonald.

In his fairy tales with children as main characters, MacDonald does not, like Fielding, point out the dangers of fantastical creatures like goblins or supernatural women to his readers. Rather, he shared Blake's and Wordsworth's organic communion of imagination and meaning. He trusted children and adults alike would garner truth naturally through storytelling's appeal to the imagination. As a former minister and as a spiritual father for his readers, MacDonald believed fantastic literature graced them with a vision of a realm beyond the natural, inspiring faith in an eternal presence. God, out of His divine imagination, creates the glories of nature, and the childlike spirit that receives his imaginative presence discerns the spiritual within God's physically created world. Writers, indwelled by God's image, are like priests and prophets—giving "fresh and compelling expression to the invisible truths of God as they are resident in the things of this world, allowing them their moral and spiritual impact."[27] This priestly-prophetic mission works naturally in one of the titles C. S. Lewis listed as MacDonald's "great works"[28]—*The Princess and the Goblin*.

In this fairy tale novel, Princess Irene lives in a large country house "half castle, half farmhouse" where she is kept safe while her father rules the kingdom.[29] Her mother died before she was old enough to remember her. When the bugle blasts announce her father's visits, she runs to his horse where he lifts her onto his saddle and folds her into his great arms. When she "hid her glad face upon his bosom, it [her father's long silvery-streaked dark beard] mingled with the golden hair which her mother had given her, and the two together were like a cloud with streaks of the sun woven through it,"[30] a beautiful image of unified distinctions, like the oneness shared between God as Father with His Son and with humanity. Between her father's visits, Irene's primary caretaker is Nurse Lootie who is anxious and self-conscious about her appearance but who deeply cares about the princess.

27. Hein, *George MacDonald*, 332.
28. From the introduction to George MacDonald's *Phantastes*, xi.
29. MacDonald, *Princess and the Goblin*, 1.
30. Ibid., 76–77.

One day Irene is drawn to ascend a staircase in the house and finds herself lost in a maze of steps and hallways until she meets an aged lady with flowing hair, smooth white skin, and wise eyes who spins invisible thread made from spider's webs and eats the eggs of pigeons roosting at her high window. The lady calls herself Irene's great great grandmother, but she also shares Irene's name, and the little girl's ascension into this supernatural Irene's home suggests the potential for the spiritual completeness that satisfies every individual's innate longing for it. When little Irene exclaims over their identical names, great Irene says, "I haven't got your name. You've got mine."[31] Princess Irene's naming from someone whose outer loveliness reflects the inner beauty of a wise and loving spirit is prophetic of the child's own becoming.

Great Irene stops her wheel to bathe little Irene's face with a soft white towel, the beginning of a greater cleansing that follows in a later scene. The cleansing and spinning, the white lamp of moon shining in great Irene's window, and the ascending room with its nesting pigeons provide a refuge for Irene from the evil stirring in her kingdom.

When child Irene descends and tries to tell Nurse Lootie about her great grandmother upstairs, Lootie is offended that the child is trying to fool her with a make-believe story and especially that Princess Irene said her great grandmother was taller and prettier than Lootie.[32] The conversation is a dialogue between the childlike and the childish. According to MacDonald, even a child may not be childlike, and an adult may be childish.[33] While child Irene has accepted the supernatural in the physical in its grace and truth, Lootie is more concerned about the princess thinking she might be ugly because she was not as pretty as Irene's made-up grandmother. Lootie's focus is on the injury to her pride, a look inward to the self that has no part in childlikeness, although this attitude might have been altered if Lootie had been in great Irene's presence. Princess Irene's thought direction moves away from self to the otherness of the supernatural being and the harmony of love deepening between them. The childlike in heart, according to MacDonald is "the truest, the least selfish."[34] Great Irene has awakened in child Irene an enlargement of her childlike heart through faith in a being who is wholly true and good but unseen and therefore doubted by others.

At this point, Princess Irene does not know that underneath the mountain goblins are planning to kidnap her and force her to marry their

---

31. Ibid., 13.
32. Ibid., 20.
33. MacDonald, *Creation in Christ*, 29.
34. Ibid., 25.

prince. She sees her first goblin when she and Lootie return late from a walk. Probably due to the nature of goblins as creatures of the night, the princess is forbidden to be out past sunset, but nurse and child walk too far before realizing the day is closing. Lootie runs wildly down the mountain holding fast to Irene, but the nurse is lost in her terror of the goblin shapes along the way. They are rescued by Curdie, a fearless miner boy who whistles and sings verses to drive away the creatures. The goblins cannot stand his rhymes, and Lootie and the princess are delivered. As a reward, Irene promises to kiss Curdie, but Lootie quickly pulls the princess inside before she can do anything so improper. The reader knows Irene's kiss was an intended act of spontaneous graciousness, and Lootie's abrupt dismissal of it prevents the harmonic love Irene seeks to gather around herself.

It is twelve-year-old Curdie who is brave enough to enter the goblins' lair and discover their intent to flood the mine and kidnap Princess Irene. The goblins are creatures who, according to legend, may have once lived above ground and looked like humans but because of their perceived oppression from a long-ago king, they disappeared into underground caverns where their bodies were distorted into hideous forms. Most notable to their appearance are heads hard as stone, like the hardness of their rationality, and the weakness of their soft feet. Although Irene's father was not the source of their reasons for going underground, the goblins still viewed the king, the miners, and all uplanders in the kingdom as enemies, and the story culminates, as many fantasies do, in a battle where vengeance wreaks havoc and is overcome by the more powerful force of good.

During Curdie's second spying excursion in goblin territory, he is caught and imprisoned in a dark cavern. In the meantime, Princess Irene has her most spiritually transcendent experience, and it prepares her to descend into the deep downs as Curdie's rescuer. One evening a long-legged cat, a pet of the goblins, jumps through Irene's room, and frightened Irene runs into the night until she is lost but is comforted by the moon-lamp of her great grandmother guiding her home. When she enters the house, she immediately rushes upstairs to great Irene's rooms where she finds the lady, not in her workroom but in her bedroom and much younger with a face "of three-and-twenty."[35] It is not uncommon for MacDonald's supernatural characters to alter their forms in size or age, as evidenced also in *The Golden Key* and *At the Back of the North Wind*. As semblances of the divine, they are unpredictable, in action and appearance, and cannot be defined by a single form. In *The Golden Key*, facets of God's revelation to humans are in both the Old Man of the Fire and a little naked child. North Wind's voice is at

---

35. MacDonald, *Princess and the Goblin*, 112.

times as comforting as a mother's, as fierce and cold as a northern gale's, and as playful and young as a child's. These shifting shapes do not contradict but rather complement characteristics of father, mother, and child within God's divine nature. According to MacDonald, God presents Himself in forms fitting to the spiritually sensitive individual's needs.

When great Irene holds out her arms to child Irene, the princess is afraid her dirty clothes and face, after having stumbled in her run from the cat, will soil her grandmother's. But "With a merry little laugh the lady sprung from her chair, more lightly far than Irene herself could, caught the child to her bosom, and, kissing the tearstained face over and over, sat down with her in her lap."[36] When the embrace is done, great and small Irenes' dresses are covered in mud from the mountain road. From her fire, the lady takes a burning rose, and passing it over her dress, cleanses it. When the rose is returned to the hearth, Irene cries out for its flame: "Won't you hold it to my frock and my hands and my face? And I'm afraid my feet and my knees want it too."[37] The child is earnest for a cleansing, no matter how fiery the rose-flame, but Great Irene smiles sadly and tells her that "it is too hot for you yet," suggesting that as Irene matures, she will be able to endure the burning roses, a sense experience illustrating MacDonald's strong belief that purging and beauty are one work in the individual. The cleansing comes, then, when child Irene bathes in a large silver oval tub with water that reflects the stars and moon shining on the walls and ceiling. Grandmother leaves the room, and child Irene settles into peace: "The child sat gazing, now at the rose fire, now at the starry walls, now at the silver light; and a great quietness grew in her heart," and the fear of her former scare is dissolved in the tranquility of the dark, blue-starred night.[38]

When Great Irene returns, she has a gift for the princess—the thread she has been weaving, rolled into a ball that "was of a sort of grey-whiteness, something like spun glass."[39] Great Irene throws it into the rose fire where it glimmers but is unburned and then places it in her drawer. Its thread is tied to a ring that child Irene will have so that the thread will always be with her as a guide. The thread is so fine it cannot be seen, but it can be felt, and great Irene assures the princess that while the child is holding the thread, her grandmother is also holding it. Cleansed in starry water and the aroma of fire roses from the fear that stumbled her into the night and with a great faith in the invisible thread, child Irene descends from the garret with

---

36. Ibid., 113.
37. Ibid., 114.
38. Ibid., 116.
39. Ibid., 117.

the quiet confidence that a great presence abides with her, and she is now well-equipped to rescue Curdie.

Irene places her finger on the thread, not knowing where it will lead her but trusting her grandmother's guide, and follows it into the unfamiliar underground, which might have overwhelmed her before the peace of the bath and moonlit night in the tower. She does not know Curdie is imprisoned nor why the thread is leading her into the darkness, but she has faith in its guiding purpose. At last she finds the rocks walling up Curdie's hole, and the two work to free him. Curdie is befuddled how the princess managed to find her way to him through the dark tunnels, having no knowledge that he was trapped there, and when Irene tries to explain the thread to him, he cannot feel it or believe in it. Irene is like the figure in Plato's "Allegory of the Cave" who ascends into the full light of the sun (representing high spiritual experience in MacDonald's work) and then descends to share with those still in the cave that a greater light exists but is misunderstood and mocked by the unbelievers. Curdie's doubt is confirmed when he, out of courtesy to the princess, climbs the stairs to the tower but finds only straw, a tub, and a withered apple.[40] He departs with an angry retort. Later, when he reflects on his experiences with his mother, he is sorry for his rudeness yet is bewildered by his and the Princess' differences of sight.

Curdie has not yet developed the imaginative, childlike sensibilities that discern the spiritual in the physical. It will take others' misunderstandings and his own suffering to work in him greater spiritual maturity. One night when he is listening for the sounds of the goblins working, the king's guards shoot him with a crossbow and accuse him of prowling about to do mischief. Curdie tries to explain himself but is locked in a room of Irene's home, disoriented and feverish from his wound.[41] He tries to tell the guards about the approaching tunnels the goblins are digging toward the house, but his speech is incoherent due to his fever, and the men ignore his warning. It is at his worst point—when his work of discovering the goblins' plan is disregarded and he is too ill to fight—that he can finally see into the spiritual realm. Curdie's experience supports MacDonald's conviction that affliction intensifies faith, and faith, purged and fortified through suffering, works through the imagination to give the Christian greater vision. Curdie, distraught that he cannot get up to protect the princess, gives a great cry. It is followed by a hand that opens his locked door, and then "he saw a lady with white hair, carrying a silver box in her hand, enter the room. She came to his bed, he thought, stroked his head and face with cool, soft hands, took

40. Ibid., 175.
41. Ibid., 201–4.

the dressing from his leg, rubbed it with something that smelt like roses, and then waved her hands over him three times."[42] When Curdie awakens from his slumber, he is well again, and hearing the sounds of the goblins in the house, he immediately picks up a sword and knife to join the battle. After the goblins' defeat, Curdie searches for the princess and finds her because he felt the invisible thread leading him to her, another indication that faith is alive in Curdie. At the end of the tale, Princess Irene gives him the kiss she promised, and this sharing of love is not only physical but also a communion of spiritual insight.

The princess' cottage is destroyed by the goblins, but she, Curdie, and the people who served there are saved. Curdie worries that great Irene will be ruined in the falling house, but as he looks up to the lighted globe at her window, a white bird descends with wings spread and circles round the king and Curdie and child Irene before gliding up again and vanishing.[43] The light and the wings personify the comforting presence of great Irene who has winged round these three humans, covering them with her feathers to protect them from physical harm but also from the selfishness that childlikeness cannot abide. At one point, even the king ascended the stair to her haven. In this final scene of wings and light and father and children, the family within God is represented. There is the loving father-king, the nurturing virtue of the mother in great Irene, and the childlike, selfless trust of truth in Curdie and child Irene. The family triune, like the doctrinal Trinity of Father, Son, and Holy Spirit, has distinct members, yet all are unified in love and in their childlike nature.

In her article on literature and a Christian worldview, Twila Brown Edwards says literary artists "creatively give birth to imaginary characters who will help us, as we read, to find the image of God in ourselves."[44] In order to be true, quality literature must represent both the Fall and the potential for redemptive human experience. Humanity's great fallenness, like heavy theater curtains confining the stage of life, may be drawn aside so that the spotlight rests on God's image in us. Great artists may incarnate the truth that evil can be slain, that it is not the final end for humanity. The redemptive elements, Edwards says, such as the transformations in fairy tales, can "shine through the Fall in us, at least partially redeeming the image of God in us."[45] Stories like *Saint George and the Dragon* assure us there is a goodness powerful enough to defeat evil. The perpetuation of this legend in

---

42. Ibid., 210.
43. Ibid., 237.
44. Edwards, "Place of Literature," 342.
45. Ibid., 362.

art and literature is testimony of our need to read again and again that the dragonish nature in us can be slain.[46]

George MacDonald tells the story once more in *The Princess and the Goblin*. The goblins, so self-focused that they are willing to harm others by flooding the miners, are conquered with the help of two children guided by a virtuous supernatural being. Even Nurse Lottie, who is so concerned someone might think she is ugly that she cannot hear the truth in Irene's story, forgets herself when her heart turns to serving the princess. Fallenness is represented, even in good Curdie when he cannot see great Irene and angrily accuses child Irene of making him look like a fool. But the story ends in redemption—the encompassing salvation of the kingdom from the goblins but also Curdie's inward transformation from doubt to belief and Princess Irene's trust linking self with the supernatural, as a thread she can feel but cannot see leads her into the darkness to save her friend's life.

Because God is childlike and we are made in His image, redemptive stories like MacDonald's are not only reshaping the good-conquers-evil motif, but they are also asking us to ascend the stair like a child and find the wonder of fire-roses, the protective wings, the lighted lamp, the bath with water reflecting the stars. With a mature spiritual imagination, we lose ourselves in the presence of the divine so that when we are called to descend into the darkness, we feel faith like a thread at our fingertips. The fairy tale is for the childlike—anyone and any age—who enters the story and finds at its end that self has faded in the glorious light of God's image.

BIBLIOGRAPHY

Blake, William. *Songs of Innocence and Experience: The Illuminated Books*, edited by Andrew Lincoln. Vol. 2. Princeton: Princeton University Press, 1991.

Edwards, Twila Brown. "The Place of Literature in a Christian Worldview." In *Elements of a Christian Worldview*, edited by Michael Palmer, 342–75. Springfield, MO: Logion, 1998.

Eliot, T. S. "Little Gidding." In *The Norton Anthology of English Literature: The Major Authors*. Vol. 2. 9th ed. Edited by M. H. Abrams et al., 1494–1500. New York: Norton, 2012.

Hein, Rolland. *George MacDonald: Victorian Mythmaker*. Nashville, TN: Star Song, 1993.

Hodges, Margaret. *Saint George and the Dragon*. Boston: Little, Brown Books for Young Readers, 1990.

MacDonald, George. *At the Back of the North Wind (Puffin Classics)*. 1871. Reissue ed. London: Puffin, 1994.

———. *Creation in Christ: Unspoken Sermons*. Abridged ed. Edited by Rolland Hein. Vancouver: Regent College, 2004.

46. Ibid., 339–75.

———. *The Golden Key and Other Stories*. Grand Rapids: Eerdmans, 1980.

———. *Phantastes*. 1858. Grand Rapids: Eerdmans, 1997.

———. *The Princess and the Goblin (Puffin Classics)*. 1872. Reissue ed. London: Puffin, 1996.

McDonald, Greville. *George MacDonald and His Wife*. 1924. Whitethorn, CA: Johannesen, 2005.

Tolkien, J. R. R. *The Lord of the Rings*. 50th Anniversary ed. New York: Mariner, 2012.

Wilde, Oscar. *The Selfish Giant*. New York: Simon & Schuster Children's, 1991.

Wordsworth, William. "Ode: Intimations of Immortality." In *The Norton Anthology of English Literature: The Major Authors*. 8th ed. Edited by Stephen Greenblatt, 1541. New York: Norton, 2006.

Zipes, Jack, ed. "Introduction to Sarah Fielding." In *The Norton Anthology of Children's Literature: The Traditions in English*, 189–90. New York: Norton, 2005.

11

Tolkien as Ethnographer:
The Role of Culture in J. R. R. Tolkien's
The Lord of the Rings

PAUL W. LEWIS

As A TEENAGER, I would go to my friend Craig Edwards' house. I remember seeing drawings of Aslan, and a poster advertising *The Hobbit*, which was some type of commercial venture in the Midwest. Craig's parents, Jim and Twila Edwards, would frequently talk with me and others in their home or our church about C. S. Lewis, J. R. R. Tolkien, Shakespeare, and many other literary figures. I remember visits to *The Tempest* in Minneapolis or the prestigious Folger Theatre in Washington DC with Jim and Craig (often with our church[1]). As I grew older, my passion for the Inklings continued, and as a foreign missionary in Asia for over nineteen years, I have developed a deeper appreciation for Tolkien. As I reread Tolkien's work, it became abundantly clear that he did not just write a story, he created a multifaceted world. I have also noticed a commonly described depth to his writings with themes including the heroic, moral values, and a love of nature.[2] Tolkien also wrote about peoples—Dwarves, Elves, Ents, Hobbits and Men—that had a depth and range which made them believable. Tolkien's description of Middle-Earth is unparalleled, with details and descriptions about geog-

---

1. With the Bible Quiz team as noted in Gary Liddle's essay in this volume.

2. There are many works on various themes in Tolkien, see for example the essays in de Koster, *Readings on J. R. R. Tolkien*, and notably the older Isaacs and Zimbardo, *Tolkien and His Critics,* and Lobdell, *Tolkien Compass*.

raphy (including the maps), climate, vegetation, population and economic systems with genuine feasibility.[3]

Tolkien's love of languages as a philologist is abundantly clear.[4] Whereas languages are fundamental to Tolkien and are inseparable from the study of culture[5], he also addresses cultures[6] (independent of language) in Middle-Earth. Tolkien embedded his narrative in a rich tapestry of mythology, history, and life. Notably, Tolkien writes like a good ethnographer. He demonstrates this in his description of cultures (like the prologue on "Concerning Hobbits" in *The Fellowship of the Ring* and descriptions of various groups in Appendix F of *The Return of the King*). Realistically, it is understood that Middle-Earth is a fictional world; however, Tolkien functionally uses what Clifford Geertz would call "thick description"[7] to unveil the cultures of Middle-Earth. In this essay, I suggest that it is not only his development of languages and mythology/history that provide a rich texture of believability, but also his description of culture. Tolkien walked a fine line of ethnographic clarity with narratival readability. Whereas too much cultural detail could side-track the story, not enough would make the peoples of Middle-Earth seem like two-dimensional subcategories of the same culture and thereby make their being as genuinely different races or peoples untenable. Therefore, the focus of this essay is Tolkien's use and description of culture. Although there are several cultures discussed in *The*

---

3. On geography, climate, vegetation and population see Fonstad, *Atlas of Middle-Earth*, esp. 179–88; on topography, geography, climate and vegetation, see also Habermann and Kuhn, "Sustainable Fictions," 263–73. Both Fonstad, and Habermann and Kuhn note that these elements have a bearing on the narrative and reflect Tolkien's moral sensitivities. On economics see Witt, "Tolkien and the Free Society." Habermann and Kuhn likewise note the accuracy of climate except in Sauron's area, demonstrating his intentional malevolence which was physically noticeable, 263–73, esp. 271.

4. On this see Fimi, *Tolkien, Race and Cultural History*, 63–115; Hostetter, "Languages invented by Tolkien," 332–44; Noel, *Languages*; Stanton, *Hobbits, Elves, and Wizards*, 147–58; among many others.

5. Noel, *Languages*, 58–59. From a cultural anthropological perspective, see Ferraro, *Cultural Anthropology*, 121–45, and Grunlan and. Mayers, *Cultural Anthropology*, 91–100.

6. Tolkien also discusses a lot about Race (Elves, Dwarves, Hobbits, etc.), however, for this essay, I will only discuss those things that are not tied to some created element of the races (e.g., Elves and immortality) unless it somehow relates to the cultural discussion. On Race, see Chism, "Race and Ethnicity," 555–56, and Fimi, *Tolkien, Race and Cultural History*, esp. on the charge of racism by Tolkien, 157–59.

7. Taken from Clifford Geertz's celebrated essay "Thick Description: Toward an Interpretative Theory of Culture," in *The Interpretation of Culture*; See also several essays in Alexander, Smith, and Norton, *Interpreting Clifford Geertz*:), especially Apter, "Clifford Geertz as a Cultural System," Clark, "Thick Description, Thin History," and Lichterman, "Thick Description as a Cosmopolitan Practice."

Lord of the Rings (*LOTR*)[8] such as the Orcs and Trolls, I will focus mainly on the Free Peoples of Middle-Earth—Dwarves, Elves, Ents, Hobbits, and Men[9]—to demonstrate not only Tolkien's ability to simply tell a story, but also the foundational cultures out of which the story flows. In part one I provide a discussion of Tolkien and culture; I examine his use of culture in line with Geertz's work. The various selected elements of culture emphasized from *LOTR* will demonstrate Geertz's "thick description" as part of Tolkien's cultural narration. In part two, I move specifically to Tolkien's usage of the *Fellowship of the Ring* as a descriptor and exemplar for overcoming cultural difference and distance.

Tolkien and Culture[10]

To be sure, as a philologist, Tolkien's usage and description of language and its diversity is both clear and enormous. Much has been much written on Tolkien's linguistic acumen. There is no doubt concerning his utilization of language to culture, such as seen in the different languages of the Dwarves,[11] the Elves with their dialects, Men's various dialects in the language of Rohan and the Wild Men of the woods, and the various unintelligible dialects of the Orcs; all of which demonstrate the diversity and interaction of language and culture.[12] The Westron or Common Speech functioned as a *lingua franca* of the Free Peoples[13] described in the tale which gave rise to the

---

8. Hereafter for this essay, I will use *H* for Tolkien, *The Hobbit*; *LOTR I* for Tolkien, *The Fellowship of the Ring*; *LOTR II* for Tolkien, *The Two Towers*; *LOTR III* for Tolkien, *The Return of the King*; *LOTR* for Tolkien, *The Lord of the Rings: One Volume*; and *S* for Tolkien, *The Simarillon*).

9. I will not deal with the intricacies (apart from cultural dynamics) of each of these Free Peoples in Tolkien that are readily found in other sources, e.g., Drout, *J. R. R. Tolkien Encyclopedia*, 134–35, 150–55, 163–64, 280–82, 414–17, respectively; Foster, *Complete Guide to Middle-Earth*, 131–32, 151–53, 159–61, 259–61, 330–31, respectively; and J. E. A. Tyler, *New Tolkien Companion*, 145–51, 176–80, 183–84, 290, 371–74, respectively; see also Stanton, *Hobbits, Elves, and Wizards* esp. 99–132.

10. There are many good works on cultural anthropology, while I have tended to follow the categorization of Grunlan and Mayers, *Cultural Anthropology*, I have also consistently consulted with Ferraro, *Cultural Anthropology*, and Hiebert, *Cultural Anthropology*.

11. It should be noted that in Tolkien's formulation, the language of Dwarves (who learned their language from the Vala, Aülë) (*S*, 43) developed differently from those of the Elves and Humans (and Ents who learned language from the Elves (*LOTR*, 468, 472).

12. See note 4.

13. Noel, *Languages* 10; *LOTR III*, 505, 513–20.

ongoing interaction and narrative progression. The Common Speech, however, functioned as a colonial language, like English, or a trade language, like Indonesian.

The various races including Elves, Dwarves, Hobbits, Men and Ents are on equal footing in that they were all under the One.[14] Each group had its own culture and possible subcultures as in the case of the Elves (West-elves and East-elves) (*LOTR* III, 505–6) and the Men (Rohan, Gondor, Dale, Corsairs, etc.). With the small pool of Dwarves and Ents, it is unclear if they had various internal sub-cultures, but they, with the Hobbits, certainly did have varying cultures in contrast to other Free Peoples.

Verbal and Non-verbal Communication

Tolkien also knew the importance of communication beyond words. What about non-verbal communication or silence? How might these modes contribute to communicative method?

In the *LOTR*, there are many examples of non-verbal communication, including gestures. The most common gesture is bowing, which is used throughout the work for introductions (especially to kings or those of higher social status), and for saying "farewell." For instance, the two Hobbits, Merry and Pippin, bowed before King Theoden when he arrived at Isengard and as he left (*LOTR*, 557–58), or when the four Hobbits greeted and offered farewells to Goldenberry (*LOTR*, 123, 135–36).

Other forms of non-verbal communication can be seen in the narration of when Celeborn was discussing the fall of Gandalf and when "at the last Gandalf fell from wisdom into folly, going needlessly into the net of Moria" (*LOTR*, 356) with Galadriel's grave response. Gimli is described as sitting "glowering and sad", yet when his eyes met Galadriel's eyes, he saw "love and understanding", and "Wonder came into his face, and then he smiled in answer" (*LOTR*, 356). Whereas Galadriel's response may be just the verbal expression or the tone, Gimli's deposition of "glowering" and his response of a smile, demonstrated non-verbal responses understood within the context.

A smile was a common gesture among the Free peoples[15] as an expression of kindness (e.g., Elrond brings Frodo to Bilbo, *LOTR* 230), pleasure

---

14. Note that although not created by the One, the Dwarves where put under the One by Aulë, see *S*, 43.

15. Note that smiles are noted for Dwarves (e.g. *LOTR*, 230, 269), Elves (e.g. *LOTR*, 82, 211), Entwives as mentioned by Treebeard, although no mention of the Ents doing so (e.g., *LOTR*, 483), Hobbits, (e.g., *LOTR*, 31, 232), Men (e.g., *LOTR*, 171, 233) and

(e.g., Bilbo at his own party, *LOTR*, 31), humor (e.g., the riders see Merry and Theoden talking, *LOTR*, 792), and good nature (e.g., Frodo after Bilbo's party, *LOTR*, 37). A smile may also have different meanings depending on the context; it could be rueful (*LOTR*, 34), grim with hardship (*LOTR*, 89, 166, 664), the wry smile of a hidden meaning or joke (*LOTR*, 157, 913), a "strange smile" of realization (*LOTR*, 680), a "pale smile" with sorrow (*LOTR*, 756), a smile with unpleasant thoughts (*LOTR*, 124) or the slow perception of someone's thoughts (*LOTR*, 163). In the *LOTR*, the smiles and laughter of the Free Peoples demonstrated true character including joy and kindness. In fact, Brian Rosebury notes that "humour . . . is almost exclusively associated with goodness."[16] Finally, still other smiles such as those of Saruman, the Mouth of Sauron, the ruffian in the Shire (*LOTR*, 1019, 890, 1005, respectively) communicate mockery.

Another similar non-verbal expression found extensively is weeping. For Tolkien, weeping functions as a common expression for grief or loss (Eowyn for Theoden [*LOTR*, 840] or the Fellowship for Gandalf after Moria, with "some standing, some on the ground" [*LOTR*, 331]). Weeping is also noted with a sad parting (Gimli leaving Galadriel [*LOTR*, 378], or Eowyn for Aragorn's leaving by the Paths of the Dead [*LOTR*, 795]), for great emotional distress (e.g. Sam's reaction to the Watcher in the Water taking Frodo [*LOTR*, 308] or to weep for joy [*LOTR*, 954]). In contrast, Gollum weeps frequently but only for himself (e.g. *LOTR*, 58, 618). Still others like the Riders of Rohan experience great hardship, but "little weeping or murmuring was heard" (*LOTR*, 802).

In the *LOTR*, Gandalf, Aragorn, Gimli, Faramir, Eowyn, Theoden, the Elves, the Hobbits, the Riders of Rohan, Tom Bombadil, and Goldberry smile and laugh; Gandalf, Eowyn, the Hobbits, Gimli, and others weep. The glaring exception to such expressions is Borormir, who did not smile except with "unfriendly eyes" when he tried to take the ring from Frodo (*LOTR*, 397) and only after Aragorn promised to go to Minas Tirith, he smiled and died (*LOTR*, 414). It is apparent that for Tolkien smiles, laughter, and weeping with and for others are not a sign of weakness, but of character and strength. In so doing, Tolkien shifts the understanding of strength and power.[17]

Wizards (e.g., *LOTR*, 63, 220). For the Elves it is frequently tied to being merry. The Elves and the Hobbits were more commonly smiling and laughing.

16. Rosebury, *Tolkien*, 43.

17. The importance of power in Tolkien's work is noted most extensively by Chance, *Lord of the Rings*; also see Chance, "Power in Tolkien's Works," 541–42, and Eaglestone, "Power in Tolkien's Works," 541–42, who notes that for Tolkien knowledge is power with Gandalf as an example contra Sauron in regards to sending Frodo to unmake the

While there are commonalities with all the Free Peoples, Tolkien also highlights distinctions in non-verbal communication, such as when Gimli, "bowed in dwarf-fashion" (*LOTR*, 356), and showed the culturally different version of bowing. Treebeard bows three times in his final meeting with Galadriel and Celeborn (*LOTR*, 981). Celeborn and Galadriel greeted the questers "after the manner of Elves" (*LOTR*, 354). Tolkien also highlighted some other culturally different gestures, such as Gondor's salute with "bowed head and hands upon the breast" (*LOTR*, 768) or at an introduction, Beregond "held out his hand and Pippin took it" (*LOTR*, 760), which is the one usage of this gesture in the work.

Touch is another important part of non-verbal communication. Tolkien has Faramir and Eowyn "clasping hands" (*LOTR*, 962) with a more romantic intent. Pippin and Bergil walked "hand in hand" (*LOTR*, 771) and Sam took his master's hand in his (e.g., *LOTR*, 624, 943), both instances of a demonstration of friendship. There are several times where kisses are given to friends (Aragorn kisses Boromir's brow as he was dying [*LOTR*, 414], Faramir embraced and kissed the foreheads of Sam and Frodo [*LOTR*, 695], or as an expression of fealty (Merry kissed Theoden's hand [*LOTR*, 777]). Kisses are also seen as a sign of compassion with resolve: Aragorn kissed Eowyn's hand but denied her request and kissed her brow when bringing her back from the brink of death (*LOTR*, 785). Foreheads and hands are kissed to express care and compassion, and general kisses show deeper emotion as when Frodo kissed Merry, Pippin, and Sam goodbye before embarking on his sea voyage (*LOTR*, 1030), or Faramir offers Eowyn a romantic kiss (*LOTR*, 1016).

For Tolkien, the role of silence in communications is important. It is common within most cultures for silence to convey as much as verbal communications. Silence may offer a sense of awe, respect, and reflection.

> Before they ate, Faramir and all his men turned and faced west in a moment of silence. Faramir signed to Frodo and Sam that they should do likewise. "So we always do," he said, as they sat down: "we look towards Númenor that was, and beyond to Elvenhome that is, and to that which is beyond Elvenhome and will ever be. Have you no such custom at meat?" "No," said Frodo, feeling strangely rustic and untutored. "But if we are guests, we bow to our host, and after we have eaten we rise and thank him." "That we do also," said Faramir. (*LOTR*, 676)

Silence can also be used to demonstrate a sense of contentment and peace among friends, "Then the companions fell silent, but a while they sat

---

one ring.

there in the high place, each busy with his own thoughts, while the Captains debated" (*LOTR*, 878), or as with Faramir and Eowyn together displaying times of speech and times of silence (*LOTR*, 961). Silence shows a depth of relationship; contentment that action and talking are not always necessary.

A common issue among cultures is the role of space and distance. The space given to each person ("space bubble") is not highlighted in *LOTR*, yet the related concept of seating arrangements at feasts or tables is clearly seen, such as the special dinner party for the 144 guests of Bilbo's (and Frodo's) birthday party (*LOTR*, 28), when Frodo sat at Elrond's table (*LOTR*, 227), by Faramir's seat in the middle of the inmost table (*LOTR*, 675), and when Frodo and Sam sat at the King's table after the defeat of Sauron (*LOTR*, 955). Seating arrangements connote social status and the importance placed on specific individuals. Feasting and food are also expressions not just of hospitality, but a developing trust, relational closeness, and honor.

Enculturation[18]

Another aspect of cultural communication is the process by which individuals acquire skills, values and attitudes that enable them to function in society. While this is one of the areas where there certainly appears to be some form of educational development, Tolkien implies as much but does not clearly develop this feature. As a whole, Tolkien created "oral rather than scribal forms that dominate the dissemination of cultural lore and traditions."[19] For one, the Elves and the Dwarves use writing and have their own scripts (Elrond is well-versed in multiple literary forms [*H*, 61]), yet it seems that the Hobbits could read and write (such as Bilbo, Frodo and Sam who learned from Bilbo [*LOTR*, 186]), although "by no means all ... were lettered" (*LOTR*, 10); it was not a key value. Yet for those who did write, they wrote many letters (*LOTR*, 10) or books, like Bilbo. Learning and wisdom were key values for the Elves. The literary dynamics of the Dwarves stems partially from the concept that their language was given by the Vala, Aulë, whereas the other languages of Elves and Men developed indigenously. The Hobbits of the Shire followed the language of the kingdom of Arnor and was part of the Westron or common speech. As such, the Men of Númenor were certainly men of learning, yet it is also surmised that other humans do not

---

18. By enculturation, I mean the way by which a person learns the skills, values, and knowledge of society.

19. Ball, "Cultural Values," part 1.

value reading and writing. It was noted that Middle-Earth had no printing; it was a "manuscript culture."[20]

As to how this learning took place (formal education) within the culture (and cultural clues), it seems that the more limited governmental Hobbits, the longevity oriented Elves, and the artisan oriented Dwarves would be more inclined to an apprenticeship/tutorial model of learning. Gondor was the one exception, as its governmental structure and population density seems better suited to a classroom approach. Albeit somewhat speculative as to the how of education, cultural values to be induced by education seem clear. Societal norms are an important object of the enculturation process using formal methods (structured learning), informal means (non-structured learning outside of the classroom/apprenticeship models) and non-formal style of education (learning in a loosely structured way). For the Hobbits, it seems that formal and informal patterns fit the culture and educational models; the Men of Gondor could conceivably function with all three; and the Elves highlight formal and non-formal styles.

A prominent form of enculturation and acculturation (the adaption to a new culture) for Tolkien is through song and poetry. As Gergely Nagy notes, "stylistic or textual details suggesting the underlying orality are therefore an integral part of Tolkien's presentation of culture."[21] Poems and songs are for Tolkien "the cultural capital and cultural identity of societies."[22] He demonstrates that songs reflect the respective cultures in style and content; there are noted Dwarven (e.g., *LOTR*, 106), Elvish (e.g., *LOTR*, 238), Entish (see *LOTR*, 477) songs, and songs of Rohan, Gondor, etc. besides the numerous Hobbit songs portrayed; each reflecting the respective cultural values and history.[23] Songs can be lighthearted, heroic sagas or laments.[24] These songs guide, teach, or enculturate in a memorable way.[25] Songs are important to remember history and inspire action. Many of the Elvish songs are sagas detailing the past, and many sagas are likewise noted in Rohan (although spanning a shorter period of time). Rohan and the Ents also have songs for going into battle (*LOTR*, 838, 565, respectively). Elves and Men sang songs of lament for loss or grief. The Hobbits had bed-songs, supper-songs, and walking songs (e.g., *LOTR*, 77). As Pippin notes, the Shire has no

20. Ibid., part 2.
21. Nagy, "Orality," 487.
22. Ball, "Cultural Values," part 2.
23. See Flieger, "Poems by Tolkien: *The Hobbit*," 520–22, and Flieger, "Poems by Tolkien: *The Lord of the Rings*," 522–32.
24. Ball, "Cultural Values," part 1 and 2.
25. See Flieger, "Memory," 413.

songs for "Great Halls or evil times" (*LOTR*, 806), but sing of food, drink and laughter (*LOTR*, 806), or Sam's informative poem about the "Oliphant" (*LOTR*, 646). Similarly, Gimli is noted to have sung a Dwarven celebration song (*LOTR*, 503). All of these examples demonstrate a universal usage of songs and poetry yet with cultural distinctiveness.

The issues of acculturation are present throughout the *LOTR* as the Hobbits adjust to their new friends, experiences and lands, such as Rohan and Gondor. Assimilation (the full adaption to a new culture) is discovered in the *LOTR*. The most prominent development of this is Aragorn's transformation from a Dúnedain Ranger to the King of Gondor. With this change came responsibilities, life-style shifts, as well as rural vs. urban shifts.

One facet of enculturation is the full life-cycle stages. The stages are: 1. Birth, 2. Puberty 3. Marriage, and 4. Death. The rite of passage or coming of age for the Hobbits is specifically stated to be at age thirty-three, which would include an inheritance (*LOTR*, 21–22, 30).[26] The coming of age for the Elves, Dwarves and Men are not noted, but certainly would be different. The role of marriage is noted for the Hobbits (e.g., Sam and Rose), Elves and Men (e.g., Arwen and Aragorn). And upon a good death, due honor is highlighted. In Rohan, the kings were buried in mounds. For Rohan's honoring of Theoden's death, there were three days of preparation; he was laid in a "house of stone" with his arms and goods, and a mound was raised over him (with grass and flowers). Riders of the royal house rode around the mound singing a song about Theoden, and Merry (and the women) wept. After the funeral there was a feast in the Great Hall to "put away sorrow" (*LOTR*, 976), including a drink to the memory of the kings (named in succession by a minstrel and lore-master), from the first king of Rohan, Eorl the Young to the most recent, Theoden (when Eomer drained the cup), and all the cups were refilled to drink to the new king, Eomer (*LOTR*, 976). As a contrast, the kings of Gondor were placed in a large tomb. For Gondor's royalty's final resting place, there was *Fen Hollen* with its mansions of the dead kings and stewards. A distance from the entry gate on Silent Street, *Rath Dínan*, there were noted empty domed halls for the dead kings and stewards, where the bodies in a wide vaulted chamber (*LOTR*, 826) were to be placed upon a table (like Aragorn at his death, *LOTR*, 1062). The Hobbits that were killed in the Battle of Bywater were put together in a common grave with a great stone and a garden and their names were specifically remembered by Shire-historians (*LOTR*, 1016). Most of the noted cases in the *LOTR* were buried (at least in a mausoleum), the clear exception being

26. Pippin notes that he himself is four years shy of "coming of age," *LOTR*, 763; thirty-three could be seen as the "coming of age" since Hobbits are long-lived, Stanton, "Hobbits," 281.

Denethor, which further shows his despair as he sets up a pyre for himself and Faramir (*LOTR III*, 153–62).

Tolkien also highlights the commonality of grief. Examples may be observed: Gimli's grief covering his face at the tomb of Balin (*LOTR*, 320), the weeping of the fellowship after the death of Gandalf (*LOTR*, 331–32), and the lament for Gandalf by the Elves at Lothlórien (*LOTR*, 359). Yet the cultural differences of the expression of grief can also be seen.

Although not cultural *per se*, Tolkien does note the created difference between Men and Elves concerning death. Upon death, Men went to another place in the afterlife for mortals, whereas Elves as immortals died to be reincarnated in the world until the end of time[27]; this makes Elrond's and Arwen's parting even more bitter, when Arwen chose a mortal life.

Kinship and Family

The diversity of kinship patterns is clear with the Hobbits and Elves. For Hobbits, genealogies were very important (e.g., *LOTR*, 2, 7) and the adoption of an heir was accepted (e.g., Frodo to Bilbo). However, while kinship and filial loyalty were important, Faramir's interaction with Denethor in regards to Frodo and Gandalf, showed his opposition to a strict filial piety (*LOTR III*, 101–6). It likewise seems that among the Hobbits, certain friendships (e.g., Merry and Pippin to Frodo) were closer than relatives (e.g., Sachsville-Bagginses to Bilbo and Frodo). While the Hobbits apparently had concrete examples of extended families living together (e.g., Tooks, Brandybucks), most lived in a nuclear family situation (e.g., Cottons).

Whereas for the kings (and stewards) of Gondor, the line was patrilineal and patrilocal (e.g., Denethor's wife moved to Minas Tiras), it is unclear about the situation for others. However, it was noted that for Númenor, the line of the kings could be a king or queen depending on the gender of the first-born (*LOTR*, 1036). For the Elves, at first glance, it appears to be patrilineal; however, Galadriel is certainly regarded equal if not higher in wisdom than Celeborn. It seems that for the Elves, wisdom and insight (and power) are more of a determining factor than gender (see below).

---

27. Devaux, "Elves: Reincarnation," 154–55, and Eden, "Elves," 150–52.

Status and Role of Gender

Status and class distinction is significant in the *LOTR*. Race is a notable element in Tolkien, for all are under the One (or *Ilúvatar*) and thus valued. Vertical status is a key concept insomuch as there is a clear class distinction (e.g., Bilbo/Frodo in contrast to Samwise/Old Gaffer).[28] Among the Elves, status is distinguished by wisdom and longevity, so Galadriel's, Elrond's, and Glorifindel's status is derivative from their living from the First Age. Other criteria are noted for the Dwarves, such as a direct lineage to Durin, the Father of the Dwarves. While status is undoubtedly recognizable, the reason for the differences of the attainment of status varies according to the respective culture.

The role of the gender and the place of women represent critical values for Tolkien. Arwen, Eowyn, and Galadriel demonstrate the importance of women, but receive various values and are diversely recognized within their respective cultures.[29] It has been noted that in spite of the size of the *LOTR*, it is "remarkable for their lack of female characters."[30] Further, Tolkien is seen as reflecting the attitude of his Inkling colleagues.[31] Some scholars argue that Tolkien demeans the role of women, at the very least by neglect,[32] while others view the complementary aspect of masculinity and femininity in a positive light.[33] The stereotypical masculine power in the *LOTR* is Boromir, but he is weak, and a moral and spiritual failure,[34] while there are successful women.[35] Galadriel, a wise and powerful elder, is an important voice on the white council. Her abilities, and even her correction of

---

28. Curry, *Defending Middle-Earth*, 40–41.

29. Ruane and James, "International Relations," 385–92.

30. Frederick and McBride, *Women Among the Inklings*, 108; cf. Aline Ripley, "Feminist Readings of Tolkien," 202–3.

31. Frederick and MacBride, *Women Among the Inklings*, 108, 114, and noted by Enright, "Tolkien's Females," 94. Tolkien reflected a traditional Victorian division of labor between genders, Stanton, 131. Leibiger notes his attitude as being influenced by his Roman Catholic, Victorian and middle-class background, "Women in Tolkien's Works," 710.

32. Frederick and MacBride, *Women Among the Inklings*, 109–14, and Stimpson, *J. R. R. Tolkien*, 18–20; cf. Leibiger, "Women in Tolkien's Works," 711.

33. Smol, "Gender in Tolkien's Works," 233–34.

34. Enright, "Tolkien's Females," 93. Although he fails in one sense, Matthew Dickerson argues that ultimately Boromir is "saved", noting the comments by Aragorn and Gandalf to that affect, *Hobbit Journey*, 151–55.

35. Enright, "Tolkien's Females," 93.

Celeborn concerning the deeds of Gandalf, demonstrate her equality if not superiority.[36] As Nancy Enright notes, female characters in the *LOTR*

> are crucial to the meaning of the tale . . . Arwen, Galadriel, and Eowyn . . . all . . . [opt] for the Christ-like power of love, healing and gentleness. . . . The kind of power associated with masculine strength and physical prowess is subverted through female characters who lay down their own power in Christ-like renunciation . . . that overturns the strongest evils in the world.[37]

Eowyn, though she is denied a place (like other women) among the riders of Rohan, was nevertheless taught how to use weapons for defense and to fight (at Helms Deep only the males were armed). Gandalf highlights the pain of Eowyn's plight living in a male-dominated society (*LOTR*, 867).[38] Arwen plays a minor role in the action itself, but is critical to the reestablishment of Gondor's royal line with elven lineage. Though women have a limited role in the narrative, I would argue that this should not be mistaken for their unimportance. Indeed the pivotal influence of Galadriel, Eowyn and Arwen all mitigate against that assumption.

General Cultural Distinctions—Politics and Society

It is true that Tolkien had embedded racial distinctions from their creation (i.e., the Elves' immortality vs. humanity's mortality) and clear cultural distinctions between groups even within a race (e.g., Gondor, Rohan and Wild Men). These distinctions operate even to the level of societal structures and values.

The Hobbits of the Shire are a pre-industrial agrarian society. In fact, while agrarian, there are some industries highlighted as farm-related—smithies and mills.[39] The primary crops mentioned for the Hobbits included pipeweed, grapes (for wine), barley (used for beer), and mushrooms. Food and eating were about more than nutrition[40] as the importance of proper preparation and the cooking process were emphasized.[41] The main social

---

36. Ibid; *LOTR*, 356.
37. Enright, "Tolkien's Females," 106.
38. Highlighted by Enright, "Tolkien's Females," 104.
39 Curry, *Defending Middle-Earth*, 28; Habermann and Kuhn, "Sustainable Fictions," 265, quoting from Curry, *Defending Middle-Earth*, 28, and Michael Stanton, "Hobbits," 281.
40. Hobbits eat six meals a day (*LOTR*, 2), while the Men of Gondor eat three (*LOTR*, 761).
41. Stanton, "Hobbits," 282. Hobbits learn to cook "before their letters (which many

unit for Hobbits was the extended family and played a fundamental role in their social life.[42] Schools were only tangentially alluded to in the literary ability of the Hobbits.[43] The Hobbits functioned with a minimal form of government—an anarchy with cooperation.[44] While fundamentally peaceful, and basically good, they are woefully ignorant of the outside world, and seem to revel in their rejection of the outside world. They are generally seen as "incorrigibly parochial."[45] The key cultural vice of the Hobbits was the isolation and championed ignorance that allowed Saruman and his henchmen's take-over of the Shire.

The Dwarves were tied to the mountains.[46] They perpetuated a rugged and secretive demeanor, as seen in the secret dynamic of their private language (*LOTR III*, Appendix F, 512–13).[47] They were lovers of gems and stones and were great miners and craftsmen (including for armor and weapons), and traders of wares. They valued industry and hard work. They also had the ability to "make a fire almost anywhere" (*H*, 44; see also *LOTR*, 292). Correspondingly, they tended to be stubborn and "fast in friendship and in enmity" (*S*, 44). The key cultural vice for the Dwarves was clearly greed.[48] This can be seen in the story of Thorin in *The Hobbit* with its implications for Galadriel's statement to Gimli, that gold will have no hold on him (*LOTR*, 376).

Elves were closely tied to nature for they were at home in the woods[49] or by the sea.[50] Elves were highly skilled, insomuch that their feats seemed like magic to the other races (e.g. their ability to heal, Sam's rope, and *lembas*).[51] The key vice or temptation for the Elves was to be caught up in the past,[52]

---

never reach)." *LOTR*, 653.

42. Stanton, "Hobbits," 282, not just the genealogies.

43. Ibid; although it can be argued that it does not necessary imply formal education, it could be in an apprenticeship model, like Sam learned from Bilbo (*LOTR*, 186).

44. Curry, *Defending Middle-Earth*, 28, Ball, "Cultural Values," part 2, and Ruane and James, "International Relations", 383.

45. Rosebury, *Tolkien*, 38; see also Colebatch, "Politics," 537.

46. Curry, *Defending Middle-Earth*, 28, Habermann and Kuhn, "Sustainable Fictions," 265, and Rosebury, *Tolkien*, 39.

47. Tolkien himself in his letters compares this secretive aspect to the Jews. Tolkien, *Letters*, 229.

48. Evans, "Dwarves," 134–35.

49. Curry, 28, Habermann and Kuhn, "Sustainable Fictions," 265.

50. Rosebury, *Tolkien*, 39.

51. Nokes, "Health and Medicine," 266, and Worthen, "Technology in Middle-Earth," 637–38.

52. Colebatch, "Politics," 537.

This seems to be a key danger throughout the *LOTR*. Where the Elves were both nostalgic and looking across the sea, they had "shown dismaying kinds of pride and defiance at various other points in their history."[53]

It is in the discussion and description of humanity that the true cultural diversity within a race is noted, although it is implied for all the races.[54] Faramir relates a taxonomy of Men as seen through his (a man of Gondor's) eyes. There are the "High" Men (Númenóreans and Edain and their descendants), the "Middle" Men (Rohan, Men of Dale), and the Wild Men (apparently all those who did not ally with the Eldar). However, according to Sandra Straubhaar, this taxonomy may not include all the tribes and peoples.[55] While humanity as a whole can be described as arrogant and proud, they can also be seen as heroic even while being wrong.[56] Pride may be a primary vice.[57] Beyond this distinction, there are clear cultural distinctions between Gondor and Rohan as noted by Tom Shippey.[58] Rohan typifies an oral culture and ritual poetry, "wise but unlearned, writing no books, but singing many songs."[59] The different procedures that Merry and Pippin followed to offer their service to Théoden and Denethor, the descriptions of the respective great halls and, the ways to bury the dead kings further reveal the difference. Faramir portrays Gondor as "a more reflective society, and one with a longer history, than the Riddermark."[60] Another culture of men, the Haradrim, who allied with Sauron, clearly had their own respective culture, which included finely made ornaments and their war elephants, *mumakil*,[61] so while they fight on Sauron's side, their humanity and, through death, their frailty are clear as humans.

Tolkien's Functional Definition of Culture

For Tolkien some things are universal for all of humanity such as isolation, division among cultural (racial) lines, distrust, subversion, dehumanization, fear, power, and control. Tolkien makes distinctions between a culture, familial eccentricities, and personal distinctiveness. Further, he views culture

- 53. Stanton, *Hobbits, Elves, and Wizards*, 101.
- 54. Chism, "Race and Ethnicity," 555–56.
- 55. Straubhaar, "Men, Middle-Earth," 416–17.
- 56. Ibid., 417.
- 57. Ibid., and Evans, "Pride," 543–44.
- 58. Shippey, *Tolkien*, 98–102.
- 59. *LOTR*, 430, noted by Ball "Cultural Values," part 2, and Shippey, "*Tolkien*, 96–97
- 60. Shippey, *Tolkien*, 102; see also Rosebury, *Tolkien*, 39.
- 61. Straubhaar, "Men, Middle-Earth," 416–17.

as the combination of material objects, behaviors and values/attitudes.[62] The type of houses, the lighthearted "banter," and the isolation (as the Shire), and family-orientation are all parts of the Hobbits' culture. For the Free Peoples (whom he discusses at length), and in particular the Hobbits, Tolkien uses two main tactics. First, he uses description as in the prologue on the Hobbits or appendices. Second, he works out the respective cultures in narrative and dialogue. Geertz's discussion of "thick description" is important here; his ethnographic description has four characteristics: 1. "[I]t is interpretative"; 2. It is in the "flow of social discourse"; 3. It moves the discourse description into "perusable terms"; and 4. It is "microscopic".[63] As such, Tolkien uses "thick description" to portray the Hobbits and the other cultures.[64]

Sauron's work and values function in the *LOTR* to help define the concept of culture in opposing Tolkien's values. Sauron's values include control, dehumanization, the exacerbation of division and strife, and the fostering of fear. An example of dehumanization comes from the Mouth of Sauron, who has a loss of identity and is isolated from camaraderie. Whereas the Free Peoples, like Sauron, have culture, Tolkien's sense of morality points to gradations and degrading culture, and Sauron demonstrates homogeneity, while the Free Peoples exude diversity.[65]

One point that needs to be highlighted about Tolkien's usage of culture is that he makes distinctions between cultural norms (e.g., Hobbits do not like to go on adventures), sub-cultural/familial practices (e.g., Brandybucks swimming and boating while other Hobbits do not) and individual practices (e.g., Frodo and Bilbo studying some Elvish). A noted theme in Tolkien includes the groups or individuals that were odd or "queer," because they were different.[66] This likewise shows the real depth of Tolkien's comprehension of culture, and that not all differences are necessarily cultural or racial.

The Fellowship of the Ring as Transcultural Remedy

I would like to argue, that as much as Tolkien notes that there are cultural (as well as personal and familial) elements of the characters, and the

---

62. Ferraro, *Cultural Anthropology*, 27–29.

63. Geertz, "Thick Description," 20–21.

64. See the sources in footnote 7; also see Starkloff, "Inculturation and Cultural Systems," 66–81.

65. Rosebury, *Tolkien*, 39–40.

66. E.g., those from Buckland, *LOTR*, 22–24, 69, and from Hobbiton from Farmer Maggot, *LOTR*, 94, as well as outlanders, *LOTR*, 45. This point is highlighted by Jane Chance in *Lord of the Rings*, 26–37.

divisiveness and distance that can be noted by these, he demonstrates a proposed remedy for these divisions by the Fellowship. The camaraderie of the Fellowship of the Ring in *The Return of the King* demonstrates the overcoming of traditional distance, especially by the Aragorn and Arwen interracial marriage[67] and the friendship that developed between Gimli and Legolas, a friendship that flew in the face of traditional enmity and distrust between the Elves and Dwarves.[68]

Tolkien does not state exactly those things that created the bond among the Fellowship, but his narrative implies several ways by which this Fellowship overcame traditional cultural distance. First, in a general sense, they simply spent time together. The time from the departure from Elrond's house on December 25, 3018 TA until the fight when Boromir dies on March 25, 3019 is a three solid months.[69] The time and space shared together, in the mundaneness of day-to-day life helped form deep relationships. Second, shared goals galvanized the expedition. The journey to destroy the Ring for the purpose of the defeat of evil was tantamount. Their respective and collective homes would be destroyed either now or in the future unless the Ring would be unmade. Third, due to this goal and their journey into the wild, they endured hardships together. As they walked in perilous lands or experienced the opposition on Caradhras, the skirmish with the Watcher in the Water, and the challenges in the Mines of Moria, their bonds solidified. The loss of Gandalf, where they all wept together, is a poignant demonstration of the developing commonality and closeness. Fourth, the role of eating together proved invaluable. Food and feasts built relational hospitality.[70] Fifth, the members of the Fellowship would on occasion be able to see life through the eyes of others. Aragorn's travels (in Rohan many years earlier, or growing up in Rivendell) helped him develop fresh perspectives. However, the clear presentation of this in the *LOTR* is when the Fellowship is brought into Lothlorien. Initially, the Elves were allowed to bring in the Fellowship, but with Gimli blindfolded. Gimli protested that he would enter in this way if Legolas would likewise be blindfolded. Legolas protests, but Aragorn steps in and states that all will be blindfolded. Later on, an order provides for all blindfolds to be removed. This event becomes a transformative event for Legolas and Gimli. From this point on, Legolas guides and accompanies Gimli around Lothlorien, and they become close friends. Whereas the whole group shares the meeting with Galadriel, the

---

67. Curry, *Defending Middle-Earth*, 44.
68. See Ruane and James, "International Relations," 383.
69. Duriez, *Tolkien and the Lord of the Rings*, 38–39.
70. See Honegger, "Food," 214.

interchange between Legolas and Gimli (and the blindfold situation) provides opportunity for Legolas to see through Gimli's eyes. Understanding and openness ensue. These relationships develop so strongly that by the end of the narrative they are comfortable together and seek out each other's company including in silence!

Conclusion

Tolkien functioned with a clear understanding of culture. While he does make personal and familial distinctions, cultures are discernible. Whereas the linguistic aspects of these divisions are often noted, I have argued that Tolkien cleverly and insistently provided a narrative with cultural distinctions in gestures, enculturation methods, status and gender, and political and societal nuances. Tolkien creates a "thick description" of these cultures; "Understanding a people's culture exposes their normalness without reducing their particularity."[71] The peoples of Middle-Earth are multi-textured. Some are described in more detail than others, notably the Hobbits, whereas the telling of the Ents' story received less detail. However, while there is little in detail about the Ents, they are no less valuable for ethnographic understanding. In so doing Tolkien employs an implied definition of culture. Though the "Free Peoples" demonstrate universal commonalities, they have unique behaviors, attitudes, values and tendencies toward a specific temptation or vice, respectively. Tolkien's *LOTR* also reveals cultural differences, historical issues between cultures, and moral decisions made based upon control, strife, and other ethical influences. He narrates not only a cultural awareness of differences, but also provides the necessary means to overcome this distance through friendship and love. For Tolkien, such an overcoming ability is made possible through time and life together in ordinary everyday life. As people eat together, share goals, endure hardships and loss, they grow not only in self-awareness, but also in relation to the perspectives of others. Tolkien's genius, indeed what makes his work so treasured, is not only the multifaceted depth of his world and story, but his mastery of the depth of the human experience. He not only highlights the reality of cultural differences, but also provides a solution to overcoming cultural distance.

---

71. Geertz, "Thick Description," 14.

BIBLIOGRAPHY

Alexander, Jeffrey C., Philip Smith, and Matthew Norton, eds. *Interpreting Clifford Geertz: Cultural Investigation in the Social Science*. New York: Palgrave Macmillan, 2011.

Apter, David E. "Clifford Geertz as a Cultural System." In *Interpreting Clifford Geertz: Cultural Investigation in the Social Science*, edited by Jeffrey C. Alexander, Philip Smith, and Matthew Norton, 181–96. New York: Palgrave Macmillan, 2011.

Ball, Martin. "Cultural Values and Cultural Death in *The Lord of the Rings*." *Australian Humanities Review* 28 (Jan–Mar 2003), part 1 and 2. Online: http://australianhumanitiesreview.org/archive/Issue-Jan-2003/ball.html.

Chance, Jane. *The Lord of the Rings: The Mythology of Power*. Lexington: The University Press of Kentucky, 2001.

———. "Power in Tolkien's Works." In *J. R. R. Tolkien Encyclopedia*, edited by Michael D. C. Drout, 541–42. New York: Routledge, 2007.

Chism, Christine. "Race and Ethnicity in Tolkien's Works." In *J. R. R. Tolkien Encyclopedia*, edited by Michael D. C. Drout, 555–56. New York: Routledge, 2007.

Clark, Stuart. "Thick Description, Thin History: Did Historians Always Understand Clifford Geertz?" In *Interpreting Clifford Geertz: Cultural Investigation in the Social Science*, edited by Jeffrey C. Alexander, Philip Smith, and Matthew Norton, 105–19. New York: Palgrave Macmillan, 2011.

Colebatch, Hal G. P. "Politics." In *J. R. R. Tolkien Encyclopedia*, edited by Michael D. C. Drout, 536–38. New York: Routledge, 2007.

Curry, Patrick. *Defending Middle-Earth: Tolkien, Myth and Modernity*. New York: St. Martin's, 1997.

de Koster, Katie, ed. *Readings on J. R. R. Tolkien*. Literary Companion Series. San Diego, CA: Greenhaven, 2000.

Devaux, Michël. "Elves: Reincarnation." In *J. R. R. Tolkien Encyclopedia*, edited by Michael D. C. Drout, 154–55. New York: Routledge, 2007.

Dickerson, Matthew. *A Hobbit Journey*. Grand Rapids: Brazos, 2012.

Drout, Michael D. C., ed. *J. R. R. Tolkien Encyclopedia*. New York: Routledge, 2007.

Duriez, Colin. *Tolkien and the Lord of the Rings: A Guide to Middle-Earth*. London: Hidden Spring, 2001.

Eaglestone, Robert. "Power in Tolkien's Works." In *J. R. R. Tolkien Encyclopedia*, edited by Michael D. C. Drout, 541–42. New York: Routledge, 2007.

Eden, Bradford Lee. "Elves." In *J. R. R. Tolkien Encyclopedia*, edited by Michael D. C. Drout, 150–52. New York: Routledge, 2007.

Enright, Nancy. "Tolkien's Females and the Defining of Power." *Renascence* 59 (2007) 93–108.

Evans, Jonathan. "Dwarves." In *J. R. R. Tolkien Encyclopedia*, edited by Michael D. C. Drout, 134–35. New York: Routledge, 2007.

———. "Pride." In *J. R. R. Tolkien Encyclopedia*, edited by Michael D. C. Drout, 543–44. New York: Routledge, 2007.

Ferraro, Gary. *Cultural Anthropology: An Applied Perspective*, 6th ed. Belmont, CA: Thomson Wadsworth, 2006.

Fimi, Dimitra. *Tolkien, Race and Cultural History: From Fairies to Hobbits*. London: Palgrave MacMillan, 2009.

Flieger, Verlyn. "Memory." In *J. R. R. Tolkien Encyclopedia*, edited by Michael D. C. Drout, 413–14. New York: Routledge, 2007.
———. "Poems by Tolkien: *The Hobbit*." In *J. R. R. Tolkien Encyclopedia*, edited by Michael D. C. Drout, 520–22. New York: Routledge, 2007.
———. "Poems by Tolkien: *The Lord of the Rings*." In *J. R. R. Tolkien Encyclopedia*, edited by Michael D. C. Drout, 522–32. New York: Routledge, 2007.
Fonstad, Karen Wynn. *The Atlas of Middle-Earth*. Boston: Houghton Mifflin, 1981.
Foster, Robert. *The Complete Guide to Middle-Earth*. New York: Ballantine, 1978.
Frederick, Candice, and Sam McBride. *Women Among the Inklings: Gender, C. S. Lewis, J. R. R. Tolkien, and Charles Williams*, Contributions in Women's Studies, Number 191. Westport, CN: Greenwood, 2001.
Geertz, Clifford. "Thick Description: Toward an Interpretative Theory of Culture." In *The Interpretation of Culture: Selected Essays by Clifford Geertz*, 3–30. New York: Basic, 1973.
Grunlan, Stephen A. and Marvin K. Mayers, *Cultural Anthropology: A Christian Perspective*. Grand Rapids: Zondervan Academie, 1979.
Habermann, Ina, and Nikolaus Kuhn. "Sustainable Fictions—Geographical, Literary and Cultural Intersections in J. R. R. Tolkien's *The Lord of the Rings*." *The Cartographic Journal* 48 (2011) 263–73.
Hiebert, Paul. *Cultural Anthropology*. Grand Rapids: Baker, 1983.
Honegger, Thomas. "Food." In *J. R. R. Tolkien Encyclopedia*, edited by Michael D. C. Drout, 214. New York: Routledge, 2007.
Hostetter, Carl F. "Languages Invented by Tolkien." In *J. R. R. Tolkien Encyclopedia*, edited by Michael D. C. Drout, 332–44. New York: Routledge, 2007.
Isaacs, Neil D., and Rose A. Zimbardo, eds. *Tolkien and His Critics*. Notre Dame, IN: University of Notre Dame Press, 1968.
Leibiger, Carol A. "Women in Tolkien's Works." In *J. R. R. Tolkien Encyclopedia*, edited by Michael D. C. Drout, 710–12. New York: Routledge, 2007.
Lichterman, Paul. "Thick Description as a Cosmopolitan Practice: A Pragmatic Reading." In *Interpreting Clifford Geertz: Cultural Investigation in the Social Science*, edited by Jeffrey C. Alexander, Philip Smith, and Matthew Norton, 77–91. New York: Palgrave Macmillan, 2011.
Lobdell, Jared, ed., *A Tolkien Compass*. LaSalle, IL: Open Court, 1975.
Nagy, Gergely. "Orality." In *J. R. R. Tolkien Encyclopedia*, edited by Michael D. C. Drout, 486–67. New York: Routledge, 2007.
Noel, Ruth S. *The Languages of Tolkien's Middle-Earth*. Boston: Houghton Mifflin, 1980.
Nokes, Richard Scott. "Health and Medicine." In *J. R. R. Tolkien Encyclopedia*, edited by Michael D. C. Drout, 266. New York: Routledge, 2007.
Rosebury, Brian. *Tolkien: A Critical Assessment*. London: St. Martin's, 1992.
Ruane, Abigail E. and Patrick James. "The International Relations of Middle-Earth: Learning from *The Lord of the Rings*." *International Studies Perspectives* 9 (2008) 385–92.
Shippey, Tom. *J. R. R. Tolkien: Author of the Century*. Boston: Houghton Mifflin, 2000.
Smol, Anna. "Gender in Tolkien's Works." In *J. R. R. Tolkien Encyclopedia*, edited by Michael D.C. Drout, 233–35. New York: Routledge, 2007.
Stanton, Michael N. "Hobbits." In *J. R. R. Tolkien Encyclopedia*, edited by Michael D.C. Drout, 280–82. New York: Routledge, 2007.
———. *Hobbits, Elves, and Wizards*. New York: Palgrave, 2001.

Starkloff, SJ. Carl F. "Inculturation and Cultural Systems (Part 1)." *Theological Studies* 55 (1994) 66–81.

Stimpson, Catharine. *J. R. R. Tolkien*. Columbia Essays on Modern Writers, No. 41. New York: Columbia University Press, 1969.

Straubhaar, Sandra Ballif. "Men, Middle-Earth." In *J. R. R. Tolkien Encyclopedia*, edited by Michael D. C. Drout, 414–17. New York: Routledge, 2007.

Tolkien, J. R. R. *The Fellowship of the Ring*. New York: Ballantine, 1965.

———. *The Hobbit*. Rev. ed. New York: Ballantine, 1966.

———. *The Letters of J. R. R. Tolkien*, selected and edited by Humphrey Carter. Boston: Houghton Mifflin, 1981.

———. *The Lord of the Rings: One Volume*, 2004 ed. Boston: Houghton Mifflin Harcourt. Kindle Edition, 2004.

———. *The Return of the King*. New York: Ballantine, 1965.

———. *The Simarillon*, edited by Christopher Tolkien. Boston: Houghton Mifflin, 1977.

———. *The Two Towers*. New York: Ballantine, 1965.

Tyler, J. E. A. *The New Tolkien Companion*. 2nd ed. New York: Avon, 1979.

Witt, Jonathan. "Tolkien and the Free Society." Lecture presented at the Acton Institute, Grand Rapids, MI, June 21, 2013.

Worthen, Shana. "Technology in Middle-Earth." In *J. R. R. Tolkien Encyclopedia*, edited by Michael D. C. Drout, 637–38. New York: Routledge, 2007.

THE LIBERAL ARTS IN PRACTICE

12

Study Abroad: A Transformative and Integrative Journey

ROBERT TURNBULL

CAN STUDY ABROAD BE a viable, indeed crucial, part of a liberal arts education in a faith-based institution? Many Christian universities include in their mission statement the ideal of forming globally aware students. Evangel University, in numerous documents, delineates its desire to provide an integrative and cross-cultural experience for all its students.[1] This worthy goal bumps rapidly into the pragmatism of coping with economic realities and of requiring an immediate return on investment; the question quickly becomes one of cost versus practical value. In the current university context of escalating tuition, one might ask if we still have the nineteenth-century luxury of sending our sons and daughters on a grand tour in order to round out their early life experience. The immediate response is often negative if we limit ourselves to the rationale of that century. The current world is vastly different and imposes a different imperative on today's graduate. Global interdependence, which influences our modern lives, shouts to us that other cultures and peoples have a direct impact on the quality of our lives. If we are to have a respected place at the international table, maintain our own society, and govern our own lives, then our children will have to participate with knowledge, skill, and personal conviction in that global interdependence.

---

1. See Evangel University website.

The Idea of the Journey

A key component in Evangel University's ethos requires all students to undergo a cross-cultural experience as an inherent part of their academic career. The decision has as its theological and philosophical basis the broader concept of the integration of faith, learning, and living.[2] Our lives are not compartmentalized; we believe that our faith informs all aspects of our existence. Christ is our center, and our learning and our living are anchored in the organizing truth of his lordship. That being said, if we determine that Christian higher education for our students constitutes a high priority and one component thereof should be a cross-cultural experience, then we must consider the personal spiritual dimensions as a compelling argument for the experience and not limit our consideration solely to its practical elements.

The study abroad experience is practical in the sense that it can improve foreign language skills, enlarge one's knowledge of other peoples, impart an understanding of the broader world to the culturally naïve, and teach stratagems for coping with unfamiliar circumstances. These results are marketable in the professional world and are arguably sufficient to justify return-on-investment thinking.[3] However, if we are to educate our students in a more holistic manner, consideration must be afforded to those elements which integrate the different aspects of the whole person and serve as catalysts for transformation. Such transformation matures a student's heart and worldview so that the student experiences convergence of faith, learning, and living beyond the secondary notion of immediate gain. In other words, the study abroad experience has the potential to affect the individual at the most profound levels through a variety of elements inherent in the journey.

In this essay, I discuss how the precariousness of liminality through the intercultural experience can foster positive results and how the labor-intensive effort of seeing beyond one's own cultural logic is essential. I consider the anxiety of being a foreigner as well as how God uses restlessness and individual choice to love us. Likewise, I address the subversive nature of study abroad and how it can become an act of worship, and show the value of a structured context and how personal assessment requires one's ongoing attention. Finally, I conclude with an understanding of the inclusive notion

---

2. See Holmes, *Idea of a Christian College*, 45–60.

3. The volume of literature describing the practical value of study abroad is extensive and continues to grow. The literature regularly addresses the role of study abroad upon the choice of career, long-term commitment to local activity, subsequent employment opportunities and graduate school admission, and the advantage of having a global mind-set.

of "whosoever will" and how Jesus' request to follow him can lead us to global awareness and the breadth of God's grace to humanity.

A Precarious Journey

Liminality is a concept that earned credibility in the second half of the twentieth century through the work of anthropologist Victor Turner. It can be defined as the precarious position between two points where the individual belongs temporarily to neither point, finds herself vulnerable, and is most self-aware.[4] This state describes the position of a student in a new cultural environment where the assumed cultural signposts are no longer visible and she has no directive to point to new acceptable behavioral patterns. Uncertainty, vulnerability, and painful awareness of one's ignorance represent the threshold (the literal meaning of the Latin word *limen*) of a potential breakthrough in the student's cultural education. Until that happens, she will feel alone. Ideally, study abroad should be disruptive to the student. Leaving one's environment is unsettling because it means changing one's routine, one's known context, and leaving one's circle of friends and family. Study abroad, in order to broaden one's horizon, should engender a creative tension that keeps one sensitized to the differences encountered on a daily basis. This heightened awareness allows learning to occur in a meaningful way because the new knowledge gained is immediately put to practical use. It allows the synthesis of previously disparate understandings to flow into cohesiveness, or as Turner puts it, "a realm of pure possibility whence novel configurations of ideas and relations may arise."[5]

The two disciples traveling to Emmaus find themselves in a liminal state (Luke 24:13–35). They have left Jerusalem after having experienced the unsettling events of Jesus' trial, crucifixion, and burial, none of which can they reconcile with their own understanding of the Messiah's mission. Analogously, these two disciples experience the destabilization that accompanies the lack of understanding and the absence of external familiarity; the disciples turn inwardly, not unlike the Christian study abroad student, who questions her own beliefs, senses her vulnerability, and becomes eminently aware of her own ignorance. This represents precisely the point of potential revelation and growth. Personal growth occurs as the hunger for spiritual stability increases. So Jesus, now traveling with these two disciples, takes advantage of the teaching moment. He retells the meaning of the Law and the Prophets according to messianic hope. The mentor's teaching coupled with

---

4. Concerning Turner, see La Shure, "About: What is Liminality."
5. Ibid.

a re-contextualization of the familiar, that is, Jesus' later act of the breaking of bread with them, leads the two disciples to experience a reordering of their thinking *and* a new understanding of their world. Their universe now contains expanded meaning, and transformation is now in progress. The logic of the new environment reveals a bit of itself, and the two disciples, like the student, stand on firmer ground when faced with the inevitable next challenge.

The state of heightened awareness and discovery cannot be maintained over an extended period of time as it is emotionally taxing and requires a deliberate choice to work at the learning and integrating process. The constant plunge into new stimuli will leave the student exhausted and confused, tempting him to return to a familiar structure in order to quell his disequilibrium. The well-meaning overenthusiasm propelling the student to make the most of a limited time presents a real danger. Fatigue will quickly set in, causing poor judgment, and the potential for serious error can sabotage the learning process. The two disciples, once Jesus had left them, came very close to this point. Of course, they were energized to share their new revelation with the other followers of Jesus in Jerusalem whom they knew to be still in shock and disbelief. In their exuberance, the two immediately set out for Jerusalem in spite of their own earlier argument that Jesus stay with them at such a late hour.

A time for reflection and for adjustments to be made in one's thinking is necessary. The evaluation of what one thinks about the new realities, and how one integrates them into one's worldview, demands a certain period of regrouping and deliberate intellectual work. Jesus knew this and appeared to the assembled group in Jerusalem again. He spent time with them, showed them his hands and feet, even ate some fish to demonstrate the reality of his flesh and bone. He then proceeded to teach and have them review the recent events in the light of the Scriptures. They began to understand. Jesus directed the disciples to remain in Jerusalem "until you have been clothed with power from on high" (Luke 24:49),[6] until they had experienced, internalized, and could implement their expanded understanding of God's promise. He wanted them to be able to act confidently and appropriately without his physical presence.

The Labor of the Journey

Why is the acquisition of expanded understanding such a labor intensive endeavor? When we are placed in a new cultural environment, our first

---

6. This and all subsequent references to Scripture come from the KJV.

reaction is to attempt to order or regularize what we are experiencing according to what is familiar. If we are unsuccessful in this attempt, or are simply unwilling to make the attempt, we tend to label the experience and other people as strange. We opt for an easy solution by slipping into the most elemental and incorrect form of cultural judgment, stereotyping. We evaluate on the basis of parochial knowledge, what is narrowly known.

Anthropologist Raymonde Carroll explains that such judgment is erroneous when based on our own cultural logic and not on the cultural logic of the society we are observing. She describes cultural analysis "as a means of perceiving as 'normal' things which initially seem 'bizarre' or 'strange' among people of a culture different from one's own."[7] It is never easy to set aside what is transparent and a given to us and assume the mindset of another culture in order to judge what is normal or bizarre in that culture. The lynchpin in doing cultural analysis is the exigency to see a behavior from the perspective of the culture in which it occurs, namely the foreign cultural logic. Without this perspective, our analysis is necessarily flawed because our native cultural logic is not relevant to the new context and will lead us to a faulty conclusion. We must refocus to be able to see in a new way. Joerg Rieger notes that "while teaching takes place regardless of whether anyone pays attention or not, learning does not happen by default."[8]

The effort required is unrelenting as life keeps moving, and the student is never outside of life's circumstances. The French philosopher/novelist Jean-Paul Sartre argues that action is always required of us because we are always "in situation."[9] Fatigue, frustration, and even anger can set in. This is the crucial point where stereotypes will surface, and override the more timid and uneasy sense of discovery. It takes courage, discipline, and the mentorship of the Holy Spirit in the life of the Christian student in order to pursue the ideal of pronouncing a valid judgment about another culture. For example, approaching a Frenchman whom one does not know, with a smile on one's face, will probably elicit a negative reaction or, at best, no reaction. The American will interpret this as rude. The American can conclude that either all Frenchmen are impolite or he can attempt to understand the cultural logic of the Frenchman for whom there exists a distinct set of social etiquette. Gaining this understanding is the hard work of cultural analysis that will ultimately ease one's entrance into the host culture. This work is thus both demanding and rewarding, and constitutes a major transformative element of the study abroad experience.

7. Carroll, *Cultural Misunderstandings*, 2.
8. Rieger, *Traveling*, 67–68.
9. Sartre, *Being and Nothingness*, 533.

In addition, if we are honest Christians, our cultural analysis will also lead to us separate what is strictly culturally-based from what is scripturally-based before we pronounce an opinion. For the true disciple of Christ, cultural analysis demands that we act Christianly in our assessments of others, which is perhaps an uncommon manner of thinking about how to put our faith into action. Study abroad becomes a true investment of ourselves in another culture as we follow the scriptural mandate to love our neighbor as ourselves. How is this possible without a certain emptying of preconceived cultural ideas in order to gain an empathetic base from which to love our neighbor? Jesus became human precisely so that he could understand us and serve us (Phil 2:1–8). It is incumbent on us to act from a position of humility and vulnerability. Saint Francis of Assisi included this idea in his *Prayer of the Morning* when he implores God to be able to "see your children as You see them, beyond appearances, and therefore, to see only the good in each one."[10] There is no guarantee the student can achieve this. The experience of study abroad can produce contrasting reactions depending on the choice of attitude a student makes. Contact with another culture can easily reinforce a person's negative views of others, usually with a concomitant superior view of one's native culture. However, it can also expose a thoughtful person to an understanding of others, and even make that person a humble advocate for the "other" among one's own people. We see the paradox of the potentially narrower cultural view being the easier or broader way, and the broader cultural view being the labor intensive or narrower way.

The Stress of the Journey

We can never fully eliminate the stress of our foreignness while in another culture. Miroslav Volf states that "the identity of a person is inescapably marked by the particularities of the social setting in which he or she is born and develops."[11] However, the very consciousness of foreignness will take the study abroad student a good distance down the path of inclusiveness found in the Gospels. The concept of "whosoever will" in John 3:16 takes on great prominence in one's comprehension of God's love for all humankind, no matter the culture of a people. Liberation from a narrow focus to a wider perspective is necessary if we are to see beyond appearances. With this perspective we can counter Jean-Paul Sartre's bold assertion that "l'enfer, c'est les Autres" (Hell is—the others).[12] Others become valuable to

---

10. Authorship is ambiguous but is most often attributed to Saint Francis of Assisi.
11. Volf, *Exclusion and Embrace*, 19.
12. Sartre, *Huit clos-suivi de Les mouches*, 93.

us not because they externally impose on us our self-image but because God loves them. Jesus did not hesitate to engage the "other" in dialog when he addressed the woman at the well (John 4:9). The outcome was that the Samaritan woman recognized Jesus as the Messiah. Jesus and his disciples stayed in the city two more days after that initial conversation, and many more acknowledged him as the Messiah (John 4:42). Foreignness, for the Christian student, does not demand inferiority or impotence. It does, however, require vulnerability, willingness to make mistakes, humility, a sense of humor, strength of character when faced with circumstances beyond one's knowledge or control, and dependence on the Holy Spirit. Moreover, these qualities will be attractive to the host person of a different culture precisely because they are not expected of the typical guest.

The Choices of the Journey

The uneasiness experienced in the liminal state can be exploited for the potential good of the student. I say "potential" because, as seen earlier, there is always a choice to make. A student can resist the invitation to learn from the host culture due to fear, haughtiness, or self-satisfaction, or she can accept the invitation and be drawn toward a practical understanding of and peace with the host culture. The study abroad student can profit spiritually from her disorientation by allowing it to direct her thoughts toward God. This uneasy spirit or restlessness is what George Herbert describes in the fourth stanza of his poem, *The Pulley*.

> Yet let him keep the rest,
> But keep them with repining restlessness:
> Let him be rich and weary, that at least,
> If goodness lead him not, yet weariness
> May toss him to my breast.[13]

Herbert imagines God pausing to muse after having poured numerous pleasurable and meaningful blessings into the creation of humanity. God determines that if he bestows the final blessing of rest, humans will be satisfied, neglect his creator, and "so both should losers be."[14] Therefore, God also gives the gift of restlessness so that a man will be led by his weariness to the breast of God. It is the wise soul who discovers his dependence on God, and therein finds ultimate peace. Thus, both humans and God

---

13. Di Cesare, *George Herbert*, 57.
14. Ibid.

experience fulfillment in their mutual communion. In his *Confessions*, Augustine conveys the same idea when he writes, "Thou awakest us to delight in Thy praise; for Thou madest us for Thyself, and out heart is restless, until it repose in Thee."[15] The student can, in his cultural and spiritual disorientation, identify significant growth in his understanding of the cultural logic of the host culture, and more importantly, experience meaningful spiritual maturity in his relationship with God.[16] The dissonance felt is to be sought and not shunned because "being a stranger does not mean to be altogether forsaken and alienated, but instead to be specially bonded to God."[17] It is the restlessness described by Herbert and Augustine that can lead to a true and personal divine revelation, and in turn to the display of God's grace toward others. This intimate relationship with God not only satisfies a deep longing of the human heart but also calls a person forth into the world.

The Subversive Call of the Journey

Study abroad becomes an educational process that is subversive to the insular mind. The student is initially drawn to study abroad as an attractive, exotic act without fully realizing that it can be the catalyst for profound change. A gradual maturing process begins to transform the individual so that the world, even his small familiar world, assumes a larger dimension. This process labors against the status quo, and challenges the individual to self-examination in the light of a differing set of values. Thus, study abroad militates against a pharisaic self-deceit, self-importance, and false superiority. The underlying goal of study abroad in the Christian context is to call the student to an expanded worldview, a more comprehensive sense of the planet and its peoples with the hope that this new perspective will lead him to live in a more generous, compassionate manner. Study abroad presents an opportunity to participate in unexpected situations and to act out one's faith practically. The transformative power of study abroad is further nuanced by examining the Latin root of the verb *to educate*, literally, *ex* meaning "out or from", and *ducere* meaning "to lead." The verb also connotes a range of meanings that include to civilize, cultivate, develop, and ameliorate. Jesus *educated* his followers in this expanded sense of the verb in that he called them out so as to lead them away from their small thinking and toward a generosity of spirit, out of individualism into solidarity with humanity.

---

15. Augustine, *Confessions*, 1.
16. Fendall, "God Appointments," 74.
17. Slagter, "Engaging Culture," 79.

A similar call is issued by the French novelist/philosopher Albert Camus. Camus called the individual to a denial of God and to a rebellion against life's absurdity that he defined as the unquenchable desire for life juxtaposed with the inevitability of death.[18] In explaining what our behavior should be vis-à-vis the absurdity of the human condition, he declares "I revolt, therefore, we are" ("je me révolte, donc nous sommes").[19] For Camus, this rebellion placed one squarely in solidarity and in common understanding with all humanity. Absurdism's rebellion changes our destiny of death not a wit, but it does place us in the company of our neighbor with the opportunity to help relieve suffering during our lifetime.

Jesus, on the other hand, calls us not to rebellion but to submission to God. This paradoxical act transforms human destiny from ultimate extinction to spiritual life, so that the opportunity to do good is realized both temporally and eternally. Jesus leads his newly-identified disciples out of an ill-fated existence into a proactive one, with practical and spiritual consequences; he leads them through a radical transformation by means of a seemingly illogical submission that would then affect thought and deed, intellect and behavior.

After Jesus called Simon, Andrew, James, and John, they were immediately immersed in activities that awed and astonished them. Matthew describes Jesus as he taught in the synagogues, preached, healed the mentally and physically sick, and dealt with crowds of the curious and the sincere (Matt 4:23–25). The abrupt thrusting of these four young students into a completely unknown universe had to be destabilizing to them. Their world suddenly took on new dimensions as they were being educated. Matthew spends the next three chapters recounting in detail the intensive teaching that Jesus lead them through. The educational process is a calling out with purpose and, for the Christian student, this is also a valid description of the study abroad experience.

Amanda,[20] a senior business major, had taken several interdisciplinary humanities courses without ever appreciating them. They were, at best, requirements to be checked off a degree sheet. During one summer she traveled on a university-sponsored study abroad trip to France and Belgium. While visiting museums, seeing the architecture, eating novel foods, hearing unfamiliar languages, she began to remark that her surroundings, the

---

18. Howard Mumma casts some doubt on Camus' atheism in his book *Albert Camus*, where he describes what he believes is Camus' later spiritual journey toward Christianity. How far Camus traveled along this road remains difficult to assess due to his sudden and tragic death.

19. Camus, *Rebel*, 22.

20. This is not her real name.

art, the sites, and the history she was experiencing had a certain familiarity, even though she had never been to Europe before. It dawned on her that what she was experiencing was the "in person", visceral connection to all that she had experienced intellectually and remotely through her interdisciplinary courses on campus. The culture she had studied was now a physical reality in her life. Her understanding became engaged. It was the difference between an earlier disinterest and a fresh start, namely the desire to relate, describe, and share insights; she was like a child at Christmas. Her new comprehension created a new imperative for her that might be expressed succinctly by the title of Francis Schaeffer's classic work, *How Should We Then Live?* or by the Apostle Paul's question after he had encountered Jesus on the road to Damascus, "Lord, what wilt thou have me to do?" (Acts 9:6). Amanda had been called out, educated, and now sensed the urgency to act. Her newly discovered realization of the broader world and the need to respond to it leads us to reflect on another element of study abroad that God can use.

The Humility of the Journey

In our personal understanding of God's modus operandi, we often limit his work to the people and the places we know. If we happen to find ourselves in an unfamiliar location, we (and particularly we Pentecostals) often conclude that we must take the initiative for God, as if he were a step or two behind us. Dare we consider, however, that another aspect of study abroad should be to observe humbly and discover what God is already doing in the "other" milieu? Even with our newly acquired sense of well-doing, should we not proceed with caution? The Holy Spirit has certainly preceded us, and our role should be to discern his work and perhaps offer assistance rather than leadership, elaboration rather than novelty.

In truth, we go finding God already at work. The challenge then becomes how best to assist in what he is already doing. Philip discovered this role when he met the Ethiopian eunuch and asked him if he understood what he was reading. The eunuch responded, "How can I unless someone guides me?" (Acts 8:31). The Apostle Paul finds himself with a little time on his hands in Athens, and in his sightseeing discovers an altar to an unknown god. At the invitation of the philosophers, he skillfully uses their intellectual curiosity and their concept of an unknown god to explain the truth of the Gospel. Some accepted his teaching and others did not. (Acts 17:22–34). Our responsibility is not to force a result but to dialogue, clarify, and proclaim. In that role, we function, not as originators of the content, but as humble conveyors of the message. We acknowledge our usefulness to God and thank him for allowing us to labor with his Spirit and his servants who are already on the job. Working alongside them, always in a secondary role to the Holy Spirit, keeps our ego in check and promotes our effectiveness. As co-workers, we quickly understand the pressures and constraints that others face. Our support, no matter how benevolent and well-meaning, becomes more acceptable when we do not set ourselves up as the norm.[21] Our desire to render assistance must be tempered with sensitivity to the Holy Spirit and a growing understanding of the norms of the host culture. As another young student stated, "A lot of my friends are talking about how they want to change the world. At this point, I just want to get in touch with it."[22]

The Structure of the Journey

Since the initial connection with the host culture is unknown territory, a structured study abroad program can greatly ease the educational, transformative process. While leaders are not able to dictate fully all encounters, the program can establish methodologies and create circumstances that will lead to culturally instructive outcomes.[23] Early on, the student needs the resources of a teacher, a mentor, a guide, and a cultural informer to supply information, emotional support, and clear instruction when questions and disappointments arise. They will inevitably arise, and in spite of the discomfort they cause, they will benefit the student. The creative tension growing out of uncertainty can spur the student to analysis and reflection, and the mentor can take this teachable moment to turn the experience into acquired knowledge. The student, lacking personal experience, must be willing to trust the mentor's knowledge and guidance until such time as her own experience validates her learning. Then she will be empowered to move into the host culture with greater confidence, enhanced critical thinking skills, and a passion for learning.[24] The cultural analysis demanded will be practiced in a "continual back and forth—'your culture,' 'my culture'—until

---

21. Rieger, *Traveling*, 83.
22. Once again, this student will remain anonymous.
23. At Evangel University, the Global Connections course is designed for this purpose. It is described on the university website in this manner: "The purpose of this class is to allow each student to explore another culture in a supervised setting with mentors who guide the process. By participating in the Global Connections experience, students will develop personal spiritual formation, experience global cultures, learn about other perspectives and world views, and actively participate in service and witness projects."
24. Hartfiel, "Go Overseas," 1.

it comes easily."[25] This process is to be carried out with humility, perhaps with occasional embarrassment, and with the encouragement of a mentor in much the manner that Paul urged Timothy to greater accomplishments in the Pastoral Epistles.

The Return from the Journey

Returning home can be one of the hardest components of the study abroad experience. Rieger describes it as "getting lost at home."[26] Friends and family can only relate to a limited number of photos and stories, no matter how life-changing they might be to the student. This student becomes disenchanted with those people closest to him, and may not understand why. There may even be a stronger sense of isolation and resentment precisely because he is home. Liminality recurs upon reentry. Crossing the threshold into a presumed familiarity, the student is shaken by an unanticipated disequilibrium. He anticipated and prepared for differences in a foreign culture, but now, even at home, the shock is that life is no longer the same. The reason? Most often, it is the student himself who has changed.

The transformative and integrative processes do not halt because he has crossed into his own country. At home, he assumes a more contemplative and introspective dimension, but nevertheless, a critical one as he is compelled once again to bring new balance to his life. He will have to do this because he is a transformed person. The student now sees his own culture as somewhat foreign given his altered perspective. I offer the following paraphrase of one such former student: "My transformation has nothing to do with looks but with an adventure that changed my world for the better. One year ago this week I traveled across the pond to Europe. I am a better person spiritually, emotionally, and made some amazing friends."

In addition to the textbooks, the mentor's teaching, and the student's personal experiences, a key resource for reflection on the time abroad is the journal. Ideally, the student has kept a running journal documenting his life abroad. Initially, this document served to keep the student aware of his daily activities and his immediate reactions to them, but now, in attempting to evaluate the impact of the time abroad and the resumption of life at home, the journal becomes his best interlocutor. Forgotten events and people will flood back to memory and be revived as he reads the narrative. He *reimages* them. Pending questions now find answers or at least pathways toward answers as the skill of cultural analysis coupled with the understanding of

---

25. Carroll, *Cultural Misunderstandings*, 63.
26. Rieger, *Traveling*, 63.

a new cultural logic leads the student past inaccurate stereotypes to valid descriptions. Lessons studied become lessons relived and may only become lessons learned upon reintegration at home. More importantly, the student takes his newly acquired skill of cultural analysis and begins to ask deeper moral and spiritual questions. He begins to contemplate the "other" through God-inspired eyes, and then to ask what his personal responsibilities should entail now that he is home.

The Assessment of the Journey

An initial response of the student is to offer her whole person and activity to God. If the concept of the integration of life, learning, and living has merit for the Christian student, then it may just find its apogee in this response through the study abroad experience. The study abroad experience with its multiple components can be the catalyst for life-long transformation. It begins with liminality, that crossing of a threshold, then engenders creative tension, which promotes heightened awareness, and finally affirms one's convictions. Bill George, Professor of Management Practice at the Harvard Business School, beautifully describes this as a *mindfulness* which creates better leadership: "You're able to both observe and participate in each moment, while recognizing the implications of your actions for the longer term. And that prevents you from slipping into a life that pulls you away from your values."[27]

Simone Weil, the French writer and devout Catholic social activist, also discusses this idea of heightened awareness. She calls it *attention*.[28] She feels that, for the Christian scholar, *attention* has the benefit of keeping her close to God. By focusing on her study, she discovers fragments of eternal truth that lead to the living Truth, to God himself. Her disciplined learning has a direct influence on the quality of her devotional life, her communion with God. She then naturally transfers the fervency of her study to the fervency of knowing Him. As her study becomes a desire to know more of God, she finds herself in a position to offer all that she does as worship to him. Weil concludes that study becomes a sacrament, a holy offering, and an act of worship. We can most certainly offer to God the study abroad experience, as described above, as an act of devotion, submission, and worship.

In our restlessness, we draw near to God and as he loves us, our false pride is laid bare, and we confess our sin in humility. We confess our cultural blindness, our self-absorption, our limited understanding of his unending

27. George, "Mindfulness."
28. Panichas, *Simone Weil Reader*, 49–50.

love for the *other*. We accept our need to be called out, to be educated, and to act in greater service to his kingdom. In the context of Christian higher education, to study abroad is certainly to acquire cultural acumen and skill, but also to understand one's own status as a child of God. It is then possible to begin to comprehend God's broader plan for all the earth's peoples. God incarnate lived among us to reveal himself and to give himself for us. Study abroad affords the student the "opportunity to observe without hasty judgment and with gracious charity the diverse manifestations of Christianity" and to witness the breadth of God's love.[29] This transformative and integrative journey of study abroad is truly powerful in its potential to shape us more fully into God's image.

BIBLIOGRAPHY

Augustine. *The Confessions of St. Augustine*. Translated by Edward Bouverie Pusey. London: Chatto & Windus, 1909.

Buteyn, Mary. "When 'Evangelisch' is not 'Evangelical': Preparing Students for a Different Religious Culture." *Journal of Christianity and Foreign Languages* 8 (2007) 61–66.

Camus, Albert. *The Rebel: An Essay on Man in Revolt*. Translated by Anthony Bower. New York: Alfred A. Knopf, 1954.

Carroll, Raymonde. *Cultural Misunderstandings*. Chicago: University of Chicago Press, 1988.

Di Cesare, Mario A., ed. *George Herbert and the Seventeenth-Century Religious Poets*. New York: W. W. Norton, 1978. Evangel University. https://www.evangel.edu.

Fendall, Lon. "Seizing the 'God Appointments': When There is Cultural Disorientation in a Study Abroad Program." In *Transformation at the Edge of the World: Forming Global Christians through the Study Abroad Experience*, edited Ronald J. Mordan and Cynthia Toms Smedley, 73–86. Abilene, TX: Abilene Christian University Press, 2010.

George, Bill. "Mindfulness Helps You Become a Better Leader." October 26, 2012. Online: https://hbr.org/2012/10/mindfulness-helps-you-become-a.

Hartfield, Lindsay. "Go Overseas." February 19, 2013. Online: http://www.gooverseas.com/blog/ways-study-abroad-changes-a-person.

Holmes, Arthur F. *The Idea of a Christian College*. Grand Rapids: Eerdmans, 1987.

La Shure, Charles. "About: What is Liminality." October 18, 2005. Online: http://www.liminality.org/about/whatisliminality/.

Mumma, Howard. *Albert Camus and the Minister*. Brewster, MA: Paraclete Press, 2000.

Panichas, George A., ed. *The Simone Weil Reader*. New York: David McKay, 1977.

Rieger, Joerg. *Traveling*. Minneapolis: Fortress, 2011.

Sartre, Jean-Paul. *Being and Nothingness. An Essay on Phenomenological Ontology*. Translated by Hazel E. Barnes. London: Methuen, 1958.

———. *Huit clos-suivi de Les mouches*. Paris: Editions Gallimard, 1947.

Schaeffer, Francis. *How Should We Then Live*. Old Tappan, NJ: Fleming H. Revell, 1976.

---

29. Buteyn, "When 'Evangelisch' is not Evangelical," 66.

Slagter, Cynthia, "Engaging Culture: Guiding Students to Reflect on Cross-Cultural Experience." *Journal of Christianity and Foreign Languages* 5 (2004) 78–82.

Volf, Miroslav. *Exclusion and Embrace: A Theological Explanation of Identity, Otherness, and Reconciliation*. Nashville: Abingdon, 1996.

13

Meeting at the Table: The Divine Intersection Between Writing Centers and the Discipline of Hospitality

JENNIFER FENTON

MY COLLEAGUE AND DIRECTOR of the Johnson County Community College Writing Center, Kathryn Byrne, uses a particularly divine quote at the end of each email she sends out. Recipients of Kathryn's emails can always expect to see the following modified quote by Mother Teresa: "I want to be a little pencil in the hand of a writing God who is sending a love letter to the world." This quote is telling, given that Writing Centers are typically places housed in universities, colleges and, more recently, high schools across the nation which serve as safe havens for student writers. Writing Center directors are often sending welcoming and supportive messages to tutors and students about the writing process. For Writing Center specialists and directors, this sentiment rings true when reflecting upon our often hectic worlds of tutor training, peer evaluation, learning assessments, faculty and student collaboration, and ongoing writing projects. Though not all Writing Center professionals claim belief in God or Christian faith, we often adopt this service-laden language of Byrne's quote when speaking about the philosophical goals of our profession. Moreover, I have often heard Writing Center specialists refer to their work as one which requires a service-oriented mindset aimed at sharing ideas or knowledge with another person.

Elizabeth H. Boquet explains that Writing Center professionals often find themselves espousing the idea that "people with common concerns benefit from sharing those experiences with their peers."[1] Yet, what this remark suggests is that many professionals involved in Writing Center work ultimately believe that their work is meaningful, service-oriented, and perhaps intrinsically requires a deeply rooted attitude of hospitality from all parties involved, whether it be a student, peer, or director.

For many in the field, an ideal writing center at a college or high school would be a hospitable space where a student could almost feel like she was home as soon as she entered, not because of an immediate visual of comfy chairs and a library which includes magazines, books, and, perhaps, e-readers; instead, she would feel an immediate sense that she had found a family ready to entertain guests due to a tutor immediately looking up from a stack of papers and cup of coffee to say hello. This feeling of belonging, in a perfect world, would continue as the tutor greeted the student and offered a cushioned seat and any refreshments; it would continue as the student offered a piece of writing to be reviewed while wondering if the tutor would remain as pleasant as first perceived. As both parties take in the writing across a table, and they ask difficult questions of the purpose of the piece while also being mindful of one another, a sense of community would also manifest within the language formed between the two peers. Ideally, as the session ended, this same student would leave knowing she had found a community of learners, a kind of pop-up family of people ready to meet her at the table. It is at the table where I see, as many others have, the conversation of hospitality beginning.

In this challenging time where educators must address fiscal, assessment, and psychological pressures, it may indeed be pertinent to explore how hospitality could ideally unfold in everyday beliefs and practices of their center, and thereby, enrich students. Conjointly, the table where the tutor and student meet is a strong locus for wrestling with the tensions that the term "hospitality" invites. Though meeting at the table with another student invites a myriad of tutoring practices and styles, I will specifically explore how the practices of active listening and Socratic questioning can inspire a hospitable interaction between a tutor and student and, in turn, harken back to some of similar hospitable practices of Jesus. By tying the stories of Jesus to how a conversation can potentially unfold between the tutor and a student, my hope is that the reader will be able to see how often the labor of grappling over the pen with a student serves not simply as practice for writing a paper, but practice for writing out and declaring the stories of their lives.

---

1. Boquet, *Noise from the Writing Center*, 29.

What problematizes this goal though is the very question of whether the character of Jesus is relevant for the modern tutor and/or student who may or may not find any relevancy to Christianity in the first place. Truthfully, evangelical Christianity has a history, as well as a current agenda by some of its believers, to force a total and unquestioning belief in all its adherents. In fact, there are self-proclaimed Christians who know that even if a person does not believe the Bible to be a literal document of truth, he may still chose to learn from various passages of either the Old or New Testament and, therefore, benefit from doing so by becoming a more well-rounded person. Likewise, I would also trust that a Writing Center tutor might explore other contexts of tutoring even if it means venturing into the world of religious practice often left open for multiple levels of interpretation. This tension reflects some of the insecurities often felt and perceived when a tutor and student sit down together in order to interpret a text, piece of writing, and perhaps, each other as well. Yet, I believe the guiding principles of hospitality may be able to help ease some of these tensions that many tutors, students, and educators may have experienced.

Writing Centers and Hospitality

To date, a great deal of Writing Center theorists already engage the function of hospitality in the daily activities of an operating center by way of a numerous foundational studies. In the last decade, a number of researchers,[2] such as Harry C. Denny,[3] Jackie Grutsch McKinney,[4] and Bonnie Sunstein,[5] have begun to question how the identity of a Writing Center may better interweave the concept of hospitality by playing with the cultural and linguistic origins of hospitality. For most Writing Center theorists, the idea of hospitality in the context of our work conjures up notions of connectedness, shared space, relieved tensions, reflective community, unassuming marginality, and as mentioned, a table of ideas, knowledge, and human experience. In fact, Bonnie Sunstein begins her essay "Moveable Feasts, Liminal Spaces: Writing Centers and the State of In-Betweeness" with a description of a

---

2. Writing Center theorists and researchers often focus on hospitality in terms of offering more to the students and/or institutions, such as stretching what services writing centers should or should not provide. Traditionally, writing centers were merely grammar labs staffed with professional tutors. Today, most writing centers offer more services, such as more comprehensive reviews of writing, peer and professional tutors, and partnership/collaboration with other services provided at colleges and/or high schools.

3. Denny, *Facing the Center*.
4. McKinney, *Peripheral Visions*.
5. Sunstein, "Moveable Feasts," 7–26.

writing center by way of Hemingway imagery: "I like to think of the writing center as a moveable feast on a transient table—sweets and savories, an interesting mix of guests, perhaps unmatched place settings. An invisible table gathering ghosts of conversations, echoes of drafts, and old assignments."[6] This image holds resonance for many as we consider how Sunstein uses some crucial references to time, limited resources, and the idea of otherness. She suggests that the Writing Center table is often set up to be ready just enough for any to sit and gather, to think and explore what it means to be human with a stranger, and defy orderliness when one is at risk of merely living out of routine practice rather than out of sincere connectedness.

Another theme concerning hospitality applicable for writing center theory and practice includes disciplines, such as composition studies, education, psychology, and even postmodern studies. Notably, John B. Bennet[7], Matthew Heard,[8] Dale Jacobs,[9] and in a co-authored work, Glenn Blalock with Janis and Richard Haswell,[10] have started to come up with their own terms for how composition studies could benefit through use of the hospitality metaphor to inform a classroom environment. Janis and Richard Haswell are currently working on a project that analyzes the philosophical constructs as well the social vehicle of hospitability within higher education institutions.[11] The Haswells' posit that hospitality is pertinent to a healthy academy as the essential framework for development of personal philosophies from what it means to be socially just, and even classically, human. In other words, they consider implications of what it means to be hospitable to the student, the teacher, and yes, even the Writing Center specialist and visitor. The idea of hospitality is a building block for creating foundational relationship within the classroom as well as institutions themselves. In an academic world of ever increasing anxieties where we are asked to institutionalize what simply cannot be, sharing knowledge across a table with a stranger or facing even a crowd of strangers in the classroom may create the

---

6. Ibid., 7.
7. Bennet, "Academy and Hospitality."
8. Heard, "Hospitality and Generosity."
9. Jacobs, "Audacity of Hospitality."
10. In their efforts to articulate acts of hospitality as part of college composition courses, Blalock and the Haswells produced an essay entitled: "Hospitality in College Composition Courses." This work is particularly valuable for Writing Center theorists.
11. The Haswells argue for a third party involved outside of the framework of guest and host, and they suggest that we should also acknowledge a "Preparer," one who allows for the guest and host to interact with one another in a healthy manner. For the academy, the "preparers" would be administrators set to manage the ties between faculty and students.

most intensely needed and felt moments of hospitality sought by both the student and the tutor.

Jacques Derrida is another important theorist who many researchers seek to unpack in order to capture the role of hospitality. Derrida serves as a valuable dialogic beginning for assessing life in a postmodern world.[12] He concludes (and resists any finality) that hospitality functions best when a person has to face the other or foreigner in an unexpected situation, and thus, a sense of egalitarianism may be achieved in this unplanned and purely incidental moment. Derrida notes how he mistrusts how hospitable a moment can be due to the ethics involved because he notes the implications of "one's dwelling place, one's identity, one's space, and one's limits."[13] Though a perfect moment of connectedness between a foreigner and a host cannot be achieved because of these problematic schemas, he considers the image of Christ to illustrate ideal moments of hospitality or to suggest that the Ideal may very well be obstructed by language. Specifically, Derrida connects the tale of Oedipus to the tale of Christ when Oedipus offers hospitality to those he should not; moreover, Derrida considers: "The host [Oedipus] thus becomes a retained hostage, a detained addressee, responsible for and victim of the gift that Oedipus, a bit like Christ, makes of his dying person or his dwelling-demanding, his dwelling-dying: this is my body, keep it in memory of me."[14] For Derrida, to give of yourself demands you speak what should be spoken or given. And yet, dwelling in such language is the power of transformation for the guest and host, a transformation powerful to raise the dead. In the end, Derrida implores others to seek out hospitality as a great act even if it cannot be achieved at a mortal table in this world, and perhaps even the next, despite what religious texts may suggest to their readership. For, Derrida asks, can society really be hospitable to the foreigners who have been stripped of agency, voice, and power and thus are not allowed to even sit at the same table with the powerful?

Immanuel Levinas, a disciple of Derrida, has inadvertently asked educators to think about what it means to be hospitable to the other/foreigner in the classroom when hierarchy and authority, at times, clash with the ability of someone to truly speak for herself. As a Jewish postmodernist, Levinas was fascinated by what hospitality might mean within the confines of ethical and political pressures. I would argue that Levinas wonders if hospitality may be more inviting than Derrida; specifically, Levinas questions whether

12. As one of the quintessential grandfathers of postmodern theory, Derrida famously dialogued about the theme of hospitality in his later work as recorded in his lecture, "Step of Hospitality/No Hospitality."

13. Derrida, *Of Hospitality*, 149.

14. Ibid., 107.

hospitality has an actual space for interaction due to social constructions and intrusions which can obstruct a vision and formation of hospitable practice in a cultural realm. In a turn similar to Derrida, Levinas creates an ethical ideal based not upon Christian ideals but on Judaic practice. Levinas needs religious belief and text to help him define what hospitality might contribute to modern society.[15]

Both Derrida's and Levinas's understanding of hospitality derive from other ancient sources such as the foundational practices of Judaism and Christianity. The vast literature on hospitality demonstrates the indelible mark that world religions have made on defining the cultural and decisive meanings of hospitality. Levinas and Derrida cannot escape how important it is to listen intently to these pivotal points of religious history. These stories whisper of the words we cannot help but hope for when meeting with the unexpected visitor, or in this case, the unexpected student who enters a writing center; we hope we would act, listen, and speak as the Great Master or the Messiah.

The Hospitality of Jesus

Given the religious importance of hospitality, I turn to a powerful and beloved story in Luke's gospel. It is by way of the act of listening where I would like to consider how a moment of hospitable silence in the life of Jesus serves as a template for the tutor and student relationship. First, when Jesus is silent, the reader may feel frustrated by His seeming lack of action or explanation. His listeners, including the disciples, sometimes hound him for more answers, for example, why such a particular judgment call, or why so slow to act? James Resseguie argues that an audience is often stunned by Jesus' actions as in the scene where an uninvited woman steps into a Pharisee's party to anoint Jesus with alabaster oil (Luke 7:36–50). It is here that "others welcome the new approaches as creative and fresh ways of reviving scriptures that long had been domesticated by more staid techniques."[16] Jesus' refusal to partake in dogged religious practice allows Him to be the silent overseer of human interaction where he can welcome the uninvited stranger, or Other, into a newer and wider space of both linguistic and physical communication.

Jesus chooses not to enter into a moral dialogue bent toward judgment and derision, but offers a hospitable defense of a woman poised to be ridiculed by others. When Simon the Pharisee fails to fulfill his responsibilities

15. Concerning Levinas, see Gauthier's "Levinas," 158–80.
16. Resseguie, *Spiritual Landscape*, 17.

as a host to Jesus, this sinful woman encounters Jesus; she begins to weep and kiss Jesus' feet while pouring her expensive oils on him. Jesus "listens" though acceptance of her gestures and allows her to sit with Him at the table. Meanwhile, Simon and other become furious with Jesus' behavior, and Simon breaks the silence by grumbling: "If this man were a prophet, he would have known who and what kind of woman this is who is touching him—that she is a sinner" (Luke 7:39).[17] In response, Jesus demands that this woman be given the opportunity for forgiveness and restores her status to community, "Your faith has saved you; go in peace" (Luke 7:50). By way of these words, the story ends, but, for readers, the questions begin.

This story breaks social constructs of moral acceptance and invites a new kind of hospitality outside of the traditional norms of Jewish law. Brendan Byrne, in fact, devoted an entire volume to the centrality of hospitality for the Lukan Jesus.[18] Jesus serves as the Great Host who constantly offers others the chance to partake in His greater vision for humankind and expands definitions of hospitality for Jewish and Gentile audiences. As Byrne explains, "Even a casual reading of Luke makes clear how often in this Gospel significant events and exchanges take place in the context of meals [or, in other words, at the table] and the offering (or non-offering) of hospitality in general. Hospitality, in a variety of expressions, forms a notable frame of reference for the ministry of Jesus."[19] Jesus establishes more than new table manners; He evokes a fresh language and narrative for those who are not supposed to have a vice in society.

Ironically, in the account above, the sinful woman does not speak. Instead, all of her communication springs from her outpouring of physical love: fervent weeping, kissing of Jesus' feet, and the lavish outpouring of expensive perfume. According to Byrne, the vocal Simon is "equally the focus of attention," and though he speaks, he fails to listen to what is happening around him. For instance, he "does not offer even the most basic gestures of hospitality: he does not wash Jesus' feet, he fails to greet him with a kiss, he does not anoint his head with oil."[20] This stark contrast between the woman and Simon allows for the reader to consider what it means not only to listen to the words of a great teacher, but be attentive to other forms of language, such as the language of the body, or perhaps, in the spirit of Derrida and Levinas, the language of God, which defies the social limita-

---

17. All subsequent references to Scripture are from the NRSV.

18. Byrne, *Hospitality of God*. See also Martin Mittelstadt's chapter on Luke's theology of hospitality.

19. Ibid., 4.

20. Ibid., 73.

tions of everyday speech. The woman who does not deserve a voice by the cultural measurements of her world is in fact invited to walk the path of peace and transcend to a new and transformed existence. She is invited to an active life of transformed existence and receives his sanctifying words: "Blessed are you when people hate you, and when they exclude you, revile you, and defame you on account of the Son of God" (Luke 6:22).

Returning to the Writing Center Table

Though tutors do not typically meet with students in the midst of life-altering occasions, we often find ourselves at a loss for words. In her book, *Unspoken: The Rhetoric of Silence*, Cheryl Glenn explains that "conversation has always been a medium for establishing oneself as an intellectual, social or financial player," which suggests that those who are not interested in a power play may be kept silent.[21] If this is indeed the case, the tutor should be wary to assume that an active conversation guarantees that active listening is indeed happening. Silence often makes tutors uncomfortable due to what is unknown in a moment of silence, and where facial expressions or body language provide no certainty of communicative efforts. Glenn notes that often silence is "perceived as emptiness," often paired with words like "barrenness" and "void," and thus refer to another kind of marginalization.[22]

This may indeed appear to be the experience in a Writing Center; for, in our modern world, many are indeed marginalized due to the common glance concerning skin color, sexual identity, economic status, and other forms of societal scorn. Anne Ellen Geller, Michele Eodice, Frankie Condon, Meg Carroll, and Elizabeth H. Boquet produce a fully co-authored work for Writing Center educators and argue that racism and marginalization often function as conversation devoid of active listening.[23] They warn that conversants need to be wary of complacency not only as subtle, but also subversive acts of racism. Such a lack of action reflects the similar inhospitable response of Simon and his guests who are not only unwilling to acknowledge a marginalized woman but unable to recognize Jesus' redemptive listening.

In a Writing Center context, the skill of active listening requires that tutors must be open to the words and the experiences of those who sit before them. Furthermore, an increasing number of Writing Center researchers continue to construct theories on why it so important for tutors

21. Glenn, *Unspoken*, 6.
22. Ibid., 72.
23. Geller et al., *Everyday Writing Center*, 87–108.

to understand their own identities. Many believe that if tutors do not see themselves reflected in those they meet, they risk missing hospitable moments with those they serve. Still others like Geller, et al. call for tutors to explore self-identify as a means for the development of the skills necessary to work amidst a vast diversity of experiences and people.[24] It is at this nexus where I believe hospitality must take place during a conversation, for active listening allows space for a diverse experience free of social and cultural assumptions of what is acceptable. Hence, a tutor who has learned the art of active listening should be able to confirm our most basic and fundamental connection: that we are human, and thus intrinsically connected. Often, as I have worked with my own tutors, I asked them to think less about the students as relatable writers but more as relatable persons who share experience of loss, laughter, and exclusion, and who deep down just want to fit in. By asking them to think beyond the confines of their roles in society or "on the job," I believe that when they sit at the table with another student, they are thereby able to listen better to what is unsaid, and open up greater space for sincere and hospitable transformation.

Revisiting the Lukan Table

To study further how to break away from the confines of expected roles, I turn yet again to the Scriptures. In another Lukan episode, readers must consider again the importance of complex linguistic contexts. As Jesus moves through a crowd of persons bent on seeing and listening to Him, one man falls at Jesus' feet and pleads for Jesus to come heal his daughter. In this moment, as Jesus begins his response and the crowd continues to press upon Him, an unidentified woman, who has suffered with physical pain and been an object of social scorn for years, touches only the hem of his garment. At that precise moment, Jesus freezes His movements and plainly asks: "Who touched me?" (Luke 8:45). His disciples insist that it could be anyone, yet Jesus insists it was one person in particular. The woman then falls at his feet, like the desperate father, explains her suffering, and how she had also been healed after touching Him. Reminiscent of the episode of the sinful woman at the house of Simon, Jesus turns to her and says: "Daughter, your faith has made you well; go in peace" (Luke 8:48). It is only as Jesus invites this woman with no social and linguistic power to identify herself that she can fully own her experience, and receives in total this divine and

24. Ibid.

hospitable encounter. She is, as Byrne puts it, able to "break through a vast barrier to gain access to Jesus" through the act of touch.[25]

Despite the power behind Jesus' act of linguistic acceptance, a reader may still be concerned with the motivations behind Jesus' reaction. Given her social location, Byrne inquires: "Would it not be sensitive to let the woman go away quietly and reenter the community in her own good time?"[26] To the contrary, Byrne demonstrates that his question is not rhetorical: "healing is never a purely private matter in the Gospel. Salvation includes restoring this person to the community, and her healing a community experience as well."[27] Byrne argues that identity actualization is intrinsic to community practice, and for the woman to be validated as a human being, she needs the experience of belonging amongst her peers. So, what we ask of each other is critical to building or destroying a person's self worth or very identity. The questions we ask of others must not fail to address the most crucial parts of what make us human. By doing so, we build hospitable space for the stranger, specifically the student, to fully explain herself, and therefore, choose what path she will take after she leaves a shared space.

This idea is very much in keeping with the authors of *The Everyday Writing Center*, who suggest that tutors "help those writers learn to make writing choices and own them, learn the questions they can ask their teachers when they're stuck, and learn the challenges they can carry back to their professors when they want to push the boundaries of an assignment."[28] These authors prompt tutors to search for space which leaves room for what is not pre-arranged; tutors are encouraged to see an experience as one which invites questions even outside of what is "normal" or previously understood. For the unclean woman, she had to touch someone to begin to know herself as a part of a larger community; our students may need to reach out with a bodily gesture in order to be validated. Though our students range from being apathetic to overly zealous about their writing, what tutors must ask is telling of their own empathetic development when faced with a student who believes she is a terrible writer, and therefore not worthy of conversation.

When preparing students for more intricate tutoring sessions, many Writing Center directors often refer to the importance of asking Socratic questions. Such questions leave room for open-ended responses that allow for students to come up with more complex and critically minded answers. Though Jesus' question to the woman may seem fairly direct, I would argue

25. Byrne, *Hospitality of God*, 83.
26. Ibid.
27. Ibid.
28. Geller et al., *Everyday Writer Center*, 80.

that He is actually asking a Socratic question; Jesus wants the woman to invest in her answer in order to search beyond an identity defined by an exclusive community. This type of question may be essential for our tutors when faced with someone like this woman with little or no societal self worth. A tutor's Socratic questions cannot simply circle around the writing at hand; they must probe the identity and wellbeing of the student. These kinds of questions can become messy due to a lack of restricted response, yet they will give the student and the tutor the ability to reach across the table, and find ways to connect beyond the confines of minimal expectations for a tutoring session. By reaching in this way, hospitality provides the necessary communal space for both parties to discover more than just how to fix a sentence. Together, they discover the joy of mutual transformation.

As a Writing Center specialist, I call upon colleagues everywhere to move beyond cultural norms, especially at the table, in order to create authentic space, which allows for unsaid communication: indeed, for a reality beyond words. We must learn to navigate through popular opinion in order to creatively invest in the lives of those who walk through our doors. If we truly believe our conversations have the potential to become an open current of questions that enliven open ethical responsibility, social acceptance, and authentic human interaction, we must encourage such interaction in even the most unexpected places. Let us talk with one another while being fully cognizant of our own humanity; at times, we may need to laugh or cry; at other times, we may simply need to be validated for who we are. May this talk be heard from the tables of Writing Centers across the world as we invite new meanings for what it means to be agents of God's hospitable transformation.

BIBLIOGRAPHY

Bennet, John B. "The Academy and Hospitality." *Cross Currents* 50 (2000) 23–35.
Boquet, Elizabeth. *Noise from the Writing Center*. Logan: Utah State University Press, 2002.
Byrne, Brendon. *The Hospitality of God: A Reading of Luke's Gospel*. Collegeville, MN: Liturgical, 2000.
Denny, Harry C. *Facing the Center: Toward an Identity Politics of One-to-One Mentoring*. Logan: Utah State University Press, 2010.
Derrida, Jacques and Anne Dufourmantelle. *Of Hospitality: Anne Dufourmantelle Invites Jacques Derrida to Respond*. Translated by Rachel Bowlby. Stanford: Stanford University Press, 2000.
Gauthier, David. "Levinas and the Politics of Hospitality." *History of Political Thought* 28 (2007) 158–80.

Geller, Anne Ellen, et al. *The Everyday Writing Center: A Community of Practice*. Logan, UT: Utah State University Press, 2007.

Glenn, Cheryl. *Unspoken: The Rhetoric of Silence*. Carbondale: Southern Illinois University Press, 2004.

Hall, R. Mark "Using Dialogic Reflection to Develop a Writing Center Community of Practice." *The Writing Center Journal* 31 (2011) 82–105.

Haswell, Janis, Richard Haswell, and Glenn Blalock. "Hospitality in College Composition Courses." *College Composition and Communication* 60 (2009) 707–27.

Heard, Matthew. "Hospitality and Generosity." *JAC: A Journal of Rhetoric, Culture, and Politics* 30 (2010) 315–35.

Jacobs, Dale. "The Audacity of Hospitality." *JAC: A Journal of Rhetoric, Culture, and Politics* 28 (2008) 563–81.

McKinney, Jackie Grutsch. "Leaving Home Sweet Home: Towards Critical Readings of Writing Center Spaces." *The Writing Center Journal* 25 (2005) 6–20.

———. *Peripheral Visions for Writing Centers*. Boulder: University Press of Colorado, 2013.

Resseguie, James. *Spiritual Landscape: Images of Spiritual Life in the Gospel of Luke*. Grand Rapids: Baker, 2003.

Sunstein, Bonnie. "Moveable Feasts, Liminal Spaces: Writing Centers and the State of In-Betweenness." *The Writing Center Journal* 18 (1998) 7–26.

14

Complexities of Learning: From Jerusalem to *Shantistan*[1]

Ruth Vassar Burgess

> "For I have singled him out that he may instruct his children and his posterity to keep the way of the Lord by doing what is right and just."
> (Gen 18:19 Tanakh)

> "Just as a person is obligated to teach his son, similarly he is obligated to teach his grandson, as it says: "Tell them to your children and to the children of your children."
> (Maimonides, Hilchot Talmud Toradh, Ch. 1, Par. 2.)

> "Let this mind be in you, which was also in Christ Jesus." (Phil 2:5 KJV)

> "And be not conformed to this world: But be ye transformed by the renewing of your mind. That ye prove what is that good and acceptable, and perfect, will of God." (Rom 12:2 KJV)

Ideological Foundations

INTEREST IN INTERGENERATIONAL TRANSMISSION of "righteous" principles and values spans the centuries. Mandates to perpetuate a people's heritage are prevalent in both the Hebrew and Christian Scriptures. The quotations

---

1. Twila and James Edwards lived a life based on biblical principles. This essay is both reflective of and represented by their models.

cited above demonstrate responsibilities for inter-generational transmission. Undoubtedly, societal emphases on sensorial and concrete learning experiences limit the ability of humans to engage in abstract and complex thinking. Too often contemporary learning models propose a static model of learning and a limited ability to change one's thought and practices.[2] In contrast, the transmitters of cultural ideas and values, particularly when one considers that humans are created in the image of God and ongoing participants in creation, should expect ongoing dynamic, progressive learning models.

To do so, one might consider the dialectic approach with its purposeful, interactive experiences between a mediator and the mediatee(-s). This approach, which rejects an alloplasticity approach to learning,[3] relies on others to make decisions for one's self. Unfortunately, this external locus approach typically promotes an unequivocal dependency and servitude to cultural expectations. On the other end of the spectrum, a *laissez faire* approach rejects the value of one's heritage. To apply the metaphor of West Texas tumbleweeds, a lack of reasoned intergenerational transmission of values and wisdom principles[4] leaves individuals longing for stability as they are being blown by society's changing "winds of whey."[5]

I would like to propose the autoplastic approach as yet another option.[6] According to this approach people must develop an inner reasoned core for learning and decision-making. A human mediator is crucial for mediated learning encounters. Reuven Feuerstein, the eminent Israeli cognitive psychologist (1921–2014) proposed an alternative in his Theory of Structural Cognitive Modifiability (SCM)[7] and his proposal for adoption of

2. Behavior modification relies on external locus of control and is known as the stimulus-to-response psychological model.

3. Alloplasty refers to when other external forces control one's thoughts and actions. This tends to limit the adaptation potential of an individual. All definitions listed in the footnotes are adapted from Feuerstein, *Definitions of Essential Concepts and Terms*.

4. Wisdom principles may be intergenerational values that initially were part of the groups' oral history and then later codified. These are often considered by the group or tribe to be transcendent.

5. Values are something of worth to a cultural or ethnic group. These beliefs determine a person's thinking, actions and character.

6. Autoplasty refers to when individuals take internal responsibility for their thoughts and actions. These occur through the development of metacognition and reasoned habits of the mind.

7. Reuven Feuerstein (1921–2014), who grew up in Romania, and later lived and taught in Israel, lived an extraordinary life. Though born into a world of hate and madness, he sought to clarity for Jews and non-Jews regarding tradition and civility. His external world consisted of warring groups, confusion, trampling, and whirling within various cultural contexts. Feuerstein emphasized focus of the mind and systematic

Mediated Learning Experiences (MLEs).[8] As a bearer of culture, a mediator bridges the abstract to the concrete, and the past to the present and into the future. This trans-temporal and trans-spatial way of living gives fuller meaning to life, particularly when developed and practiced in conjunction with the Judeo-Christian context of one created in God's image.

So how does one teach and apply the autoplastic approach? Thus far I have provided a foundational context and vocabulary for this model. In the second section of this essay, I propose an overall curriculum design that addresses the complexity challenge, namely the "Learning Star," a four-pointed Bethlehem star design, whereby MLE serves as the central conduit for curriculum development. In the third section, I introduce the role of Enabling Learning Encounters and in the fourth section, I apply and extend the Reuven Feuerstein Cognitive Map as a contemporary curricular framework. The Cognitive Map components assist in the curriculum development and analysis of learning encounters. In the fifth section, I provide further guidelines relating to Feuerstein's Mediated Learning Process. Such focused and intentional interaction encourages and enables the development of metacognition, critical thinking, and cross-modality networking of cognitive modalities and functions. In the final section, I encourage Mediated Culture Bearers to engage in intergenerational transmission of values and wisdom principles. I create *Shantistan* as a modern sample for curriculum built on the Feuerstein Theory of Structural Cognitive Modifiability and thereby illustrate the intentional import for complexities of learning.[9]

---

order, regardless of the circumstance.

For many years he was a lone prophet in the desert advocating for the oppressed and those deprived of their reasoned heritage. Then, standing steadfast in a world of suppression, came this human-enabling empowerment. Into a world of sorrow, Feuerstein gave hope. Into a world of limitations and acceptance of a predetermined status quo, comes a man demonstrating possibilities. Into a world of egocentric relativity comes this man insisting on the strength of multiple perspectives. Into a world promoting sensory pleasures comes a man advocating internal control principles. Into a world living for the present comes Reuven Feuerstein, declaring the reality of transcendent values and wisdom principles (Burgess, *Changing Brain Structure*, 186–87). Blessed be his memories.

8. Mediated Learning Experiences (MLEs) represent a formula for learning. Stimulus-Human-Organism-Human-Response: The intentional qualified adult mediates the mediated learning experience by selecting, framing, focusing, intensifying, and feeding back environmental experience in such a way as to produce appropriate learning sets and habits. See Feuerstein, *Instrumental Enrichment*. In this essay, MLE refers to Mediated Learning Experience, and MLEs to Mediated Learning Experiences.

9. I first developed this idea for a workshop that I lead in India in 2004.

The Bethlehem Learning Star[10]

In the twentieth century, the dominance of a new industrial revolution led to a parallel transmission of information based upon literacy and emerging technology. Unfortunately, new developments undercut the value of the Habits of the Mind and Habits of the Spirit, particularly in relationship to the transformation of one's heritage. All too often one's heritage became less and less valuable in educational systems. The products of direct instruction and *laissez faire* practices did not necessarily yield principled individuals with reasoned outcomes. Throughout this season, as public surveys continued to indicate, students remained deficient in critical thinking, pedagogical approaches struggled to adapt.

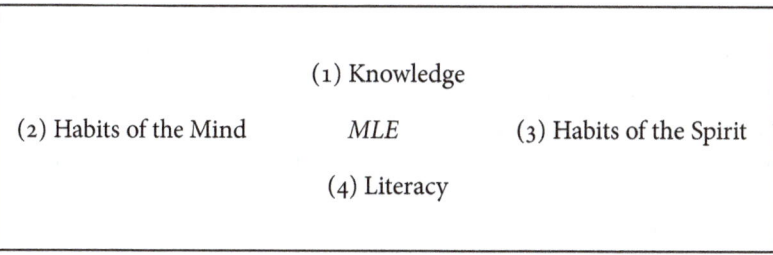

In order for a curriculum to support the possibility of an intergenerational transmission of values and wisdom principles, I created the above diagram as a model for pedagogy. MLEs radiate from the center and produce interaction between a mediator and mediatee. I argue that all components of the Bethlehem Learning Star are critical to the selection, adaptation, and implementation of curriculum. Feuerstein proposed innovative learning structures and programs through MLEs. However, while he emphasized Habits of the Mind (reason, critical thinking, decision making) over the Habits of the Spirit (affect or emotions),[11] I argue, to the contrary, that successful mediated learning requires implementation of the four points of the Bethlehem Learning Star.

Feuerstein argues that humans are modifiable based upon cognitive developments that adjust human feelings, motivation, and behavior. These habits are physiological modifications that occur in brain structure and the nervous system, in other words connected to a biologic theory. Feuerstein suggests that cognition occurs through three venues: (1) transformation by

---

10. I first presented this approach while in Israel in 2006 and later applied the model for course design at Regent University, Virginia Beach, Virginia.

11. See Feuerstein, *Instrumental Enrichment*, 9.

way of heritage; (2) learning from experience; and (3) scientific learning.[12] Through his inclusion of scientific learning with the teaching of one's heritage and the value of experience, he establishes a foundation for the complexity of learning. From this multidimensional model caregivers become intentional culture bearers. The teacher is not only a dispenser of information, but must be given to the development and integration of multifaceted levels and networks of meaning.

Enabling Learning Encounters

"There is one God, and one mediator between God and men, the man Jesus Christ." (1 Tim. 2:5 KJV)

For many years I understood Paul's use of mediator in his letter to Timothy to mean that Jesus Christ functions much like an attorney. Jesus takes our human failure and pleads with God the Father and Magistrate not to punish us for our sins. Similarly, through our emotionally laden prayers we ask forgiveness and request that we be restored to God by his grace. It was not until I studied under Feuerstein in 1986 during a sabbatical at the Hadassah-Wizo-Canada Research Institute in Jerusalem, that I became acquainted with alternate meanings for "mediator" in the context of MLE.

For Feuerstein, MLEs serve as primary channels for cultural transmission and may occur among people of all languages, social classes, and cultures. Indeed, one who is not afforded such learning components becomes "culturally deprived" and limits the potential for greater alloplastic development. Scholars propose varying components and directions for successful MLEs.

Alex Kozulin assesses the success or failure of MLEs to four quadrants.[13] In the first quadrant is an individual who has received positive MLEs through internalization of higher order psychological tools and applied the benefits of heritage transmission. The second quadrant includes the individual with exposure to MLEs but devoid of higher order psychological tools, such as a non-literate culture, but rich in its transmission of heritage. In the third quadrant, learners receive little or no transmission of heritage, though skilled by way of other tools. This person does not receive the opportunity to integrate tools based learning with transmission of heritage. Finally, in the fourth quadrant, individuals receive no MLEs or exposures of higher

---

12. Ibid.
13. Kozulin, *Psychological Tools*.

order psychological tools. Examples might include the dire situation experience by those displaced by war, famine, or other major social upheavals.

Another theorist, Lev Vygotsky, wrote of two zones that illustrate cognitive development.[14] First, the Zone of Proximal Development distinguishes between unassisted and mediator-assisted behavior. Both Vygotsky and Feuerstein insisted that cognitive growth is dynamic and occurs by way of ongoing mediated encounters. Second, Vygotsky proposed a Zone of Distal Development, where the mediator considers the mediatee's future and possibilities. Vygotsky emphasized the intentional necessity of intergenerational transmission of one's heritage. It follows that cultures more intentional at transmission of their heritage would be more successful at doing so.

The Reuven Feuerstein Cognitive Map: A Template For Curricular Design

Feuerstein promoted that humans, created in the image of God, could be modified in a positive direction. He refuted the idea that distal etiological factors determined one's outcome. Distal influences were identified as heredity and organicity, emotional disturbances in the parent or child, low educational level of parents, poverty of stimulus, cultural differences, and even normal interactions, but with an absence of MLEs. Feuerstein insisted that "Never shall we make decisions based on etiology,"[15] but upon MLEs to provide the foundation for positive outcomes, namely, Habits of the Mind.[16]

Using a grounded research approach over several decades, Feuerstein devised a seminal template for learning by way of his Theory of Structural Cognitive Modifiability.[17] Initially, this dialectic reciprocal pedagogy, now referred to as mediated learning, was not viewed as a seminal contribution, for it was commonly applied in Jewish homes. When the Instrumental Enrichment Curriculum was first utilized in the United States, most of the teachers applied minimal use of mediation, and reverted to direct instruction, behavior modification, or *laissez faire* approaches in their classrooms or therapy sessions. Many of these educators had not received the benefits of

---

14. Vygotsky, "Mind in Society"; Vygotsky, *Thought & Language*; and Vygotsky and Luria, *Essays in the History of Behavior*.
15. Feuerstein, Public Discourse, 1986.
16. Feuerstein, *Instrumental Enrichment*.
17. Cognitive modifiability is an approach that is not directed at the remediation of specific behaviors and skills but at changes of a structural nature that alters the course of cognitive behavior and opens the system to learn.

MLEs, whereas today, mediated learning instruction plays an integral part of Feuerstein's Instrumental Enrichment Curriculum program.

Feuerstein began to develop a template with cognitive intervention instruments and dynamic assessment tools, which would assist in curriculum development. His work was first applied to adolescents displaced by the Holocaust. Subsequently, the Theory of Structural Cognitive Modifiability and its applications have spread globally. Even he was surprised at its potential for global application: "I didn't realize the Theory of Structural Cognitive Modifiability had so many degrees of freedom."[18]

Feuerstein produced his Cognitive Map in order to help a mediator identify problem areas experienced by the mediatee. In so doing, the Cognitive Map becomes a tool or template used to develop curriculum, evaluate instructional activities, and assess progress towards cognitive modifiability. By utilizing six components found in the Cognitive Map, interactive mediation strives to discover and address an individual's difficulties. For Feuerstein, the following components address Habits of the Mind.

1. Cognitive Content

According to the Feuerstein, human beings process life experiences through heritage, experience, and scientific contexts. These three categories assist in understanding organization and integrative skills. Since an unmediated individual may not recognize significant differences between these contributing contexts, successful MLE planning and curriculum must focus on the convergence of these three contexts.

2. Modalities of Presentation

Cognitive modalities are the codes or learning styles by which the brain decodes and encodes information. Learning forms may include verbal, pictorial, numerical, figural, symbolic, graphic, or a combination of these and other codes. These forms must not be confused with intelligence, for someone may demonstrate proficiency in problem solving by way of one modality, but less so with another. If this is the case, it seems reasonable to consider flexibility of cognitive modalities for intervention.

3. Cognitive Operations

Once the mediator perceives the learning task, she then determines what cognitive operations are needed to complete a successful learning process. Such operations include sets of internal, organized actions that assist in acquisition and expansion of higher-order thought. The mediator employs various cognitive operations to assist in understanding the complexity of

---

18. Feuerstein, Public Discourse, 1992.

mental formation from basic (i.e. identification, seriation) to complex (i.e. analogical thinking, logical multiplication, syllogisms, metaphoric thinking) development.

4. Cognitive Functions or Dysfunctions

Whereas some educators might believe that Habits of the Mind are simply "caught not taught," Feuerstein classified various habits according to input, elaboration, and output functions. Cognitive dysfunctions are the counterpart of cognitive functions. Dysfunctions may be understood as being undeveloped, poorly developed, arrested, or impaired cognitive functions. This lack of development is seen as a peripheral deficit, rather than central cognitive incapacity. These cognitive dysfunctions interfere with one's ability to learn from direct experiences as well as to modify or to transfer Habits of the Mind and Spirit to other contexts. Such reversibility of cognitive dysfunctions enables mediatees to experience positive alternatives and is supported by clinical and experimental studies.[19] The following tables and commentary reveal three levels of cognitive dys/function:[20]

Level One *Input Level*

Cognitive Functions	Cognitive Dysfunctions
1. Clear perception	1. Blurred & sweeping perception
2. Systematic exploration	2. Impulsive & unplanned exploration
3. Precise understanding of words	3. Impaired receptive verbal labels
4. Use of spatial referents	4. Impaired use of spatial referents
5. Use temporal referents appropriately	5. Impaired use of temporal referents
6. Use object permanence & conservation of essences	6. Impaired use of object permanence & conservation of essences
7. Recognize need for focus & precision	7. Deficient need for precision & accuracy in data gathering
8. Use more than one source of information	8. Deals with information in a piecemeal / episodic manner

---

19. Feuerstein, *Don't Accept Me as I Am*; and Feuerstein, *You Love Me!!*
20. Developed by Burgess in 2011 and adapted from Feuerstein's general works.

Thoughtful attention must be given to the use of functions and dysfunctions, for such data illustrates the manner in which one receives, collects or absorbs information.

Level Two   *Elaboration Level*

Cognitive Functions	Cognitive Dysfunctions
1. Recognize & define a problem	1. Inability to perceive a problem
2. Determine relevance of issues & problem/s	2. Inability to discern relevant problem-solving cues
3. Engage in broadening of one's mental field	3. Sustain a narrowness or fixed mental field
4. Use spontaneous comparative behaviors	4. Lack comparative skills
5. Use spontaneous summative behavior	5. Impaired need to summarize
6. Project relationships	6. Inability to project relationships
7. Need for logical evidence	7. Lacks need to seek logical evidence
8. Interiorize the *gestalt*	8. Limited interiorization of *gestalt*
9. Use hypothetical thinking	9. Limited hypothesis testing
10. Check hypothesis during the process	10. Impaired / non-reflective implementation of hypothesis
11. Use goals & planning behaviors	11. Impaired goal & planning behaviors
12. Project relationships & patterns	12. Exhibits an episodic grasp of reality
13. Categorize efficiently	13. Limited use of categorization

Positive Elaboration Functions (Level 2) reflect higher order thinking. These are built on the Input Cognitive Functions (Level 1). But if the data has been collected inadequately in Level 1, then additional impairments may be seen at this level. Examples of errors can be found during critiques, synthesis, metaphoric thinking, logical multiplications, and other higher order thinking skills.

COMPLEXITIES OF LEARNING 239

Level Three   *Output Level*

Cognitive Functions	Cognitive Dysfunctions
1. Overcome egocentric communication	1. Use egocentric communication
2. Overcome blocking of communication	2. Display blocking behaviors
3. Overcome trial & error communication	3. Use trial & error communication
4. Use clarity & precise lexicon	4. Impaired use of lexicon
5. Efficient use of visual transport	5. Impaired visual transport
6. Give precise, accurate, & thorough responses	6. Impaired need to be precise in communication
7. Restrain impulsive behavior	7. Exhibit impulsivity & acting out
8. Consider the context	8. Oblivious to contextual cues
9. Actions support civil community	9. Neglect responsibility for civil community

The Output Cognitive Functions (Level 3) relate to expressive skills. Scholars proposed that impulsivity and blocking of thoughts were behavioral issues. These functions were noticed initially and thought to be a subject's primary problem. Instead, underlying cognitive dysfunctions in the Input Level (1) were impacting the Output Level (3). Dynamic assessments must address these three levels individually and as inter-related in order to plan mediation. Certainly, there are interactions occurring between and among the three Cognitive Functions levels.

Finally, cultural differences may also influence how output cognitive functions are expressed. Moreover, "egocentric communication" may be defined differently in various cultures, and pragmatic miscues may be deemed as differences rather than deficiencies.

5. Abstractions, Complexity, and Novelty

The mediator skillfully monitors the cognitive contents, cognitive modalities, and cognitive operations with regard to abstraction, complexity, and novelty of the learning task. The levels of complexity consist of the number of units of information on which the learning act centers. Novelty refers to the familiarity of information to the subject, whereas the level of abstraction denotes the cognitive distance between a mental act and the object or event on which it operates. These variations sustain interest and challenge.

6. Learning Efficiency

Cognitive efficiency relates to the ease in which one processes and uses cognitive functions and performs mental operations. Learning efficiency highlights the progress being made by an individual.

Mediated Learning Process

What are the characteristics of a clean heart in concert with Habits of the Mind? In what manner do these changes occur? And how does one assess such changes? The Apostle Paul proclaims the value of Habits of the Spirit and Habits of the Mind when he states: "You were taught to put away your former way of life, your old self, corrupt and deluded by its lusts, and to be renewed in the spirit of your minds, and to clothe yourselves with the new self, created in the likeness of God in true righteousness and holiness" (Eph 4:22–24 KJV). As a bright light in the twentieth century, Feuerstein advocated that it was through MLEs one became cognitively modifiable. The following four Habits of the Mind provide a contrast between the old mind and the new mind. These conclusions are not to minimize the influence of the Habits of the Spirit. The differences between an untransformed and transformed mind would include the following: 1) whereas the old mind is sensorial based, the new mind uses flexible, logical, and abstract thinking habits; 2) the old mind is scattered, disorganized, and impulsive, but the new mind is organized according to precepts, wisdom principles, and transcendent values; 3) according to Autoplastic or Alloplasticity Thinking Practices, the old mind remains self-centered, but the new mind exhibits service and selflessness; and 4) the old mind remains egocentric, the new mind seeks relationships and plans for intergenerational transmission of values and wisdom and principles thereby balancing change and continuity.

For Feuerstein, MLE is the interaction process between the developing human and an experienced adult mediator who frames, selects, and focuses environmental experience in such a way as to create appropriate learning sets.[21] To the contrary, in non-mediation learning approaches, the developing person learns only by chance or by direct spontaneous experience of an object. Instead, mediated learning does not depend on chance confrontation with objects, but on the intentional intervention of the mediator. The mediator seeks to sensitize the developing individual, and does so through

---

21. Feuerstein, *Instrumental Enrichment*.

differentiation between mediated and non-mediated learning experiences. MLEs prove to be a prerequisite to effective independent and autonomous use of environmental stimuli by the mediatee. Reflective thinking, inner representations, and the gradual emergence of operational behavior are by-products of this approach.

Cognitive dysfunctions may exist because of any one or a combination of negative factors expressed in familial interactions. Sociopolitical circumstances may cause vast disruptions in the lifestyles of families and culture-bearing communities so as to interrupt the transmission of values and their ethnologic.[22] Such dysfunction causes the young pupil to be deprived of adequate transmission of ethnic and cultural identity. These pervasive cognitive deficits will affect problem-solving and result in the mediatee's inability to utilize an inherited ethnologic. Finally mediators inevitably and intentionally employ their primary belief systems throughout the MLE. Feuerstein employs the following twelve MLE components:

1. Intentionality and Reciprocity occur when the mediator and mediatee engage in the purposeful focusing of the mind.
2. The Search for Meaning is achieved with clarification and intensification of general and specific understanding.
3. Transcendent Values and Wisdom Principles fulfill a basic purpose to identify values and implement such concepts, principles, or laws to a specific place, time, circumstance, and situation.
4. Mental Competence is strengthened when interaction enhances a person's ability to contribute to cognitive competence by engaging in problem-solving and the demonstration of thoughtful decisions.
5. Self Regulation and Control of Mental Activity encourages intentional self-regulation and self-control. Through metacognition, an individual reflects on her thinking, regulates the speed, and owns the nature of the thought process (e.g., "What thoughts guided the process while you were working on this project?" or "What happens when you reflect and regulate your thinking?").
6. Sharing refers to willingness to share thoughts, energies, personhood, and resources for self-understanding and mutual benefit.
7. Psychological Differentiation seeks to foster constructive individualization and group identity. A prime example might be a new ability for Holocaust survivors to learn of a past and heritage beyond only

---

22. This can be defined as how a person within their cultural-linguistic-ethnic group creates meanings.

the travesty of their primary experience and recollection. In so doing, the survivors will discover an enlarged and rich group identity formed and enhanced by extended family and community.

8. Engagement in Goal Behaviors promotes futuristic thinking. Mediatees must be encouraged to plan beyond the moment and develop habits that address multiple cognitive functions. These habits should include goal seeking, setting, planning, achieving, evaluation, and celebration of goals attained.

9. The shift between one's current self-identity versus understanding of self as a Changing Entity recognizes the intentional acknowledgment, monitoring, and planning of positive modifications to assist in acceptance and appropriation of change as an integral part of the human experience.

10. Appropriate Challenge occurs when the mediatee willingly wrestles with abstract or complex unknowns. The mediator encourages positive reflection and assessment of current struggles with life challenges.

11. Belonging refers primarily to a mutuality, whereby an individual applies appropriate skills to be self-aware and connected in a family, group, or crowd.

12. Optimistic Alternatives refer to the articulation of possibilities beyond one's current situation and recognizes the need for ongoing reassessment of personal development.

In order to assess the stability and cognitive modifiability of a mediatee (and in fact a mediator) Feuerstein provided six mediation questions:

1. What *qualities of interactions* brought about structural cognitive modifiability that is sustaining and self-regulatory?

2. What *types of interactions* brought about structural cognitive modifiability that is sustaining and self-regulatory?

3. What *types of interactive environments* brought about structural cognitive modifiability that is sustaining and self-regulatory?

4. What *agents of interactions* brought about structural cognitive modifiability that is sustaining and self-regulatory?

5. What *engaging stimuli* brought about structural cognitive modifiability that is sustaining and self-regulatory?

6. What *interactive activities* brought about structural cognitive modifiability that is sustaining and self-regulatory?[23]

When an individual demonstrates sustainability and regulation of these six elements, the individual exhibits "autoplasticity." At this point, attention shifts to the development of a culture bearer.

Mediated Culture Bearers

I conclude with the creation of a fictive place called *Shantistan* literally "the land of peace." I use *Shantistan* as a place where individuals and communities become culture bearers based upon peace. Such peace building must employ the following four elements: First, humans must seek a land of peace and appreciate commonalities among cultures. Second, a thorough understanding of historical precedence assures recognition that different groups adopt various ways of making meaning ("ethnologic"). Third, collaborative consultation requires that humans seek understanding by way of mediated learning principles. Finally, collaborators resist impulsivity and instead analyze cultural similarities and differences through higher-order thinking processes.

What do we hold in common? I suggest we share varying degrees of common symbols. Through reasoned and principled behavior we have the opportunity to identify symbols to sustain *Shantistan's* worldview. We are blessed with a tradition, a collection of stories, that should be told and retold. Such unfolding narratives of days current and gone by help to define and refine our existence. Familiarity and appropriation of our heritage strengthens our individual and community identities. In a *Shantistan* curriculum, students are encouraged to explore their personal stories and identify core concepts such as integrity, brotherhood or sisterhood, faith and forgiveness, protection of life, sacrifice, and reconciliation.

The *Shantistan* community explores the value of ethnologic, namely, the way individuals discover meaning and apply historical precedence. All peoples and cultures strive to perpetuate their beliefs through formal and informal stories. To do so requires understanding of another's, and possibly multiple, perspectives. Such discovery may strengthen or create the necessity for alternative meaning and behavior.

Application of this belief was realized recently in Ahmedabad, India, the city where more than two thousand Hindus and Muslims were killed over sacred space issues. A team from three religions volunteered to

---

23. See further Burgess, *Changing Brain Structures*.

participate in a mediated learning pilot study. It was a novel curriculum entitled *Shantistan*. The goal of this encounter was articulated that the inter-religious team would replicate the curriculum at a high school where both teachers and students held a variety of religious beliefs. I was unsure if they would be able to do this.

At the end of *Shantistan* study, as I gathered my belongings there was a knock at the door. There stood a well-respected attorney, Mr. Bhatt. He came to say farewell and to give an assessment of the *Shantistan* experience.

"Dr. Burgess, I want to share something with you. First, I did not think you would come to Ahmedabad. But you came. Second, I thought you were coming to change my religion. But you did not. Third, then I began to study your materials and I questioned my daughter who was in your class. I began to learn. You have become my guru."

After the monsoon rains broke, I received the message that the *Shantistan* team had replicated the experience at a high school among Hindus, Sikhs and Muslims. In addition, one of the students had presented two more applications in southern Gujarat among Hindus and Christians.

To summarize, *Shantistan* is an example that supports a peace building philosophy, an interactive and constructive process called mediated learning and a context-based curriculum that believes humans have choices. Peace building is enhanced when we share life stories, engage in collaborative consultation with mediated learning interchanges, and show respect for the use of representational thought. We learned that the complexity of learning is a gift from our heritages that can be implemented presently, and we have an obligation to carry it into the future. Our duty is to transmit one's heritage into the future. This mandate relates basically to human survival. Indeed "learning-to-learn" is a complex endeavor.

BIBLIOGRAPHY

Ben-Hur, Meir, ed. *On Feuerstein's Instrumental Enrichment: A Collection*. Palatine, IL: IRI/Skylight, 1994.

Burgess, Ruth V. *Changing Brain Structure Through Cross-Cultural Learning: The Life of Reuven Feuerstein*. Lewiston, NY: Edwin Mellen, 2008.

———. "Reuven Feuerstein: Propelling the Change, Promoting Continuity." In *Experience of Mediated Learning, An Impact of Feuerstein's Theory in Education and Psychology*, edited by Alex Kozulin and Yaacov Rand, 147–65. New York: Pergamon, 2000.

Feuerstein, Reuven. "Cognitive Modifiability in Adolescence: Cognitive Structure and the Effects of Intervention." *Journal of Special Education* 15 (1981) 269–87.

———. Public discourse. Hadassah Wizo Canada Research Center, 1986.

———. Public discourse. Soresh Conference Center, Israel, 1992.

———. "Structural Cognitive Modifiability and Native Americans." In *To Sing Our Own Songs: Cognition and Culture in Indian Education*, 21–36. New York: Association on American Indian Affairs. 1985.

Feuerstein, Reuven, et al. *Definitions of Essential Concepts and Terms, Working Glossary*. Jerusalem: ICELP, 1998.

———. *Don't Accept Me as I Am*. New York: Plenum, 1988.

———. *The Dynamic Assessment of Cognitive Modifiability*. Jerusalem: ICELP, 2002.

———. *The Feuerstein Instrumental Enrichment Program*. Rev. and enlarged ed. Jerusalem: ICELP, 2006.

———. *Instrumental Enrichment*. Baltimore, MD: University Park Press, 1980.

———. *You Love Me!! Don't Accept Me as I Am*. Jerusalem: ICELP, 2006.

Kozulin, Alex. *Psychological Tools: A Sociocultural Approach to Education*. Cambridge, MA: Harvard University Press, 1998.

Litz, Carol. "Mediated Learning." Presentation at the International Association of Cognitive Education, Calgary, Canada. July, 1999.

Sharron, Howard. *Changing Children's Minds, Feuerstein's Revolution in the Teaching of Intelligence*. London: Souvenir, 1987.

Sigel, Irving, et al. "Beyond Questioning: Inquiry Strategies and Cognitive and Affective Elements of Jewish Education." *Journal of Jewish Education* 73 (2007) 51–66.

Vygotsky, L. S. *Mind in Society: The Development of Higher Psychological Processes*. Edited by M. Cole, V. John-Steiner, S. Scribner, & E. Souberman. Cambridge, MA: Harvard University Press, 1978.

———. *Thought & Language*. Rev. ed. Cambridge, MA: MIT Press, 1986.

Vygotsky, L. S., and A. R. Luria. *Essays in the History of Behavior*. Moscow: Sozekgiz. 1930.

Wertsch, James V. *Vygotsky and the Social Formation of Mind*. Cambridge, MA: Harvard University Press, 1985.

Index of Authors Cited

Abeysekera, Fred, 136n61, 138
Aldrich, H. E. , 72, 73n14, 74n17, 80
Alexander, Jeffrey C., 182n7, 198
Allen, C. Leonard, 96n48, 97nn51–52, 105
Appleby, Blanche, 126, 126nn11–12, 138
Apter, David E., 182n7, 198
Aquinas, Thomas, 27, 38–39
Aristotle, 25–26, 37–40
Armstrong, Nancy, 110n9, 121
Augustine, 24, 24n2, 26–27, 38, 210, 210n15, 216
Aviad, Janet O'Dea, 69nn7–8, 81
Awbrey, Diane, 9, 107–22
Bailie, Annie, 129, 129n30, 138
Baird, Lula Ashmore, 134n52, 136–38
Baker, D. Hugh, 135n56, 138
Ball, Martin, 187n19, 188nn22&24, 193n44, 194n59, 198
Bartleman, Frank, 100, 100n74, 103–4, 104n88
Barton, S. C., 156, 157n8, 165
Barzun, Jacques, 85, 85n1, 95, 97n53, 102n81, 104
Bell, E. N., 65, 65n1, 80
Bellinger, W. H., 144–50, [144nn10,11&15], 153
Benedict of Nursia, 28
Bennet, John B., 221, 221n7, 228
Benois, Alexander, 91n22, 94n36, 104
Berg, Robert, 85–106
Blake, William, 171–73, 172n24, 179

Blalock, Glenn, 221, 221n10, 229
Blumhofer, Edith L., 98nn59&62, 103n87, 104
Boethius, Ancius, 25–28, 25n4, 34, 37
Boquet, Elizabeth H., 218, 219n1, 225, 225n23, 226, 226n24, 227n28, 228–29
Bowlt, John E., 91n24, 98n60, 104
Brennan, Michael G., 142n4, 153
Brown, Laura, 110n8, 121
Brueggemann, Walter, 144, 144n13, 149, 153
Bundy, David, 127n17, 138
Burgess, Ruth, 10, 230–45
Buteyn, Mary, 216, 216n29
Byrne, Brendan, 224, 224n18, 227, 227nn25–27, 228
Camus, Albert, 211, 211nn18–19, 216
Cantor, Norman F., 25n3, 34n41, 36n47, 40n59, 41
Capella, Martianus, 24–25, 28, 34
Carlow, Margaret, 133n46, 139
Carmichael, Christine, 128n24, 139
Carrier, Roch, 154n2, 155, 155nn4–5, 156, 165
Carroll, Meg, 225, 225n23, 226, 226n24, 227n28, 229
Carroll, Raymonde, 207, 207n7, 214n25, 216
Carter, Craig, 50n9, 63
Cashman, Sean Dennis, 97n55, 104
Caton, Eva Mae, 127, 127nn19–20, 139

247

Chadwick, Henry, 27n16, 41
Chance, Jane, 185n17, 195n66, 198
Chase, Betty, 65n2, 81
Chekhov, Anton, 91n24, 104
Chism, Christine, 182n6, 194n54, 198
Cibber, Colley, 9, 111-12, 117-21, [118n16]
Cicero, 25, 34
Clark, Stuart, 182n7, 198
Clemenson, Pamela, 133n47, 139
Colebatch, Hal G. P., 193nn45&52, 198
Collins, James, 27n13, 41
Comenius, Jan Amos, 9, 54-58, 55n15, 58n18, 63
Condon, Frankie, 225, 225n23, 226, 226n24, 227n28, 229
Corey, Barry, 4, 4n6, 8-9, 14n7, 16n12, 65-81
Craft, Robert, 90n20, 94n35, 95nn42&45, 105
Crouch, Andy, 45n4, 48, 48n6, 50n9, 50-52, 52n10 63
Curry, Patrick, 191n28, 192n39, 193nn44&46&49, 196n67, 198
Cyert, Richard, 76, 76n20, 81
D'Avenant, William, 111n13
Dales, Douglas, 30n27, 41
Dalton, Adele Flower, 126n10, 139
Dayton, Donald, 99n69, 100n70, 104
De Bruyn, Jan, 110, 110n12, 121
De Koster, Katie, 181n2, 198
Denny, Henry C., 220, 220n3, 228
Derrida, Jacques, 222, 222nn13-14, 223-24, 228
Deutch, Miriam, 88n12, 105
Devaux, Michël, 190n27, 198
Di Cesare, Mario A., 209n13, 216
Dickerson, Matthew, 191n34, 198
Diepeveen, Leonard, 86n3, 104
DiMaggio, Paul J., 76nn20&22, 81
Dorff, Marcella, 131, 131n40, 139
Drane, Frances, 32n33, 41
Drout, Michael D. C., 183n9, 198
Dryden, John, 111n13

Dufourmantelle, Anne, 228
Duriez, Colin, 196n69, 198
Durkheim, Emile, 69, 69n9, 79, 81
Eaglestone, Robert, 185n17, 198
Eden, Bradford Lee, 190n27, 198
Edwards, Jim (James), 11-19
Edwards, Michael, 16, 16n4, 19
Edwards, Twila, 11-19, 15nn9-11, 16n12, 178-79, 178nn44-45
Eksteins, Modris, 92nn27&29, 94, 94n39, 95n44, 105
Eliot, T. S., 167, 167n4, 179
Enright, Nancy, 191nn31&34&35, 192, 192nn37-38, 198
Eodice, Michele, 225, 225n23, 226, 226n24, 227n28, 229
Evans, Jonathan, 193n48, 194n57, 198
Fairclough, Norman, 148n20, 153
Feldman, Martha S., 77n24, 78, 81
Fendall, Lon, 210n16, 216
Fenton, Jennifer, 10, 218-29
Ferraro, Gary, 182n5, 183n10, 195n62, 198
Feuerstein, Reuven, 10, 231-37, [231nn3,7, 232n8, 233n11, 234n12, 235nn15-16, 236n18, 237n19], 240-42, [240n21], 244-45
Fielding, Sarah, 172-73
Fimi, Dimitra, 182nn4&6, 198
Fitzgerald, J. T., 157n9, 165
Flam, Jack, 88n12, 105
Flieger, Verlyn, 188nn23&25, 199
Fonstad, Karen Wynn, 182n3, 199
Foster, Roger, 183n9, 199
Frederick, Candice, 191nn30-32, 199
Freer, Coburn, 141n1, 153
Friesen, LaDonna, 10, 166-80
Gaebelein, Frank, 12, 12n1, 19
Garau, Marius, 47
Gauthier, David, 223n15, 228
Geertz, Clifford, 10, 182-83, 182n7, 195, 195n63, 197n71, 199
Geller, Anne Ellen, 225, 225n23, 226, 226n24, 227n28, 229
George, Bill, 215, 215n27, 216

INDEX OF AUTHORS CITED 249

Gies, Frances & Joseph, 29n20, 41
Gill, Deborah M., 18, 18n19, 18n22, 19, 123n1, 137n65, 139
Glenn, Cheryl, 225, 225nn21–22, 229
Goldingay, John, 2n3, 6
Gottwald, Norman K., 144, 144n15, 153
Graves, Frank P., 27n17, 30n23
Grunlan, Stephen A., 182n5, 183n10, 199
Guneratnam, Prince, 134–35, 135n55, 139
Gunkel, Hermann, 143n9, 144, 144nn10&12, 153
Habermann, Ina, 182n3, 192n39, 193nn46&49, 199
Hartfield, Lindsay, 213n24, 216
Haskins, Charles H., 35n43, 37nn50–51, 41
Haswell, Janis, 221, 221nn10–11, 229
Haswell, Richard, 221, 221nn10–11, 229
Heard, Matthew, 221, 221n8, 229
Hein, Rolland, 168n7, 169n11, 170nn17–18, 171, 172n22, 173n27, 179
Herbert, George, 9, 141–53, [142n2], 209–10
Hiebert, Paul, 183n10, 199
Hill, Peter, 90n19, 94, 94n37, 105
Hittenberger, Jeffrey, 8, 14n7, 16n12, 43–64
Hodges, Margaret, 166n2, 167, 179
Hodgkins, Christopher, 145, 145n16, 152, 152n22, 153
Holmes, Arthur, 4, 13, 13n5, 15, 19, 50n8, 63, 204n2, 216
Honegger, Tom, 196n70, 199
Hostetter, Carl F., 182n4, 199
Howe, Elizabeth, 108n2, 121
Hughes, Richard, 96n48, 97nn51–52, 100n71, 105
Hunter, Sam, 90n18, 102n81, 105
Hus(s), John, 54
Isaacs, Neil D., 181n2, 199
Jacobs, Dale, 221, 221n9, 229

Jacobus, John, 90n18, 102n81, 105
James, Patrick, 191n29, 193n44, 196n68, 199
Jeauneau, Edouard, 33n35, 34n38, 41
Joachimides, Christos M., 89n17, 105
Johnson, Luke Timothy, 159n11, 165
Jones, Wilma, 132n45, 139
Juergensen, Marie, 132, 132nn43–44, 139
Ketcham, M. L., 125n9, 134n54, 135, 136n59, 139
Knowles, David, 29n21, 30nn24–25, 31n28, 33n34, 36n34&48, 38n52, 40n58, 41
Kozulin, Alex, 234, 234n13, 245
Kruger, Joan, 131n36, 139
Kuhn, Nikolaus, 182n3, 192n39, 193nn46&49, 199
La Shure, Charles, 205n4, 216
Lacy, John, 111n13
Lawrence, B. F., 99n69, 100, 100n73
Lederman, Minna, 92n28, 93n33, 94n34, 95n43, 105
Leff, Gordon, 23n1, 36nn45&49, 39, 39nn54–57, 41
Leibiger, Carol A., 191nn31–32, 199
Leighten, Patricia, 89n14, 105
Levinas, Immanuel, 222–24, 223n15
Levinson, André, 92n28, 94n34
Lewis, C. S., 15–16, 173
Lewis, Paul W., 7–10, 17n16, 181–200
Lewis-Anthony, Justin, 146n18, 153
Lichterman, Paul, 182n7, 199
Liddle, Gary, 8, 11–19, 181n1
Lins, Joseph, 31n30, 41
Lobdell, Jared, 181n2, 199
Loomis, Majorie, 130n34, 139
Loscocco, Karyn, 76n21, 81
Lovelace, Richard F., 12, 12n2, 16n15, 16–17, 19
Luria, A. R., 235n14, 245
Luyken, Jan, 3
McBride, Sam, 191nn30–32, 199
Macchia, Frank, 54, 54n13

INDEX OF AUTHORS CITED

MacDonald, George, 10, 166–80 [167n3, 168n5, 168–69nn8–10, 169n13, 170nn15–16, 171nn19–20, 173–178nn29–43]
MacDonald, Greville, 169, 169n12, 172n23, 180
MacKinney, Loren C., 33n37, 41
Macrobius, 34
March, James G., 71, 71n13, 76, 76nn19–20, 77n24, 78, 81
Marenbon, John, 25–27, 41
Marsden, George M., 98nn58&62, 105
Marsden, Jean I., 108–11 [108n4, 109n6, 110nn8&10–11, 111n14], 122
Marshall, I. Howard, 159n11, 165
Mayers, Marvin K., 182n5, 183n10, 199
McGee, Gary B., 18, 18n22, 124nn3–4, 128n22, 139
McInerny, Ralph, 26, 26nn6&8–9, 27n15, 35n42, 41
McKinney, Jackie Grutsch, 220, 220n4, 229
Milton, John, 15–16, 142
Mitchell, Donald, 102n82, 105
Mittelstadt, Martin W., 1–6, 9, 154–65, 224n18
Monteux, Pierre, 93, 93n33, 95, 95n43
Moorhead, John, 26n7, 42
Morris, Edmund, 97n54, 105
Morrison, J. C., 135n57, 140
Mother Teresa, 218
Mumma, Howard, 211n18, 216
Nagy, Gergely, 188, 188n21, 199
Nelson, Nathan H., 9, 141–53
Nelson, R. R., 76, 76n21
Niebuhr, H. Richard, 50n9, 63, 79, 81
Noel, Ruth S., 182nn4–5, 183n13, 199
Nokes, Richard Scott, 193n51, 199
Noll, Mark, 13n6, 19, 48n5, 63
Norton, Matthew, 182n7, 198

O'Connor, Flannery, 16, 164, 164n13, 165
O'Dea, Thomas F., 69nn7–8, 81
Olsen, J. P., 76, 76n19, 81
Ortberg, John, 12, 13n4, 19
Otto, Rudolf, 69, 69n10, 81
Paine, Thomas, 96, 96nn49–50, 105
Palmer, Michael, 8, 16, 16n12, 19, 23–42
Panichas, George A., 215n28, 216
Parham, Charles F., 98, 99n65, 101n75, 102, 103n84, 105
Parks, Barbara Cavaness, 9, 18, 18nn21–22, 19, 123–40
Patch, Howard, 26n12, 42
Patrides, C. A., 142, 142n3, 153
Perry, Gill, 86n6, 105
Pervo, Richard, 162n12, 165
Pfeffer, Jeffrey, 72, 73n14, 74n17, 80
Piaget, Jean, 56, 56n16, 64
Pierson, Paul, 124n2, 140
Plato, 25, 34, 177
Pohl, Christine, 156n7, 165
Pollak, Ellen, 109, 109n7, 111, 122
Porphyry, 26, 37
Powell, Walter W., 76nn20&22, 81
Quitslund, Beth, 142, 142n5, 153
Repko, Allen, 5, 5nn7–8, 6
Resseguie, James, 223, 223n16, 229
Reynolds, Myra, 107–8, 108nn2–3, 122
Richardson, John, 86n6, 105
Riché, Pierre, 30n26, 32n31, 42
Rieger, Joerg, 157n10, 165, 207, 207n8, 213n21, 214, 214n26, 216
Ripley, Aline, 191n30
Robeck, Cecil M., 49n7, 64, 98n63, 99n66, 101nn77–79, 105
Roberts, Jeanne Addison, 107n1, 122
Rosebury, Brian, 185, 185n16, 193nn45–46&50, 194n60, 195n65, 199
Rosenblum, Robert, 88n13, 96n46, 105
Rosenthal, Norman, 89n17, 105

INDEX OF AUTHORS CITED 251

Ruane, Abigail E., 191n29, 193n44, 196n68, 199
Rubin, William, 85n3, 88n11, 89n15, 105
Rumsey, Mary, 133, 133nn48–49, 134, 140
Said, Edward, 47
Salmon, André, 86n8, 88nn10&12, 105
Sartre, Jean-Paul, 207–8, 207n9, 208n12, 216
Schaeffer, Francis, 212, 216
Schwarze, Richard, 129n29, 140
Seymour, William, 98, 99nn64–65, 100, 101nn75–76, 103n85, 103–5
Shakespeare, William, 107–9, 111–18, [113n15], 120–21, 121n18, 122 168, 181
Shippey, Tom, 194, 194nn58–60, 199
Sidney, Sir Philip, 142, 142n4, 153
Slagter, Cynthia, 210n17, 217
Smith, James K. A., 1, 1n2, 6, 59n20, 60n28, 64
Smith, Philip, 182n7, 198–199
Smol, Anna, 191n33, 199
Southern, Richard W., 33n36, 34n40, 42
Spence, Inez, 126n13, 140
Spencer, Christopher, 118n16, 120n17, 122
Spenser, Edmund, 167
St. Francis of Assisi, 208, 208n10
Stanton, Michael N., 182n4, 183n9, 189n26, 191n31, 192nn39–40, 193n42, 194n53, 199
Starkenberg, Alma, 127, 127n18, 128, 140
Starkloff, SJ. Carl F., 195n64, 200
Stimpson, Catherine, 191n32, 200
Stone, Lawrence, 109n5, 108, 111, 122
Straubhaar, Sandra Ballif, 194, 194nn55–57&61, 200
Stravinsky, Igor, 90, 90nn20-21, 92–96, 94n35, 95nn42&45, 96n46, 105

Sunstein, Bonnie, 220, 220n5, 221, 229
Tarushkin, Richard, 90n20, 91nn23&26, 98n60, 105
Tate, Nahum, 111n13
Taylor, G. F., 100, 100n70,
Taylor, Gary, 107n1, 122
Thompson, James W., 31n29, 42
Tolkien, J. R. R., 10, 167, 180–200, [183nn8&11&13, 184n15, 189n26, 192nn36&40–41, 193nn43&47, 194n59, 195n66]
Tomaseck, Anna, 130, 130n35, 140
Trask, Ray, 136, 136n60, 140
Trueman, Carl, 13n6, 19
Tucker, Ruth, 137, 137n66, 140
Turnbull, Robert, 10, 203–17
Turner, Victor, 205, 205nn4–5
Turner, William, 38n53, 42
Tyler, J. E. A., 183n9, 200
Valla, Lorenzo, 27
Van Laar, Timothy, 86n3, 104
Varnedoe, Kirk, 89n15
Volf, Miroslav, 208, 208n11, 217
Von Bracht, Thielem J., 3, 6
Vygotsky, Lev S., 235, 235n14, 245
Wach, Joachim, 70n12, 81
Wacker, Grant, 48n5, 64, 98n61, 99n67, 100nn71–72, 101n78, 103n86, 105
Wagner, David, 33n36, 42
Wall, John N., 143, 143n8, 153
Warncke, Carsten-Peter, 86n7, 89n16, 96n46, 106
Weber, Max, 69, 69n11, 70, 79, 81
Weil, Simone, 215
West, Shearer, 102n80, 106
Westermann, Claus, 144
Wheeler, Daniel, 90n18, 102n81, 105
White, Eric Walter, 95n41, 106
Wilcox, Helen, 141–43, 142nn2&7, 143n8, 146–48, 153
Wilde, Oscar, 166n1, 167, 180
Winter, S. G., 76, 76n21
Witt, Jonathan, 182n3, 200
Wohlers, Charles, 146n19, 153

Wordsworth, William, 171, 171n21, 173, 180
Worthen, Shana, 193n51, 200
Wycliffe, John, 54
Yarustovsky, Boris Mikhailovich, 96n46, 98n60, 106
Yong, Amos, 6, 6n9 60n28, 64
Youn, Ted I. K., 76n21, 81
Zald, Mayer, 73, 73n15, 78, 78n26, 81
Zimbardo, Rose A., 181n2, 199
Zipes, Jack, 172nn25–26, 180

www.ingramcontent.com/pod-product-compliance
Lightning Source LLC
Chambersburg PA
CBHW051518230426
43668CB00012B/1656